Australia's Italians

Culture and community in a changing society

Edited by
Stephen Castles
Caroline Alcorso
Gaetano Rando
Ellie Vasta

ALLEN & UNWIN

Fondazione
Giovanni Agnelli

The preparation of this research and its publication in book form were generously assisted by the Fondazione Giovanni Agnelli of Turin, Italy.

First published in 1992
Allen & Unwin Pty Ltd
8 Napier Street, North Sydney, NSW 2059 Australia

National Library of Australia
Cataloguing-in-Publication entry:

Australia's Italians.

Bibliography.
Includes index.
ISBN 1 86373 170 9.

1. Italians—Australia—Ethnic identity. 2. Italians—Australia—Cultural assimilation. 3. Italians—Australia—Social life and customs. 4. Italians—Australia—Intellectual life. I. Castles, Stephen.

305.851094

Set in 10/11 pt Times by DOCUPRO, Sydney
Printed by SRM Production Services Sdn Bhd, Malaysia

Contents

Foreword

This book is the outcome of a research project commissioned by the Giovanni Agnelli Foundation. The project brought together a large group of Australian scholars, co-ordinated by the Centre for Multicultural Studies at the University of Wollongong under the guidance of Stephen Castles and Gaetano Rando. I would like to thank all the authors and co-ordinators. The book's purpose is to present a vast and varied picture of the social, cultural, political and economic reality of the community of Australians of Italian origin.

I will briefly illustrate the reasons which have led us to launch this project. First of all, I think it is important to stress that this is not an occasional initiative. On the contrary, the Agnelli Foundation has been interested in communities of Italian origin for more than twelve years and it has launched an extensive and detailed program for research and cultural relations. For some years the Foundation has been publishing a journal entitled *Altreitalie* [Other Italies], the editorial board of which includes an Australian scholar, Professor Gianfranco Cresciani, which is intended as a forum for debate and communication for all scholars interested in communities of italian origin throughout the world. The publication in Italian of three volumes under the title *Euroamericani: La popolazione di origine italiana negli Stati Uniti, in Brasile, in Argentina* [Euroamericans: Communities of Italian Origin in the United States, in Brazil, in Argentina] (Turin: Edizioni della Fondazione Giovanni Agnelli, 1987) represented a first summing-up of some of our studies. The Foundation has also now launched a new series, *Popolazioni e culture italiane nel mondo* [Italian Populations and Cultures in the World], which will publish the Italian version of this book.

The principal reason for the Agnelli Foundation's interest lies in the exceptional importance of Italian migrations. Between 1876 and 1985 the total number of overseas migrants, mainly directed towards the Americas and subsequently to Australia, amounted to a net outflow of approximately 12 million Italians: one of the largest migrations in modern history.

The size of the phenomenon, its intensity, its relevance to Italian and world history, and its lasting consequences, is sufficient to make it a culturally interesting phenomenon requiring study from a historical, sociological and anthropological point of view. But in addition to these factors, there are others which lead us to consider the presence of world-wide communities of Italian origin as an issue which is important beyond a retrospective or merely academic interest.

A brief quotation taken from the great French historian Fernand Braudel can be used as an introduction to this subject: it has been a constant source of inspiration in the research and reflections of the Agnelli Foundation. Braudel writes:

> In the nineteenth and twentieth centuries we find an element which is important but which is discreet, almost lost in the artificial noise of Great History, the vast human expense represented by Italian emigration from which the peninsula has not been able to benefit. But this migration, which started at the end of the last century, has significantly contributed to the take-off of human development in the Americas: the Portuguese, the Spanish, the Anglosaxon Americas. This has been no mean feat on a world scale. Is it simply a beginning? The issue is still undecided.

Braudel does not mention Australia, which is in many respects the most recent, and probably the last addition to the migratory history of Italy—a country which now *receives* foreign immigrants. But this only strengthens Braudel's comments: to examine the issue in terms of research and intellectual debate is an extremely important task for an Italian cultural institution. In effect, given the modesty of the imperial role which our country has had, and the end of the hegemony or at least the primary position of Italian culture in Europe since the 17th century, migration and its legacy, that is to say the overseas growth of communities of Italian origin, has really been the only form of international diffusion which modern Italy has had.

From the beginning, our intention has been to study not so much migration as such, but rather post-migratory conditions: following the paths which lead from migration to the formation of an ethnic group, analysing relations between Italians and their descendants within the new multi-ethnic or multicultural realities, following the contributions which Italians and their descendants have made to the development of these societies, to a large extent formed as a consequence of European migrations. It is no longer possible, and is indeed misleading, to talk of 'migrants'. The actual Italian overseas emigration is a process which may be considered finished. The legacy for the future of Australian and American society is left instead to the descendants of the great migration: full citizens of these countries, and therefore first and foremost, in this case, Australians.

With the end of primary identities (that of being born in Italy, or being Italian citizens), the persistence or the emergence of some form of 'Italian identity' in the post-migratory generations becomes more important. With the passing of generations, and the increasing distance from those who have a direct memory of migration, this secondary identity becomes increasingly voluntary and less automatic.

One of the most interesting aspects of these processes has been the emergence of a Euro-Australian koiné, i.e. a community of ethnic groups of European origin, inside which special conditions, personal strategies, specific institutions or historical, political and cultural circumstances will strengthen or weaken the tendencies towards strong and specific ethnicities. 'Australian of Italian origin' is therefore an appropriate term for statistical and sociographic use, but it will be increasingly associated with identities of an ever more voluntary and even non-exclusive nature, in the now frequent case of mixed families. In this sense Australians of Italian origin (as a socio-cultural category and not merely a statistical–descriptive category) will be those who will feel they are so, those who will want to feel so and those who will be induced to be so.

Just as in the case of Italians living in Canada, it is possible to forecast in the case of Australians of Italian origin that cultural identity will be preserved in some form by the institutionalised multicultural nature of these societies. The decision taken by Australian governments to follow a multicultural policy, instead of one of assimilation, the vitality of the local ethnic *intelligentsia,* and the relatively recent nature of the migratory flows, are all factors which confirm the belief that some form of specific identity has a good chance of survival, even in the future.

This is not a matter of reviving the simple 'third generation theory', which presupposed that the forms of ethnic camouflaging which belong to the first and second generations, striving for acceptance in the society of arrival and therefore often rejecting their origins, were typically followed by positive assertions of ethnic identity in the third generation. What matters is, rather, the new and inexhaustible features of the processes of cultural definition in multi-ethnic societies, and the numerous and subtle relations between current ethnic identities and more or less remote national origins.

This is precisely the field in which the connection between the objectives and interests of contemporary Italian society and those of the most aware sectors of Italian overseas migration may emerge more clearly. And, once again, in this light we can understand to what extent, together with the research and strictly scholarly objectives which are its inspiration, we have always been accompanied by a political and cultural objective.

Interest in the growth of a more qualified and less fragmentary or marginal Italy, is in fact mutual. The reasons are obvious in the case of our country. But for Australians of Italian origin the importance of being able to identify with a reality which is appreciated and is in any case respectable is part of the essential requirements for self-esteem and social esteem. Dialogue with Australians of Italian origin and with their institutions and organisations is therefore an important part of the Agnelli Foundation's program and represents an important aspect of cultural relations between Italy and Australia.

A hundred years after the beginning of the historical process of the great Italian migration, and two hundred years after the beginning of the first, timid contacts between Italy and the new continent, revisiting the story, the big and small stories of Italian migration in Australia and its legacy, is a way of establishing a new meeting point in a field which is at least partly common.

Marcello Pacini
Director, Giovanni Agnelli Foundation

Illustrations

Tables and figures

Tables

Figures

Acknowledgments

Producing this work has been a long and complicated task, in which many people have generously given help and guidance. The editors and authors wish to thank all who have given assistance, not all of whom can be named here. In particular we would like to express our recognition for the information and advice given to us in personal conversations by many Italo-Australians from all walks of life.

We would especially like to thank the Fondazione Giovanni Agnelli for providing the financial support which made the project possible. The Director, Dr Marcello Pacini, and the Deputy Director, Dr Piero Gastaldo, gave us a great deal of encouragement and assistance.

We thank Claudio Alcorso, who made the original suggestion which led to this book.

Research assistance and editorial support throughout the project were provided by Cesare Giulio Popoli, while Colleen Mitchell and Maureen Dibden were responsible for the meticulous editing of the manuscript for the Italian version. Colleen Mitchell co-ordinated and edited the text for the English version. Wendy MacFarlane, Kim McCall and Tina Kungl typed large parts of the text, and provided administrative support.

Michael Arrighi, Kathy Gibson and Tim Turpin read some of the drafts and made useful comments.

Finally, the editors would like to thank all the authors for their contributions, and for their willingness to co-operate in the arduous and lengthy process of producing this work.

The Editors
Wollongong, May 1991

Authors

Caroline Alcorso was born in Hobart, Tasmania, in 1958. She has a BA from the University of Tasmania and an MA from Cambridge University. She has worked as a research fellow at the Centre for Multicultural Studies, University of Wollongong, as well as for government and the labour movement. Caroline Alcorso has two daughters, and has recently been working as consultant on ethnic affairs issues to government and women's organisations. She is currently co-authoring a book on migrant women and work.

Claudio Alcorso AO studied economics at the University of Rome, and did postgraduate work at the London School of Economics and the Harvard School of Business Administration. After emigrating to Australia, he established one of Australia's first textile firms, Silk and Textiles Ltd (weaving, dyeing and printing of fine fabrics). He remained Chief Executive until his retirement in 1973. For many years he was a member of the executive committee of the Australian Elizabethan Trust. He has been Foundation Chair of the Australian Opera, Board Member of the Australian Ballet, Foundation Chair of the Tasmanian Arts Advisory Board, and Foundation Chair of the Sullivan's Cove Development Authority (Hobart Waterfront).

Stephen Castles is a professor at the University of Wollongong and Director of the Centre for Multicultural Studies. He previously taught political economy at the Fachhochschule, Frankfurt am Main, Germany. He has been involved in research on migration and ethnic relations for many years. Stephen Castles' books include: *Immigrant Workers and Class Structure in Western Europe* (with Godula

Kosack); *Here for Good—Western Europe's New Ethnic Minorities; Mistaken Identity—Multiculturalism and the Demise of Nationalism in Australia* (with Bill Cope, Mary Kalantzis and Michael Morrissey); and *Migrant Workers and the Transformation of Western Societies.*

Jock Collins is Associate Professor of Economics at the University of Technology, Sydney, where he is Head of the Department of Economics and Director of the Centre for Labour Studies. He has been writing and commenting on Australian immigration policy since the early 1970s. He is currently carrying out research on ethnic small business. Jock Collins is author of *Migrant Hands in a Distant Land: Australia's Post-War Immigration.*

Al Grassby AM PhD (HC), the 'father of multiculturalism', was Minister for Immigration in the Whitlam government from 1972 to 1974 and was Commissioner for Community Relations from 1975 to 1982. His career spans journalism, agricultural extension, immigration, multiculturalism, community relations, politics, international affairs and race relations. For his services to the Australian community he has been awarded many honours. His major publications are *The Morning After, The Spanish in Australia, Tyranny of Prejudice* and *Six Australian Battlefields.*

Bernadette Kelly is a lecturer in sociology at Charles Sturt University, Wagga Wagga, New South Wales. Her main research interests are ethnic studies and women's studies. She has published several chapters and articles on the Italian population of Griffith, a city in rural New South Wales. Her recent research has been on the early settlement needs of newly arrived migrants in rural areas. Bernadette lives on a small farm on the outskirts of Wagga Wagga with her husband and two young sons.

Franko Leoni comes from Rome, and was a journalist before coming to Australia. He is a lecturer in Italian at the University of New England, Armidale, New South Wales. Franko Leoni wrote his PhD thesis on *Australitalian: The Language of Italian Migrants in Multicultural Australia,* and has written several articles on this topic as well as a book, *Vocabolario Australitaliano.*

Michael Morrissey grew up in (old) South Wales and emigrated to Australia in 1976, having previously taught at the Universities of Exeter, Sierra Leone and Glasgow. Since 1980 he has been a research fellow at the Centre for Multicultural Studies and is currently Associate Director of the Centre. His major interests are workforce issues, nationalism and ideology.

Frank Panucci was born in Sydney, Australia, of Italian parents from Calabria. He has an Honours Degree in Economics from the University of Sydney and is currently undertaking a Masters in Industrial Relations at the same university. He has been involved in the Sydney branch of the Italian Federation of Migrant Workers and their Families (FILEF) since 1980; he was co-ordinator for five years and then editor of its monthly magazine *Nuovo Paese* for over two years. He is still a member of its executive.

Robert Pascoe is Dean, Faculty of Humanities, at the Western Institute, a part of the Victoria University of Technology. He attended the University of Melbourne before undertaking his doctorate in history at Murdoch University in Perth. In 1982 and 1983 Robert Pascoe was a visiting scholar at Harvard University. His research on the Italian community of Boston's North End provided the theoretical structure for his subsequent Australian work. Among his nine books are *Buongiorno Australia, Our Italian Heritage, The Recollections of Luigi Grollo* [Italian: *Luigi Grollo: Elementi di memoria*], and *Open for Business: Aboriginal and Immigrant Entrepreneurs Tell their Story.* He is presently writing a social history of Treviso and the *trevisani.*

Cesare Giulio Popoli was born in Naples in 1960, where he graduated in modern languages. He came to Australia in 1988, and has worked as a teacher and as research assistant at the Centre for Multicultural Studies.

Gaetano Rando is a senior lecturer in Italian at the University of Wollongong, and previously taught at the universities of Western Australia, Auckland (New Zealand) and Griffith (Queensland). He has carried out extensive studies on Italo-Australian language and literature, and is currently President of the Italo-Australian Writers Association. His many interests include ethnic broadcasting (he was foundation president of the ethnic radio station 4EB in Brisbane), interpreting and translation, and the application of artificial intelligence in language teaching. On the occasion of the Australian Bicentenary he organised an international conference on Italians in Australia. His books include: *Italian Writers in Australia: Essays and Texts, Dizionario degli anglicismi nell'italiano postunitario* and *Language and Cultural Identity.*

Ellie Vasta grew up in the Italian community of Fairfield in Sydney. Her parents migrated as teenagers to Australia in the 1920s and 1930s. Ellie Vasta is a lecturer in sociology at the University of Wollongong and recently completed her PhD thesis entitled *Australia's Post-War Immigration Policy: Power, Identity and Resistance.*

She has conducted research among second generation Italo-Australian youth, has completed a study for the Department of Immigration and Ethnic Affairs on the Italian community in Brisbane, and has recently published work on Italian migrant women in Australia.

Abbreviations

STATES AND TERRITORIES OF AUSTRALIA

ACT	Australian Capital Territory
NSW	New South Wales
NT	Northern Territory
QLD	Queensland
SA	South Australia
VIC	Victoria
WA	Western Australia

OTHER ABBREVIATIONS

ABC	Australian Broadcasting Corporation
ABS	Australian Bureau of Statistics
AGPS	Australian Government Publishing Service
ALP	Australian Labor Party
ANU	Australian National University (Canberra)
BHP	Broken Hill Proprietary
BWIU	Building Workers Industrial Union
CA	California
CHOMI	Clearing House for Migration Issues
CIRC	Catholic Intercultural Resource Centre
COASIT	*Comitato Assistenza Italiani* (Italian Committee of Assistance)
CPA	Communist Party of Australia

CSE/CSER	Centro Studi Emigrazione
CSIRO	Commonwealth Scientific and Industrial Research Organization
EPT	Electric Power Transmissions
ESL	English as a Second Language
FCI	*Federazione Cattolica Italiana* (Italian Catholic Federation)
FILEF	*Federazione Italiana dei Lavoratori Emigrati e delle Famiglie* (Italian Federation of Migrant Workers and their Families)
MA	Master of Arts
MIA	Murrumbidgee Irrigation Area (NSW)
NESB	Non-English Speaking Background
NY	New York
NZ	New Zealand
PhD	Doctor of Philosophy
RSL	Returned Servicemen's League
SBS	Special Broadcasting Service
TAFE	(Department of) Technical and Further Education

Introduction: Italian migration and the emergence of a 'post-European' society

This book is about Italian migration to Australia, about the emergence of an Italo-Australian community, and about the way Italian settlement has helped shape Australian society. Italo-Australians are the largest group of non-British origin in Australia. The 1986 census showed that 262 435 Italian-born people were resident in Australia, and that 76 per cent of them were Australian citizens. There were 300 997 people who had been born in Australia, but whose parents (either one or both) had been born in Italy—we refer to this group as the 'second generation'. The Italian language was used in the home by 415 765 people, which gives some idea of transgenerational cultural maintenance. Italian-born people made up 1.7 per cent of the total population, while Italian speakers made up 2.7 per cent of the total population. These numbers may not seem very large, but they are sufficient to have a significant economic, social and cultural impact on Australian society.

This book is a shorter version of a work entitled *Euroaustraliani: La popolazione di origine italiana in Australia,* which is being published in Italian by the Fondazione Giovanni Agnelli of Turin. *Euroaustraliani* is a companion volume to three books on *Euroamericani*—which examine Italian settlement in the United States of America, Argentina and Brazil—published by the Fondazione in 1987. Indeed, the idea for our work came when we first saw the three volumes of *Euroamericani.* By contrasting the experience of another new world continent with the Americas, we hoped to increase knowledge not only of Italian migration, but also of the dynamics of international migration and settlement, and of the evolution of post-colonial societies. The project, which started in 1988, has throughout been generously supported and encouraged by the Fondazione Giovanni Agnelli.

This work was co-ordinated by the Centre for Multicultural Studies at the University of Wollongong. Three of the editors—Stephen Castles, Ellie Vasta and Caroline Alcorso—are sociologists. The exception—Gaetano Rando—teaches in the Modern Languages Department. He is of Italian birth, while Vasta and Alcorso are second-generation Italo-Australians. This is an edited book, with authors of differing backgrounds, opinions and experience. They represent various social scientific disciplines and use different theoretical approaches and methodologies. Nonetheless, we feel that an overall statement does emerge. This is partly because of the co-operative discourse between the authors during the process of writing, which was particularly encouraged by a two-day symposium held in Wollongong to discuss first drafts in December 1989. Important contributions to the Italian book were made by authors whose chapters or sections have had to be excluded from the English version for reasons of space: Tito Cecilia, Silvia Stefanoni, Joe Lo Bianco and Paolo Totaro. Although their specific writings are not to be found here, their ideas and knowledge remain significant in this work.

Italian migration to Australia is mainly a modern phenomenon: the overwhelming majority of settlers came after 1945. Here it differs from Italian migration to the Americas, which mainly took place before 1914. There were only about 7000 Italian-born people in Australia in 1911. Italians started coming to Australia in somewhat larger numbers in the 1920s, mainly because entry to the USA was barred, but the Great Depression and Australian mistrust of foreigners soon reduced the flow to a trickle. In 1933 there were still only 27 000 Italians in Australia. The early history of Italian settlement in Australia has been well documented, both through the chronicles of writers of the time, and by modem scholars.

This book is not primarily about the history of Italian migration to Australia. It is above all a sociological study of the dynamics of social interaction and cultural change, and the ways these affect contemporary Australian society and its future perspectives. This means describing the living and working conditions of Italians in Australia; studying processes of community formation and institutional development; examining the participation of the immigrants in Australian social, economic and political structures; and looking at Italo-Australians' cultural expressions of their experience of the migratory process. All these aspects must be put in a more general context: we examine Australian society at the start of the postwar immigration program and its historical trajectory in the last half century; and ask how non-British immigration in general and Italian immigration in particular have affected that trajectory.

The dynamics of societal and cultural development cannot be understood exclusively at the national level, nor even just in terms of the bilateral relationship between Australia and Italy. International communicative networks arise through return migration and through maintenance of links with the area of origin. These developments are part of the process of globalisation, which is affecting all types of economic, political and cultural relationships. As Pacini pointed out in the Introduction to *Euroamericani* (1988:23), a world perspective rather than a Eurocentric one is essential if we are to understand the emerging international cultural relations. Eurocentrism—in the even more restricted guise of Anglocentrism—was the way most Australians saw the world until recently. Some still do: the reluctance to abandon allegiance to the British monarchy and to become an independent republic is symptomatic of this. British traditions, culture, economic links and political interests have been central to the definition of the nation. After 1941, the link with the USA was added—Australians saw themselves as part of an Anglo-Saxon family of nations. This post-colonial mentality has long isolated Australia from the new dynamism of the Asian–Pacific region.

At the beginning of the 1990s, the nation is at last beginning to wonder whether its future lies in the region, rather than in being a distant outpost of the continent whence most of its settlers came. Italian migration has been a movement of Europeans, to a country already colonised by another European nation. Has it served to reinforce the Eurocentric blinkers, or has it helped open an insular and conservative British culture to new influences? Has the Italian link reinforced European culture as a boundary marker against the cultures of Asia, or has it provided a flair for innovation, which will help Australia create a distinctive position as a post-European society in the Asian–Pacific region?

The structure of the book and the approaches it embodies are best introduced by briefly outlining the 15 chapters.

The first three chapters present the historical and sociological background, which is a precondition for understanding today's Italo–Australian community and its position in a changing society. Chapter 1, by Caroline Alcorso, starts with early white settlement and the destruction of Aboriginal society, and looks at economic growth and the development of class relations in the 19th century; at the emergence of a racist definition of national identity through the White Australia policy; and at Italian migration and reactions to it up to 1939. In Chapter 2, Claudio Alcorso and Caroline Alcorso examine the fate of Italians in Australia during World War II, when they became 'enemy aliens', to be treated as potential spies and saboteurs. The centrepiece of the chapter is Claudio Alcorso's personal account of internment, and of the racist attitudes among Australians which surfaced in this period.

Chapter 3, by Stephen Castles, describes the mass Italian migration which started at the beginning of the 1950s, showing how it arose from the aftermath of fascism and war, as well as the failure to develop the *Mezzogiorno* (the south of Italy). The main type of movement to Australia was a chain migration of people of rural background, mainly from the south. Most settled in major cities like Melbourne and Sydney, where they, like other southern Europeans, became the 'factory fodder' of Australia's postwar manufacturing expansion. Chapter 3 goes on to present statistical data on the current demographic and social situation of the Italo-Australian population. Finally, Italian migration and settlement is linked with Australian attitudes and policies towards immigration and ethnic diversity. Until the 1960s, assimilationist policies were designed to preserve Anglo-Australian cultural dominance. Assimilationism broke down because it did not present a viable strategy for responding to the economic and social segmentation and cultural differentiation arising from mass immigration. Since the 1970s, Australian governments have developed various forms of multiculturalism in order to manage social policy and cultural identity. Italo–Australian community formation has contributed to the emergence of multiculturalism, and has in turn been influenced by it.

Chapters 4 to 11 examine various aspects of Italian settlement and of Italo-Australian involvement in Australian society. Chapter 4 looks at how Italians have helped build Australia as construction workers, factory hands and farmers. Frank Panucci describes the hard and dangerous toil of Italian workers in the Snowy Mountains Hydro-Electric Scheme, and then presents some case studies of the situation of women factory workers. Bernadette Kelly shows how Italians used their farming skills and family solidarity to build successful agricultural enterprises where others had failed. The last section of the chapter presents a statistical picture of the contemporary labour market position of Italian migrants. Italian enterprise, both small and large, is the theme of Chapter 5. Jock Collins discusses its economic and social role, and shows how the move into small business was often a reaction to the discrimination and lack of opportunities for upward mobility encountered in factory work.

In Chapter 6, Robert Pascoe examines the different phases of Italian immigration, and shows how they have been integral parts of the overall migratory process. His emphasis is on the way Italians have formed communities, developed their neighbourhoods and constituted spaces and rituals. Chapter 7, by former Minister for Immigration, Al Grassby, presents an example of the reconstruction of informal social networks in the new country, and the way this is sometimes misunderstood by Anglo-Australians, due to lack of knowledge of other cultures. Chapter 8, by Caroline Alcorso, Cesare Giulio Popoli and Gaetano Rando, examines a variety of more formal social institutions of the Italian community: the Church, the media, welfare organisations and clubs. Together these three accounts give a graphic impression of complex processes of community formation. Chapter 9, by Castles, Rando and Vasta, examines the political and trade union participation of Italians in Australia, showing how they have on the whole become incorporated in mainstream organisations, rather than setting up autonomous structures.

In Chapter 10, Ellie Vasta analyses the experience of Italian women in the migratory process, showing their special situation and the way it is often ignored. Italian women have made major contributions in manufacturing industries as well as in agricultural work. Moreover, women have been the custodians of Italian culture, especially within the family—a role which has been crucial to the maintenance of a strong sense of Italian community identity. Chapter 11 deals with a question of great significance for the future of the Italo-Australian community: the educational, socio-economic and cultural situation of the second generation, and the extent to which it maintains a distinct identity. Here Vasta examines the social and historical links between Italian and Australian culture and identity, and the way these have been renewed and transformed by young Italo-Australians.

If Chapters 4 to 11 present a sociology of Italian settlement, Chapters 12 and 13 concentrate on the lived experience of migration and community formation, as embodied in language, personal accounts and artistic expression. Chapter 12, by Gaetano Rando, focuses on Italian as a language of education at school and university, and as a community language, with special consideration of the relationship between regional dialects and standard Italian. A section by Franko Leoni deals with the linguistics of the emerging new variety of Australian Italian. In Chapter 13, Rando shows how the migratory experience has been expressed in various artistic forms, often by people lacking the formal education normally seen as a precondition for literary endeavour.

Chapter 14 provides a cross-national perspective with Michael Morrissey's comparison of Italian settlement in Argentina and Australia. Despite some apparent similarities in the character of the migrations and of the receiving societies, the different situations during the periods of migration and the diverging dynamics of the receiving societies have led to quite different results.

Together with the three volumes of *Euroamericani,* our book is an element of the complex worldwide mosaic of the Italian diaspora. It is a mosaic as yet incomplete, since exhaustive accounts of Italian settlement in Canada, western European countries and elsewhere have yet to be written. Similarities and differences begin to emerge. Italian settlers have almost invariably at first encountered hardship, rejection and racism. Everywhere, hard work, struggle, family and community solidarity have led to success, and a respected place in society in the long run. On the other hand, the varying economic, social and political structures have led to substantial differences in settlement patterns in different countries. This in turn has helped shape the Italian impact on the wider society. For instance, as Pacini (1988: 109) points out, it was easier for Italians in Latin America to play a determining role, than in the USA. In the former they arrived as initial colonisers, in the latter they entered established social structures, dominated by people of British origin. Moreover, the Latin cultures of South America did not have the same negative stereotypes of Italians as did the white Anglo-Saxon Protestant culture of the USA. Clearly, the Australian case is similar to that of the USA.

In the concluding chapter, the four editors summarise the many facets of Italian community formation presented in the book. We explore the transformations in Italo-Australian and Anglo-Australian identities, as they emerged through lived cultures in Australian communities. This leads on to a discussion of the consequences for both Australia and Italy, and the links between them. Italian migration and community formation have been intertwined with dramatic changes in Australian society and its relations to the rest of the world. Italian migration to Australia took place at a time when the nation's previous identity as part of the British Empire was becoming untenable. By the time Italian communities were becoming established, Australia was enfranchising the Aboriginal people, dropping the White Australia policy and admitting Asian immigrants.

In the early 1990s, as the second generation of Italo-Australians are taking over from their ageing parents, the country is at last beginning to realise that its future lies in an opening to the Asian–Pacific region. This is not just a political and economic problem, but also a cultural one. Past contempt for anything non-European has erected barriers which hinder effective communication in trade, education and international relations. Australians now face the task of overcoming these barriers, changing entrenched attitudes and learning to understand other cultures. We argue that Italian settlement has contributed to an opening up of consciousness, a new willingness to learn from the rest of the world, and an acceptance of a wider and more diverse cultural universe. Paradoxically, the Italo-Australian presence has helped prepare Australia not only for a post-colonial but also for a post-European future.

The Editors
Wollongong, April 1991

Valle
d'Aosta
(Aosta)
(Turin)
Piedmont
Lombardy
(Milan)
Trentino-
Alto Adige
(Trento)
Veneto
Friuli-Venezia Giulia
(Trieste)
(Venice)
Emilia-Romagna
(Bologna)
(Genoa)
Liguria
(Florence)
Tuscany
(Ancona)
The Marches
(Perugia)
Umbria
(L'Aquila)
Abruzzi
Molise
(Rome)
Latium
(Campobasso)
Campania
(Naples)
(Bari)
(Potenza)
Apulia
Basilicata
Sardinia
(Cagliari)
Calabria
(Catanzaro)
(Palermo)
Sicily

1 Early Italian migration and the construction of European Australia 1788–1939

Caroline Alcorso

The Australian continent is one of the oldest sites of human habitation in the world. In 1788, the Aboriginal population is estimated to have been somewhere between 500 000 and one million people, who made up 600–700 clan-based political units, each with a different language or dialect (Australian InFo International, 1989: 1–5). Skilled at surviving in the marginal geographical and ecological conditions of Australia, Aborigines built a culture where many different groups were involved in a complex series of relationships with their environment and with each other.

Although there had been considerable contact between Australia and her near northern neighbours, as well as with European countries, in the preceding 1000 years, it was the British who established the first foreign settlement in Australia in 1788. The following century saw the British and British-Australian colonialists extend their hold over the rest of the Australian continent and several nearby islands.

This process involved a statement of ownership and sovereignty vis-à-vis two sets of other potential claimants. One set was the other imperial European powers who were interested in establishing South Pacific colonies: France in particular was actively investigating the possibility of colonising the south-east and the west of Australia in the early 19th century. The other, much more serious, threat to British sovereignty was the Aborigines. Although the British designated Australia *as 'Terra Nullius'* it was in fact thoroughly occupied, and the process of British settlement therefore involved a long struggle with the original inhabitants, who were not prepared to accept British claims to ownership.

The dispossession of the Aborigines

More than 20 000 Aborigines were killed in the ensuing guerilla wars over this supposedly unowned, empty land; wars that, despite the massive technological superiority of the British weaponry, at times threatened the viability of individual British settlements and colonial communities, and resulted in considerable loss of European lives (Reynolds, 1987: 1). The basic problem was not simply the intrusion of the British onto the Aborigines' land, but also the disastrous effect of their intrusion on the continent's fragile ecosystems and their ultimate refusal to share the land with the Aborigines.

As the pastoral frontier moved deeper into the hinterland, many Aborigines made the desperate decision to attempt to drive the invaders away completely. The result was a cycle of violent conflict, massive retaliation and eventually the crushing of black resistance. As the British invasion continued, starvation, destitution and being driven off the land were the most important factors that impelled Aborigines to approach white settlements from the mid-19th century. Once Aborigines moved into the urban fringes, new and powerful forces—in particular alcoholism and disease—limited their ability to leave, and they typically became semi-permanent fringe-dwellers.

The Aborigines who took this path—of reluctant accommodation to European culture—received few benefits from white society, while sacrificing much in terms of their previous way of life. The imported diseases of smallpox, measles, syphilis, influenza, tuberculosis, whooping cough and dysentery were more lethal to Aborigines in the long run than was white warfare. Deaths from the cumulative effects of disease, infant mortality and the sharp drop in birthrates that characterised the remaining miserable Aboriginal communities, meant that by 1878 the black population had fallen to only about 50 000 in total.

Today the Aboriginal population is around 227 000, most of whom are of mixed descent (Australian InFo International, 1989: 1). In addition to continuing conflict over Aboriginal rights to land ownership and self-determination, the late 20th century has been marked by an escalation of ideological struggle over the form and content of Australian history. What is the relevance of the history of contact between the Australian Aborigines and the British colonisers for Italians in Australia? First and foremost, the struggle between the colonisers and the Aborigines is important because it was a major determinant of the racism that has characterised European Australia ever since.

Clearly, the racism of the European settlers predated their arrival in Australia. Established ideas about the intellectual and cultural inferiority of the Aborigines had already been developed in the context of centuries of European trade, warfare and political domination of other non-European populations, especially in Africa. As Robert Miles has argued, by the 18th century, the 'African' had become the key 'other' in British racist discourse (Miles, 1989: 29). It was an 'other' signified above all by black skin colour and nakedness, two characteristics that early settlers immediately identified in the Aborigines.

However, the relationship between Europeans and Aborigines as it developed in the 19th and 20th centuries, and in particular the strength of Aboriginal resistance to both dispossession and assimilation, reproduced Australian racism and gave it a dynamic of its own. It can be argued that the European–Aboriginal encounter laid the foundations of a collective Australian tendency towards racism, what Bourdieu calls a *habitus* (Bourdieu, 1977). A key element of this racism is the obsession with 'whiteness' as a measure to define relations of inferiority and superiority between all ethnic and racial groups and, most importantly, to assess who can, and who cannot, be assimiliated into mainstream society (see Burgmann, 1978:25).

A second aspect of the British–Aboriginal interaction that is important to the history of Italo-Australians concerns the issue of labour power. It seems that overall, the use of Aboriginal men as stockmen and Aboriginal women as domestic labourers in 19th century Australia has been underestimated (Wright, 1982). Nevertheless, the fact remains that on the whole the British did not, or were unable to, incorporate Aborigines into the emerging industry and commerce of the towns in 19th-century Australia. Their exclusion from capitalist relations of production has continued to be a feature of Australian society. Instead, continuing immigration was required from the earliest days of settlement to sustain the working and petit-bourgeois classes (Miles, 1989: 91).

Immigration

Since 1788, the history of Australia has been the history of continuous immigration. In the early years of settlement, production in the colonies was dependent on the use of bonded convict labour from Britain. As Manning Clark wryly observed, 'once again the European discovered to his regret that to transplant a civilisation it was necessary to use a slave or semi-slave labour force to lay its foundations' (1986: 59). The convict settlers were predominantly British, though other Europeans also arrived as sailors or prisoners on those early ships.[1]

It was with the onset of free immigration in the 1830s that major ethnic differentiation started to occur within the European population of the Australian colonies. Among the first mass migration of over 200 000 British workers under assisted passage schemes were a large number of Irish Catholic immigrants, who added to the number of Irish convicts already in Australia, to form European Australia's first culturally distinct ethnic minority.[2]

As transportation was phased out (by 1853), chronic labour shortages and the militancy that this lent to the available workforce became major continuing problems for colonial employers. By the 1840s the demand for workers in the countryside was insatiable; as one settler wrote '[t]he fact is, we must have Labour in some Shape or other—Free Labour if we can get it—if not Prison Labour, and failing either, Coolie Labour' (quoted in Clark, 1986: 78).

Aware of the way North American colonialists had benefited from the importation of African labour, some squatters acted to introduce Indian and Melanesian labourers to the colonies. Ben Boyd, a prominent New South Wales pastoralist and whaler, first recruited shepherds from the Pacific islands in 1843 to break a strike, and other squatters followed his example although the schemes were mainly unsuccessful (Saunders, 1988: 721).

In the debate that followed Boyd's actions there was, for the first time, an organised working-class response to attempts by colonial capital to replace local workers with foreign labour, thereby reducing labour costs. Setting the tone for the years to come, this response took a racist form. The Aboriginal dimension of British-Australian racism noted above could be seen as having cross-class appeal; despite the other divisions between 19th-century convicts and labourers and the colonial gentry, it was in the interests of both to dispossess the Aborigines and smash their resistance. However, the second major component of Australian racism—the fear of cheap labour and the ideal of a 'White Australia'—emerged primarily as a working-class ideology, and until the 1960s was strongly associated with the radical Australian nationalist tradition (see McQueen, 1986). In the 19th century, plans to import immigrant workers were seen as a ploy of the traitorous upper classes who wanted to transpose the evils of Old World class oppression from Britain to Australia and thus preserve the gulf between rich and poor. The working class's identification of national pride with racism, chauvinism and xenophobia was encapsulated in the phrase which the radical newspaper the *Bulletin* took as its motto: 'Australia for the White Man' (McQueen, 1986: 37).

The exclusivist attitude of the working class and the comparative material advancement possible for workers in Australia were both strengthened by the events that took place after the discovery of gold.

The gold rush and Chinese labour

The first Australia gold rush took place in New South Wales in 1851. Subsequently, new, richer fields were discovered in Victoria and overnight the colonies became famous as a place where fortunes could be made. The gold rushes continued spasmodically for the rest of the 19th century and had a major impact on all aspects of colonial society. The 1850s became a decade of sudden mass immigration. Sixty thousand people on average migrated each year during the period, five times as many as during the preceding decade (Knott, 1988: 48). Among these were large numbers of assisted migrants from Britain, but also over 60 000 from Continental Europe. The first numerically significant group of migrants of Italian stock arrived at this time—2000 *ticinesi* fleeing agricultural depression and lured by gold. Australia's first Swiss-Italian community, complete with pasta factory, began to form near the goldfields at Daylesford in Victoria; other Lombard and Piedmontese emigrants also arrived in the late 1850s and 1860s, some later re-emigrating to California.

The timing of the gold rushes was fortuitous for European radicals; in addition to impoverished peasants and workers, the Australian gold attracted political activists and revolutionaries, displaced and disillusioned by the failure of the 1848 revolutions. The Urbino-born Raffaello Carboni has subsequently become one of Australia's best-known Italian migrants as a result of his role as participant and chronicler of the Eureka Stockade uprising of 1854 (Carboni, 1855).[3] Not untypically, he was a temporary migrant, leaving Australia to return to Europe in 1856.

Of particular importance to the social development of the colonies and the nature of Australian identity was the arrival of a new ethnic group to Australia during the gold rushes. Forty-two thousand Chinese emigrated to Australia in the 1850s, making them by far the largest non-European group in the colonies (Knott, 1988: 51). They were the first group of immigrants to be subject to widespread discrimination, both of a formal and informal nature. The Chinese were seen as unfair competitors on the goldfields, and as the gold became more scarce, were blamed for the miners' ill luck. White violence and hostility eventually forced the governments of Victoria, New South Wales and South Australia to restrict the entry of Chinese to the colonies and to make them the subject of special taxation. These measures were followed, in the period 1855–88, with further discriminatory legislation against Asians in all colonies, covering not only immigration but also various types of commercial activities and employment (Markus, 1988b: 930).

White Australia

Apart from the Chinese, the labour movement's other immediate target for exclusion was indentured Pacific Islander labourers. Their sporadic early use by the pastoral industry has been noted above. The major sustained importation of Pacific Islander labour, however, was in Queensland in the second half of the 19th century, where a plantation-style sugar industry had been developed. Over 60 000 imported male workers provided an exploitable labour force for the industry for 40 years before its structure altered and the large plantations were broken up (Saunders, 1988: 722). Organised labour in Queensland, led by the socialist William Lane, fought a bitter struggle against the use of so-called 'kanaka' labour, excluding Islanders from trade unions and virulently attacking their alleged racial and moral impurity (Hunt, 1978: 80–95). After fifteen years of campaigning, anti-'kanaka' candidates were elected in most electorates in the federal election of 1901 and a Labour victory on the issue was assured.

While the ideology of racial purity, and the desire to exclude 'coloureds' were most vehemently articulated by the trade unions and their political representatives, the Labor parties' racist views about non-Europeans were espoused by all sections of the society at the time. After Federation in 1901, the first Australian Prime Minister stated that he represented 'overwhelming public opinion' in immediately announcing measures to prevent the immigration of Asians and Pacific Islanders and to deport and/or discriminate against those already in the country (Hunt, 1978: 82). The *Immigration Restriction Act,* and other legislation, was warmly welcomed by virtually all commentators, the Melbourne *Argus* stating '[i]t is good for the world, good for the empire, good for ourselves that this dream should be realised. That a White Empire should grow up in these Southeast Asian seas, as a counterbalance to the great Asiatic empires of China and Japan with all their mysterious possibilities' (Crowley, 1973: 6).

It is clear that the policies known collectively as the White Australia policy were about more than safeguarding workers' rights, and indeed should not be seen simply as a defensive victory for organised labour. In addition, as the comments by the *Argus* make clear, they constituted a fundamental statement of national identity. Creating Australia as a 'white' society (it was assumed that the

Aborigine would die out) was identified as the basis for building a free, homogeneous, consensual and democratic community. Indeed, for some it was a precondition for the building of a nation. Alfred Deakin, the first Commonwealth Attorney-General, contrasted the new 'white' Australia with the strife-torn US:

> Cost what it may, we are compelled at the very earliest hour of our national existence . . . to make it positively clear that . . . these sacrifices for the future of Australia are nothing when compared with the compensating freedom, from the trials, sufferings and losses, that nearly wrecked the great republic of the west . . . The unity of Australia is nothing if it does not imply a united race. A united race means not only that its members can intermix and intermarry without degradation, but implies one inspired with the same ideas, of a people possessing the same cast of character, tone of thought—a people qualified to live under this constitution—the broadest and most liberal perhaps the world has yet seen reduced to writing—without abusing it, and to develop themselves under it to the full height and extent of their capacity (Crowley, 1973:16–17).

The idea of a 'White Australia' was thus at the core of Australian nationalism in the period from 1860 to World War II and it gave this nationalism its characteristically contradictory nature: on the one hand, radical and liberating, on the other hand, bigoted and racist. The employers' attempts to introduce cheap labour into the colonies were seen as actions which frustrated democracy (McQueen, 1986: 268). As McQueen has commented, '[w]hat needs to be understood is that "racial purity" was the pivot of an ideal which embraced an enlightened and self-reliant community' (1986: 270).

The White Australia policy remained in place between 1901 and the late 1960s. While its main stated aim was to prevent Asians from emigrating to Australia, the philosophy of White Australia had implications for all non-British immigrants, including Italians. Because it encompassed a set of beliefs about what Australia was and therefore about who Australians should be, it could also be used as a measure of the ability of any people to become 'Australian'. At specific historic moments, when certain powerful interests were served by marginalising a particular section of the population, the loose racist assumptions of the White Australia policy provided handy ideological categories with which relations of inequality between people could be justified.

Italian settlement and racism

How, then, were 19th-century Italian immigrants to Australia regarded, and what were their experiences? Were they considered 'white' as opposed to the 'black' Asians and Aborigines, or as the feared 'other', non-British, foreign labour? In fact the nature of relations between British–Australians and Italian immigrants varied regionally and temporally. To answer these questions we need to examine briefly the nature of Italian settlement in the period. I will argue that the class background of Australia's Italian migrants and the way that they were incorporated into the Australian class structure made them at times the target of such racism. Yet they had an ambiguous 'cultural location', particularly in the 19th century, for Italians were also seen as representatives of a country which symbolised antiquity and the traditions of a glorious civilisation.

As noted above, travellers and adventurers from the principalities and duchies that (after 1870) made up modern Italy began arriving in the Australian colonies with other Europeans from the late 18th century. As well as the early sailors and convicts, the 1840s saw the arrival of political refugees and professionals, such as the pharmacist and inventor, Giuseppe Bosisto, together with other free settlers from Europe (Cecilia, 1992). In addition, Italian Catholics were present among the religious orders who established missions in the first 50 years of European settlement in the hope of proselytising the Aborigines and educating their children. Indeed, some of the Italian pioneer priests and nuns had relatively progressive notions about the rights of Aborigines as well as an anthropological interest in those whom they proselytised. In 1846 Father Angelo Confalonieri built a mission in the extreme north of the continent (Port Essington, later Darwin) with the help of the local Aborigines. He not only spoke certain Aboriginal languages and prepared translations of several sacramental documents, including the New Testament, but also mapped the Coburg Peninsula and classified the seven Aboriginal peoples living there (Cecilia, 1992). However, the total number of these early sojourners was small, they were dispersed across the continent and many eventually returned to Europe.

It was only from the 1850s on that there were sizeable settlements of Italian migrants in Australia. It should be noted, however, that the total number of Italian immigrants to Australia before World War II was always fairly small; in 1868, for example, when the Victorian population was around 600 000, the Italian consul Biagi estimated that there were some 1600 Italians living there (Cresciani, 1986a). According to the first national census in 1901, the population of Australia was 3 773 801; of these, approximately 7000 (or less than 0.2 per cent) were estimated to be of Italian origin (Cresciani, 1985a). Alternatively, we may note of the first major wave of emigration from Italy between the last quarter of the 19th century and World War I, that departures for Australia amounted to

This photograph from the late 1800s shows Antonio and Angelina Pezzutti displaying their grape harvest and an earlier vintage of their wine. Their son, Marco, on the right, was the first child born in New Italy. (*Richmond River Historical Society*)

only 0.13 per cent of the 14 million Italians who left their native land (Cresciani, 1986b: 4).

As economic opportunities opened up in the colonies, chain migration (the process whereby whole families and even villages followed an original pioneer to a certain area in Australia) became the dominant form of migration. Because the community was the main source of assistance and support for new arrivals, Italian migrants became concentrated in certain areas. As well as the *ticinesi* settlements in Victoria described above, a large settlement of northern Italians (mainly *veneti* and *furlani*) developed in the 1880s near Woodburn, in northern New South Wales. These were the survivors of the failed New Guinean colonising expedition of the Marquis de Ray, and their rural settlement, New Italy, survived until the 1950s. In the late 19th century, *siciliani* and *pugliesi* seafarers and fishermen began to arrive in the southern tip of Western Australia, building up strong communities based on regional and family ties, with the result that by 1905 a local commentator noted that they had 'monopolised the fishing industry of Fremantle' (Zunini, quoted in Cecilia, 1992). Similarly, but this time as a result of conscious industry and government policy, 335 *lom-*

bardi and *piemontesi* immigrants arrived in North Queensland in 1891 to work on the cane fields. By the late 1930s, one-third of all Australia's Italian migrants lived on the Queensland cane fields and 40 per cent of Queensland's 'Granite Belt' market gardeners were Italian (Randazzo, 1987: 198; Papalia, n.d.: 9). This type of regional and occupational concentration allowed them to be seen as competitors for jobs and resources by other workers and small farmers.

In addition, factors relating to their pre-migration circumstances as well as to their time of arrival meant that Italians were sometimes found in areas where resources were scarce, labour organisation strong and economic competition fierce. Italian migrants, like other Australian workers, exhibited high rates of geographical mobility and frequently moved to states or regions where labour was scarce and wages consequently high (Pascoe, 1987: 112). One example is in the mining industry, where relatively large numbers of Italians settling in the Kalgoorlie goldfields became conspicuous targets of attack during the impoverished depression years. Another example is the sugar industry, where Italians began to appear just as the labour movement had successfully expelled the previous 'foreign' labourers, and consequently immediately perceived Italians as a threat. This perception received support when the Colonial Sugar Refining Company, which had been instrumental in facilitating the introduction of Italians into Queensland in the first place, then sought to use them as strike-breakers during the prolonged 1911 sugar workers' strike (Saunders; 1988: 98–9).

Some commentators have identified features of pre–World War II Italian internal community relations as part of the explanation for their becoming objects of suspicion for Anglo-Australian workers. Indentured migration, for example, which operated at times from southern Italy, was resented by other workers in the mining and sugar industries because it resulted in the newcomers working for under-award wages and conditions (Pascoe, 1987: 110). While the two Royal Commissions into this practice found little conclusive evidence for it or for its contribution towards eroding union standards, it seems that patron–client bonded migration (both formal and informal) did take place and provoked opposition from Australian-born workers.

More significantly, however, it appears that patterns of communal co-operation, usually built on the basis of kin or village ties, led the endeavours of Italian migrants to flourish in the mining, horticultural and agricultural industries. The economic success and rapid consolidation of farm ownership among Italian *paesani* using the 'gang system' in the sugar industry is one example (Pascoe, 1987: 116). Another is mining in Western Australia, of which Pascoe comments '[t]he Italians were not materially more successful than the rest, but were certainly conspicuous on the goldfields for their high level of cooperation' (Pascoe, 1987: 173, 132–3). The 'New Italy' episode mentioned above, which resulted in a prosperous agricultural settlement on land the English colonialists had rejected as infertile, is a poignant example of the power of co-operative work, in the context of the 'innate frugality and tenacity' of the Venetian peasant farmers (quoted in Randazzo, 1987: 44).

Indeed, the argument about Italians' cultural propensity to co-operate is frequently linked to (and sometimes confused with) the observation that migrants often displayed an acceptance of higher rates of exploitation, or self-exploitation, than did local workers, thus making them more desirable workers from the point of view of employers and/or more successful small farmers in their own right. This characteristic derived from the high aspirations and economic vulnerability of the migrant, but was facilitated by cultural factors such as the strength of patriarchal structures and the consequent way in which the family unit could be utilised in production. While the argument has been made in relation to 19th-century labourers and farmers, we shall see in Chapter 5 that these factors have been crucial to the success of Italian small business in the 20th century.

As noted above, Australia's history as an outpost of the British Empire established on Aboriginal land was the basis for the emergence of a strongly racist *habitus*, or collective consciousness, amongst its citizens. This consciousness became incorporated into the radical nationalist ideology of the labour movement as a strong, organised working class sought to defend its position against the possible importation of cheaper labour from less economically advanced countries. Thus, any distinct group of migrant workers in Australia has been historically viewed with suspicion. At the same time, the specific geographical, historical and cultural aspects of Italian settlement in Australia discussed above have contributed to Italian migrants being seen as economic competitors, or threats, to Anglo-Australian and locally born workers and have therefore led them to be recurring targets of racist attack through the 19th and early 20th centuries.

In addition, phenotypical attributes of Italians have been readily seized on as both a reason for and justification of their inferior status. Their 'darkness' has been identified and understood in terms of the dominant racist beliefs. Echoing the north–south prejudices of the Italians themselves (see, for example, Barzini, 1964: 234–51), Australian characterisations of Italians have sometimes focused on this division. In early 20th-century Queensland, which was, as we have seen, a crucible of Australian racism, public commentators laboured to distinguish northern Italians from their allegedly 'darker' southern Italian brothers and sisters. The popular journal *Smith's Weekly* actually constructed two species of Italian that appeared throughout its editions: 'White Italians' and 'Black Italians' (Henderson, 1978: 338). Moreover, the report of the 1925 Ferry Royal Commission elaborated and legitimated this distinction, finding that:

> [t]he northern Italian is a very desirable class of immigrant. He [sic] is thrifty and industrious, law-abiding and honest . . . and is much superior to the southern Italians and the Mediterranean races generally . . . It is certain that the growing animosity against all foreigners is, in particular, due to the different and inferior types arriving (cited in Henderson, 1978: 337).

Italian culture

Another prevalent ideology coloured the way British-background Australians viewed Italians in the years up to World War I, placing Italians in what was described above as an ambiguous 'cultural location'. This second ideology reflected the central position of the Italian city-states in the flowering of the Renaissance in Europe, and more generally the role of successive societies of the Italian peninsula in the formation of Western civilisation. For the British bourgeoisie and aristocracy, the 19th century was a period of rediscovery and adoration of the Classical and Renaissance heritage of Europe. Like Greece, the Italian peninsula was a place of ancient ruins, museums and refinement; a place to which to make pilgrimages (Pascoe, 1987: 78).

Similarly, reverence for Italy and symbols of Italian culture was reflected in the attitudes of middle- and upper-class Australians in the 19th century and in their predilection for purchasing Italian goods and mimicking Italian cultural styles. Along with French and German, the Italian language was learned by the educated classes, and Australian graziers and merchants furnished their new colonial country mansions with Italian or Italianate statues, marble and furniture.

Gold wealth and the related population increase provided a major impetus to capital accumulation in Australia, and in the 1850s and 1860s considerable urban and rural development took place. The expanding economy not only created further labour scarcity, but also produced the wealth that made the practices described above possible. It created a large rich elite who desired the services of skilled crafts and tradespeople, and as Pascoe comments, '[the) set of [British] expectations put certain occupations of professional migrants at a great advantage in colonial Australia!' (1987: 78).

As we have seen, in the first half of the 19th century, Italians were spread geographically across the colonies and also across a range of occupations. While many early Italian arrivals were hapless peasants and unemployed proletarians, at the same time, some distinguished intellectuals, scientists, craftspeople, artists and tradespeople settled in Australia and were seen as the epitome of the sophisticated cultured Italian. Perhaps the best-known of these is the Tuscan political émigré, Count Girolamo Carandini, who with his London-born wife, singer Maria Burgess, successfully implanted Italian opera as a popular form of entertainment in the Australian colonies in the 1840s and 1850s. The success of the Carrara Marble Stores, founded by Alessandro Martelli and Luigi Veroli in Melbourne in 1865, is an example of Italians bearing valued bourgeois commodities to the colonies, and in the process underlining their own association with the high culture of Europe. The Stores imported marble artefacts and distributed them across Australia, and the local newspaper, the *Age*, noted that the marble 'instead of being the inferior sort which was usually imported to the colonies, was such as would be sent to London or Paris' (Cresciani, 1986a: 3). Pascoe notes that three successful engineers who emigrated to or sojourned in Melbourne in the 1870s quickly became 'household names' (1987: 84).

Thus, because of the skill shortages and because things Italian were 'fashionable', these early middle-class 'Italians' in the colonies were able to have an important cultural impact, out of proportion to their numbers, and directly linked to their image as transmitters of European 'high' culture.

As more Italian peasants migrated to Australia, becoming incorporated into the lowest ranks of the working class, the gap between the Italy of the bourgeois imagination and actual Italians in Australia became more obvious. The writings of the Italian Socialist, Francesco Sceusa, in a centenary pamphlet where he seeks to prove that Italians are of equal status to the British *vis-à-vis* other 'uncivilised' races, bear testimony to this reality. Sceusa is concerned to oppose those who are deriding Italians as the 'Chinese of Europe' (1888: 15). On the contrary, he argues, Italy is the 'Mother' of all civilisation and learning, the mother indeed of the British, 'who has breathed into [their] nostrils the breath of intellectual life' (1888: 21). For Sceusa, unfair denigration of Italians by British-Australians is linked to the recent arrival of working-class Italian migrants in Australia; to the 'organ-grinders and fruit hawkers', the 'lazy sturdy beggars' who are 'no longer fed in Italy' but who in Australia 'swarm' (1888:18).

The major changes seemed to occur during the 1890s, when gold and sugar cane brought Italian peasant migration to Western Australia and Queensland respectively, and economic depression reduced the market for professional services and luxury goods. One such poor worker from Umbria, who followed his father to Australia in the first years of the 20th century, witnessed how the shifting images of Italian migrants were reflected in the attitude of the manager of a Western Australian sawmill where he worked:

> Mr Smith couldn't understand why we [migrants] didn't even read the newspaper . . . Before he met us Italian workers, he'd thought all Italians were artists, tenors and renaissance men . . . When he came in contact with us illiterates, he couldn't imagine how paradise could be populated by such donkeys (Strano, 1986: 51).

As peasant and proletarian migration continued to grow during the 20th century, however, Sceusa's appeal that Italians should be seen as representatives of 'the founders of Europe and her colonies' (1888: 22) fell increasingly on barren ground. In the 1920s, the sudden imposition of quotas on Italian entry to the USA led to considerably augmented Italian migration to Australia, resulting in over 36 000 immigrants in the decade (Cecilia, 1992). Most were, as in the earlier years of the decade, agricultural workers, miners, labourers, fisherpeople and tradespeople. The majority were men who arrived alone, either as single men or married with wives and children who joined them later.

With the exception of some doctors, few professionals emigrated, deterred by the non-recognition of their qualifications in Australia (Cecilia, 1992). Racism and marginalisation became the common experiences of these mainly male Italian workers, especially in times of economic downturn when they and other non-Europeans became convenient scapegoats. In the Western Australian goldfields such racism flared into anti-Italian riots in the goldfields centre, Kalgoorlie, in 1919 and 1934, when Italian families were driven from their homes and their property looted and burned. Oral historical research conducted recently in this area (see Gabbrielli, pers. comm.) reveals here too the ambiguities of the Italian position. While the Italians, like the other European settlers in Australia, sexually exploited Aboriginal women, who were of course in an even more vulnerable and powerless situation than non Anglo-Australians, interviews with surviving Aborigines suggest that in at least some cases the liaisons between Aboriginal women and Italian men were positive ones, resulting in permanent relationships and paternal responsibility for their mixed-descent children.

Among those Italians who migrated in the 1920s were many single men who could not eke out a living with their family in Italy. Below is an account of the experiences of some young Italian migrants of the time.[4]

Luigi Grollo arrived from Treviso in 1928 at the age of eighteen. As a boy in Italy, he had started to do all the work of a *contadino*

This 1930 photo shows a group of Italian workers during the construction of a bridge at Ballan in Victoria, (*Centro Italiano Rinnovamento Cattolica, Victoria*)

(peasant), but there was little relief from the poverty of the time; it was 'mainly . . . a sad life, consisting only of work, work and work. And for little result' (Grollo, quoted in Pascoe, 1988: 40). After arrival in Melbourne, Grollo began working as a cook for a camp of men, then irrigated trees for a farmer, dug canals with pick and shovel, broke stones in a quarry, and worked on a sewerage system in Melbourne. From 1928 to 1940, Grollo lived in a tent:

> . . . twelve years under canvas; twelve years spent in all sorts of places, always looking for work which, when the Depression arrived, became even more rare . . . I had no confidence as far as the Australians were concerned, and so I spent twelve years of life as a 'slave', without understanding what this life really was. I met only men: if you were not speaking English the women did not even say a word to you (Pascoe, 1988: 76, 92).

In 1940, Grollo moved to Melbourne and began to work as a *'cementista'* and in 1941 married Emma Girardi. During his spare time from paid work, Grollo set up his concrete business in 1948 and Emma kept the books of the business in its early days. In 1952 he was able to devote himself entirely to his own business, which later grew to a multimillion dollar concern when in 1969 his two sons '. . . transformed the company into something grander in scale' (Pascoe, 1988: 122). (The story of this transformation by the second generation is contained in Chapter 5.)

Orazio Vasta and Salvatore Torrisi, both aged sixteen, arrived from Sicily in the 1920s to work in the sugar cane plantations of northern Queensland. These young boys, who had lied about their age on their application forms to emigrate, had been nominated by relatives and on arrival began the back-breaking job of cane-cutting with the technology of the day, the cane knife. Although they occasionally shifted to other jobs such as clearing thick bushland in areas such as Tully in north Queensland and droving, they cut cane for the best part of 30 years before they moved to Sydney.

The stories of their lives are full of the complexities and contradictions of migrant men of that time. They started work in the cane fields at 3 a.m. to beat the semi-tropical heat of the day, wearing work clothes which, although washed in boiling water, were so stiff from molasses they stood up on their own. They had problems learning the English language and, for the most part, felt a strong sense of belonging to the Italian community. The racism of the Anglo-Australian community drove the Italians to stick together and this contributed to their sense of Italian identity. But they also noted Anglo-Australian racism towards Aborigines, who were treated 'worse than dogs', and who were prohibited from drinking in the pubs. As a result, Italian men would go out to drink with Aborigines on the verandas of the pubs. They spoke of the kindness towards them by Anglo-Australian neighbours and of the jealousy of Anglo-Australians towards Italians who worked hard and long to buy their

The cane-fields of northern Queensland employed many Italian workers. This group of cane-cutters at Ingham was photographed during a tea-break in the fields in 1929. (*Centro Italiano Rinnovamento Cattolico, Victoria*)

own farms. Many early migrants remained 'Italian' through and through. Even after they had lived in Australia for 50 years, these two men spoke and understood only enough English to get by and they socialised only with the Italian community. They resisted assimilation and continued many of their own symbolic and cultural traditions (for example, meetings with *'compaesani'—'il parlamento a la piazza'*). They also passed on to their children their Sicilian dialect and they provided them with a good education; and, like many of that generation, they never returned to Italy, not even for a visit.

As this chapter has shown, Italian migration to Australia before World War II was small in volume. Yet it was sufficient to lay down the foundations of the Italo-Australian communities that were later to emerge. Moreover, these early migrations helped shape Anglo-Australian attitudes—in all their ambivalence—to the postwar Italian influx. The rest of this book examines in more detail the various faces of Italian settlement in Australia in the 20th century, enlarging on the diverse and sometimes contradictory themes that have been touched on in this chapter.

2 Italians in Australia during World War II

Claudio Alcorso and Caroline Alcorso

In the years leading up to World War II, sections of both the conservative and Labor parties viewed fascism as a positive political force with the potential to defend the established order against the communist menace. However, Australia saw itself as part of the British Empire, and had no independent foreign policy. So when Britain declared war on Germany, the Australian government automatically followed suit. Throughout the war years, Australian government policy was to assist the 'mother country' as best she could by providing troops, foodstuffs, and supplies to Britain. Several direct confrontations between Australian and Italian troops took place in the Middle East. Australian Sixth Division troops defeated a much larger contingent of the Italian army at Bardia, and inflicted heavy losses on the Italians in the defence of Tobruk (Fitzgerald, 1981: 4). Clearly, these events had significant repercussions for Italians in Australia.

The war led to a dramatic increase in state surveillance and regulation of the lives of ordinary Italian migrants. All Italians (along with Germans, Japanese and nationals of other Axis-linked countries) were officially classified 'enemy aliens', which meant the denial of ordinary civil rights. Anyone of Italian origin was considered potentially dangerous. In some places, 'enemy aliens' had to report weekly to the police. They were forbidden to lease or buy land, to obtain bank loans or to travel. All torches, radios, cameras, trucks and tractors in their possession were confiscated.

All Italian males in Australia were scrutinised and categorised by the security service (Cresciani, 1980: 172) and detention was deemed necessary for those considered by Military Intelligence to be in the highest-risk categories. This meant imprisonment in one of the specially designed military camps around the country or conscription into the 'Civil Aliens' Corps', a national labour force. The numbers of people interned varied considerably from state to state, and depended on the state's strategic position as well as the political climate, and the role of the Catholic Church. For example, in Victoria the pro-Italian and pro-fascist Archbishop Mannix was able to intervene on behalf of many Italians to prevent their internment. Just over 10 per cent of Australia's Italian population (4727 people) experienced internment during the course of the war (Cresciani, 1988a: 611). In total, 7711 'enemy aliens' of all nationalities were interned (Fitzgerald, 1981: 5).

The following section is Claudio Alcorso's personal history of internment. It gives an insight into the day-to-day running of the camps and the attitudes of the security and armed forces towards Italians.

Internment: a personal account

'The thought that I might be interned in the event of war between the Allies and fascist Italy never entered my mind. I had left Italy because I found life under a fascist regime intolerable and I wished, together with my parents and brother, to establish a new life abroad. I had made my beliefs clear from the moment I arrived in Australia at the end of 1938. I agreed with the often repeated assertion by democratic leaders that the war against fascism transcended nationalities and that anyone who believed that Hitler's victory would be a tragic backward step for the whole of humanity had the duty to offer his or her services to the common cause. When war broke out with Germany, I volunteered to join the Australian Airforce. I was told that for my application to be accepted "it would be necessary to have the support of several citizens whose integrity could not be impugned . . ." I followed up with a letter to the minister for Airforce giving the names of several citizens ready to vouch for me. His reply gave me hope that the fact that I was not a British subject could be overcome.

'On 4 July two policemen arrested my brother and me and took us to our flat to pack a few clothes. They confiscated two empty suitcases covered with the labels of French and Swiss hotels as well as a number of books. One of them asked "Why do you have so many books?" I did not know what to answer. The books were mostly books of poetry, history, classics and novels, but there were also a few official books portraying the regime in a favourable light. The two suitcases and the few "incriminating" books were put on show in a "fifth column" exhibition staged in Sydney a few months later. It was a stage exercise in war propaganda, difficult to understand then or now. The concept of "fifth column" had been recently invoked in Australia in a speech delivered in July 1940 by the then Premier of New South Wales, Alex Mair, who advocated the internment of all Italians. His view was that ". . . it was the aliens against whom no suspicions or proof could be gathered who were dangerous. The true components of a fifth column operate in the dark; they are the most serious danger" (quoted in Cresciani, 1985a: 53).

'After being arrested my brother and I were taken to the venereal diseases section of Long Bay gaol, which had been emptied of its inmates and was being used as a transit depot for internees. I could not believe it; I could not accept it. The grim environment compounded the shock. I had seen this type of gaol in American movies but they were pictures and they related to criminals; this was real and it related to me. It was a grim, repugnant, unknown world. My individuality did not count. I can still feel the sting of the slap on my hand from one of the guards as we queued up for the evening meal. I knew that I would not eat the revolting-looking stew being dished out from a table at the right of the queue, so I raised my hand to take a slice of bread from the table on the left side. I was out of turn; bread could be taken after we had passed the stew, not before. The slap on my raised hand told me firmly what my new status was.

'After a week or so, we were transferred to the Royal Showground at Orange. It was temporary, makeshift accommodation, but an enormous improvement on Long Bay. The people who had been interned before us were already there, housed in corrugated iron huts with stretchers along the walls. We ate in one of the Agricultural Halls equipped with a kitchen. There were showers but no hot water. Orange is cold in July and the water was icy. I came out frozen after my first shower but soon warmed up kicking the ball around an improvised soccer field, the first of many to follow. Visits were allowed on Sunday mornings and took place on the steps of the showground's grandstand. Wives and children came by train from Sydney bringing parcels of especially cooked food and warm clothes. It was a time for embraces, and after the first flow of information had dried up, for silences and a few tears.

'After a couple of months we were transferred to Hay, in western New South Wales, where a permanent camp had been built. We travelled during the night. As light appeared I looked outside the train's window to see a perfectly flat, almost treeless plain. I had never seen such a landscape. It looked eerie, immense, hostile. The camp was completely bare; whatever grass or shrubs might have been present were destroyed during construction—only pale beige clay, light timber huts, a grey barbed-wire ring and a blue sky. It was, however, adequate and functional and I imagine it was built on the same blueprint as army camps, except for the double row of barbed wire and the sentry towers surrounding it.

'Our beds had to be made by 10 a.m., when roll-call and hut inspection took place. We swept and cleaned our own huts on a roster basis. Nothing else was required of us, but one could seek employment, for a shilling a day, in special duties squads doing cooking, sanitation work, common room cleaning, firewood splitting or first aid. Work outside the camp was later available for the same rate of pay.

'The camp was located close to the gorge where the Murrumbidgee flowed and where occasionally we could go in groups for a swim. Thanks to the good water supply, the spaces between the huts were soon covered in small, beautifully kept vegetable gardens. A rivalry developed as to who would grow the best, biggest vegetables. Strangely enough the man who produced the champion cauliflowers, carrots, lettuces and cabbages was not one of the many peasants who had been engaged in farming before internment. It was Phil Bossone, a big strong man, a metal worker, and a devoted anti-fascist who was later released through the representations of his trade union. His simple secret for growing the best vegetables was abundant fertilisation. He got up during the night to collect the human manure, solid and liquid, which accumulated prior to the arrival of the early morning sanitation squad! In addition to growing vegetables, many started to use the firewood which was supplied to the kitchens in large chunks to carve practical objects (bowls, spoons, boxes) and sculptured forms.

'The more I got to know my fellow prisoners, the less I could understand the policy of internment. Apart from a handful of declared fascists, plus a few wool-buyers temporarily in Australia, all the interned Italians had migrated to Australia to improve their status in life and had no intention of ever returning to Italy. They were good workers and willing to work. Some of them were skilled and Australia was short of manpower; it did not make sense. I had not understood the various forces which had shaped the history of my new country. I had not been aware of the colonial conditioning against all non-British people or of the special conditioning against Asians—the so-called "yellow peril". I had vaguely heard about the "White Australia" policy and of the dictation test used by immigration authorities to stop unwanted immigrants; but I had not realised that racist attitudes were strong in all sections of the community and prevalent in the army and in returned soldiers' organisations.

'Eventually I realised that there was no single Australian policy on internment; it had been left to the states and each state had acted differently. Victoria had taken a realistic view. Labour was needed and the Italians had been law-abiding, quiet citizens. Victoria interned only a handful of avowed fascists. Queensland seemed to have interned a random sprinkling from the numerous Italian communities in the north, but New South Wales was by far the most chauvinist state. The New South Wales police commissioner, W. J. Mackay, and the Premier, Alex Mair, were obsessed with the idea of sabotage by foreigners who would link up with the enemy in case of invasion. People of Italian descent born in Australia and naturalised Australian citizens were still foreigners in the eyes of Mr Mackay.

'However, notwithstanding all the anti-Italian propaganda, Australia still had a human heart, and the federal government established the Aliens' Appeals Tribunals to consider the cases of people who claimed to be unjustly interned. Naturally, Orlando (my brother) and I promptly lodged an application to be heard by the Tribunal. Early in February 1941 we were transferred to Sydney for the hearing, back to Long Bay gaol; but this time I did not mind! Legal counsel was allowed and on the advice of our Australian friends we retained Clarrie Martin, the Attorney-General in the new state Labor government. When he was approached, Mr Martin stated that he would take up our case providing he could first satisfy himself that we were anti-fascists as we claimed to be. So we had a dress rehearsal with him and answered all questions to his satisfaction. His concluding address to the court, which I read in the transcript of the hearing, 45 years later, was excellent. Our case started on 5 February and concluded on the 24th. On the 4th I had been transferred to the cell at Darlinghurst police station as the court wanted to ensure that there would be no communication between me and my brother Orlando during the course of the hearing.

'Many witnesses were called to give evidence before the judge; others volunteered to testify, although this was unknown to me at the time. The transcript of the case covers more than 300 pages plus a large amount of evidence made up of letters and other documents. All are now located in Canberra, in the National Australian Archives, Police Intelligence Section. Forty-five years later, and after overcoming considerable opposition from the intelligence service, I finally convinced the bureaucracy to let me see my files. I read my friends' testimonies with emotion and gratitude. They had believed in me. Not one of the friends I had made in my new country spoke against me or even abstained, notwithstanding the war propaganda and the so-called fifth column exhibition. My assertion that the war transcended national boundaries was not after all a poetic illusion.

'Although Army Intelligence clung to the books and the suitcases, the barrister for the Crown prosecution understood that they had no relevance, and thus resorted to rubbishing all assertions that we were ideologically opposed to fascism, or indeed that there might be, in this war, an ideological content. In the words of the barrister "[the war] is not a war of ideologies, or of the economics or the philosophy of fascism. It is a war against a country . . . and the country, Italy, is fighting the British Empire". His case was simply that we were enemy aliens and that was enough to keep us interned.

'However, the Tribunal was unconvinced and wrote a fourteen-page summary of the trial, dated 3 March 1941 and ending with the sentence: "for the above reasons we are all of the opinion that the objectors should be released from internment".

'We returned to Hay full of hope. Again, I had misjudged the mentality of Army Intelligence. I had believed that a favourable recommendation from the Tribunal would mean release from internment and a change in my status which would permit me to enlist and do my share in the war. But I had been put on show as a fifth columnist. The rabidly anti-foreign and scurrilous newspaper *Smith's Weekly* had written an article on the show adding its usual insults on the 'dangerous Wog'. How would Intelligence look if the man portrayed as a wily enemy was released because he turned out to be in fact an ally? I would have to endure another two-and-a-half years of unjust and unjustifiable imprisonment.

'After the objections of Intelligence had been considered by the Minister, the Tribunal was invited to reply. It refuted the Army's objections to our release one by one. The Secretary for the Army then followed with a minute paper for the Minister in which he admitted "I do not believe that the Alcorsos are agents . . . I should very much like to know how they have behaved themselves in their internment camp. It would be interesting to see how strong their democracy really is and whether it is real enough to make them avoid the Nazi and fascist element in the camp. Perhaps you would call for an urgent report".

'The report of the camp commander duly arrived, stating that "[t]he behaviour of the above internees was exemplary", that our camp associates appeared to be internees favourably known to the camp commander. It concluded "[w]hat is upsetting to me is that there are any number of Italians interned on much slighter grounds than those which exist in this case. On the whole it would perhaps be playing safe to keep them interned." So because they had committed injustices by interning perfectly innocent, diligent Italian settlers, we, who were also innocent (but potentially more dangerous because "intellectuals"?), had to stay in.

'A few months later we were transferred from Hay to Loveday Camp in South Australia, a much larger establishment with four compounds, each holding approximately 2000 people, around a circular block where the hospital was located. Two compounds were occupied by Italians and by various other groups which I shall mention later. The other two were empty when we arrived but later became occupied by Japanese prisoners of war.

'As at Hay, at Loveday volunteers were called for to perform different duties—orderlies at the hospital, splitting firewood, garbage collection etc. The fascist leaders had accepted the fact that certain work inside the camp was necessary for the comfort of the internees, but they disapproved of going to work outside the camp, which they said meant co-operating with the authorities. Therefore the volunteers for outside duties were either openly or tacitly anti-fascists.

'The various non-Italian groups in our camp were a mixed bunch. The military sent to the Italian camp all groups and individuals that they did not know what to do with. They found that the Italians would be more tolerant and easy-going than the Germans and so all oddments finished up with us. We got the Vienna choir boys, who had been caught by the war as they were touring Australia. They also sent us a few merchant seamen, mostly Danish, Norwegian and Swedish—taciturn, good people who spoke in simple sentences of their experiences when their ships had been torpedoed and many of their mates had drowned.

'We got the "Australia First" boys, a mixed group, some old, some young. Their movement claimed to put Australia first, which meant before England. In fact, they were Nazi supporters. I was intrigued and struck up an acquaintance with one of them, a pleasant young man of Irish descent. I vividly remember walking around the perimeter of the camp with him, questioning him about his reasons for supporting the Nazis; his answers were vague. He really knew little about Germany, but said: "Claudio, you will never understand what the English have done to us!" So it did not matter that he and his father before him were born in Australia: the memory of what England had done to the Ireland of his forefathers was never to be forgotten or forgiven. The Irish priests who visited the camp also perturbed us by seeking out the fascists and gloating with them over English defeats.

'Towards the middle of 1941, an Official Visitor to the camp was appointed in accordance with the Geneva Convention. In his report of 25 November 1941, he wrote " [i]n my report I called attention to the presence in the camp of several men who claimed to be anti-fascists, and who went in actual danger of violence" (Australian Archives CRS Accession A1533, Item 54/3092: 1). He concluded "[i]n any case it seems somewhat unwise to leave them amongst fascists where they are exposed to ill-treatment, and remain a constant provocation to the untidy elements in the camp''.

'The warnings of the Official Visitor were ignored and as the tide of war turned against the aggressors, the fascists inside our camp became more bitter and vindictive. The anti-fascists in the camp could not help smiling or showing pleasure as they read the newspapers reporting Allied victories on all fronts. The defence of Stalingrad seemed a turning point. It is true that we, the anti-fascists, showed pleasure, walked erect, with confident strides, smiled to each other; but on the whole we were far more subdued by comparison with the bravado and the shouts of the fascists at the beginning of the war, when they thought they had won.

'On 16 November 1942 a committed anti-fascist, Francesco Fantin, was murdered in our camp at Loveday. He was struck a blow on the back of his head when he went to a water tap for a drink. He was unconscious by the time they carried him to the camp hospital. As I was serving as an orderly at the time I saw him being brought in. The story of the Italian camp leader, Dr Piscitelli, who accompanied the stretcher, was that it had been an accident. He said that Fantin had been pushed and had hit his head on the tap as he fell down. Fortunately the Italian doctor in charge of the hospital was honest. He could not save Fantin's life but he proved his death had been caused by a blow struck at the back of his head with a heavy stick of wood, fracturing the lower part of the skull. After he had fallen on the ground his assailant had jumped on him and kicked him, breaking many ribs.

'After Fantin's murder the fascist leaders went around the camp whispering "those who speak will die . . . there are six more communists to be killed". The military authorities, faced with Dr Muggia's unequivocal diagnosis of the cause of death, realised that they could not risk going along with the assertion of the fascist camp leader that it had been an accident. A court of inquiry was held. It showed that Fantin had already been attacked by fascists three months before his death and that the reason for the attack was that he had proclaimed his anti-fascist beliefs (Australian Archives Accession A373). The inquiry showed that Fantin and the murderer did not know each other. Casotti, the assassin, had been the instrument of the fascist camp leaders. Behind the fascist leaders there stood the ignorance, the indifference and the prejudice of Army Intelligence. They were aware of mounting representations being made to the new Attorney-General, Dr Evatt, querying the keeping of anti-fascists in internment and asking that they be immediately separated from the fascists pending their release.

'Casotti was transferred to the court in Adelaide. He was on a charge of manslaughter rather than murder as Intelligence felt that it would attract less attention and prompt fewer "difficult questions" about what was happening in internment camps. There were two levels of justice: one for British and a lower one for "aliens". In a letter, the South Australian Deputy Director of Security assured his superior that matters had been resolved favourably.

> The Crown proposes to take the line that since the adjournment further investigations have shown that the accused's actions strongly point to murder, *but that on account of the majority of the witnesses being aliens* it has been considered advisable to proceed with the charge of manslaughter (my emphasis, Australian Archives Accession A373, Item 10913).

'At the court hearing Giuseppe Casotti was found guilty of manslaughter and sentenced to two years hard labour. He was deported to Italy on 21 January 1947.

'Three-and-a-half years of internment made me understand how human beings in confinement gradually become transparent. What is inside each one of us, our real self, at least the self that is real at the time, surfaces and cannot be hidden. My upbringing had isolated me from previous contact with workers or peasants. In the camps, though, day after day I heard ordinary people recount their lives. One big group were the cane cutters from north Queensland. They cut the cane by hand. I learned how the cutting gang, called *la ganga* (all their language was full of Italianised Australian words[1]) was put together, the knives they used, how they sharpened them, the tons of cane each man cut in a day, the loads they carried, the burning of the undergrowth before cutting and the soot that covered them, the catching of beetles with a reflector and a board behind it and the great importance of the gang's cook. A smiling, lovable man called Tati had been one of the best cooks and he described the food he prepared and the enormous amounts they ate. They recalled the money that each member of a good gang would accumulate by the end of the season, and the habit of going south, of depositing the money with the licensee of the pub where they stayed, and then played, fucked, drank, enjoyed it, until being told that it was all spent. They had adopted the habit of drinking huge amounts of beer at the pub and, with it, another peculiarly Australian institution: *il fait,* the fight, that seemed to be an inevitable component of the drinking ritual.

'Politics were never mentioned; they were abstractions alien to their lives. The terms fascism, democracy, freedom, and even newspapers, belonged to the world of the *padroni,* the bosses. Anti-fascists? These men did not have to say it, they had been anti-fascist for 2000 years, ever since dominant, privileged classes had been formed.

'When the Aliens' Appeals Tribunals heard their cases, the judges were perplexed; they had difficulty in understanding the peasant mentality. Most Italian migrants had come either from southern Italy or from the poorer areas of the Veneto region. They had started to work after three or four years of school, when they were still children. The only realities they knew were their families, their work, the land. The war had nothing to do with them; they looked at it as a disaster thrust upon them by the *padroni*—Italian and Australian. When answering the judges' questions they all stated that they wanted to remain in Australia, against all odds, and that their only interest was their families and their work. One of them, more vocal than most, told the judges ". . . he who wins, wins; he who loses, loses; I will always have to work the land" (quoted in Cresciani, 1985b: 4). In the transcript of one of many similar appeals, the Crown prosecutor thought that he had at last understood it all and exclaimed ". . . the Italian migrant has not the slightest interest in books . . . these (holding up a bank passbook) are the only books that he knows!" (quoted in Cresciani, 1985b: 6). Was that a good reason to keep them behind barbed wire? A minority were politicised and stated that "Mussolini was bad for the working class"; they generally expressed socialist principles mixed with anarchist ideals, but Intelligence lumped them all together as communist sympathisers.

'In July 1942 the secretary of *Italia Libera,* with whom I had been corresponding since the association had been authorised in Melbourne, wrote asking me to prepare a paper which could be used in the free Italian movement. I wrote a paper on the Abyssinian war because fascist propaganda had used that war to enlist support and obtain donations from Italian migrants overseas. Italian communities were told that Italian soldiers had been sent to Abyssinia to secure a legitimate "place in the sun" for overcrowded Italy. Many innocently responded and made donations. The facts were rather different and I set them out to the best of my ability. The district censor stopped my paper and referred it to Security. My paper never reached *Italia Libera* and another year passed before my release. A year is a long time when you are in gaol. When the great day came it did not seem to be the result of any belated feat of understanding by the Intelligence Service. Most Italians were being released at last, following Mussolini's downfall. The army had discovered a simple formula to distinguish those to be released: "who is for Mussolini, who is for the King?" It was not difficult to guess which reply would lead to release; the camps were emptied and a sad chapter was closed.

'Only a handful of Italians, too compromised with fascism or too bitter, opted for *Il Duce* and remained in confinement. We others were sent in batches to Adelaide for medical inspection and relocation. Most were sent to work with the Civil Aliens' Corps in central and northern Australia. I was among a smaller group who were given tickets to go home and report to the police for further instructions. I found myself on a train bound for Sydney. It was 9 October, 1943. A final punctuation was contained in a memo from the Deputy Director of Security for New South Wales dated 26 March 1943, saying that "it would seem to me that the Alcorso brothers' case should be permitted to fade into oblivion" (Australian Archives Accession A1533XM Item 54/3092). Well, 46 years later I would be the first to agree that my unjust internment was insignificant when compared to the tragedies which happened every day during the war. But the behaviour of the people responsible for the policy, both inside and outside the army, was and remains significant. Just like Hitler and Mussolini they scorned and despised democratic beliefs; indeed they considered them dangerous and subversive. They were fascists without knowing it.'

Australia and Italian fascism

A major theme of Claudio Alcorso's account is the ironic tragedy of being treated by the Australian authorities as an enemy, and by implication, a fascist, after leaving his country of birth because of opposition to fascism. This paradox was experienced by many. Historians of the Italian community during the 1920s and 1930s have discussed to what extent fascism had active support and whether Australian government policy was appropriate, or at least comprehensible. The most usual judgment is that reached by Robert Pascoe: 'the internments were, on balance, a pointless exercise, instigated by irrational fears' (1987: 146).

However, Cresciani, the foremost Australian historian of the period, seems more ambivalent. On the one hand, he points out that while many Italian migrants in Australia reacted favourably to the rise of Mussolini, this had little to do with them being fascists in the political sense of the word and was rather an assertion of national pride in the context of an unfriendly Australia. On the other hand, in documenting the strength of fascist-influenced organisations and community structures in Australia in the 1930s, he portrays the Australian government as being duped by years of fascist propaganda. It is not surprising, he suggests, that by the early 1930s, Italians in Australia were 'widely suspected' of being fascists (Cresciani, 1981: 38).

It would be useful to reformulate the questions: we need to ask to what extent the internment policy was a response, irrational or otherwise, to potential fascists in Australia and to what extent it had

A group marching behind the Italian flag in the May Day parade in Melbourne in 1954 is led by Omero Schiassi, an intellectual prominent in the anti-fascist movement. (*Italian Historical Society, Melbourne*)

other motivations. There are many indications that the government's concerns did not lie primarily with repressing fascism. Both the Conservative Bruce government of the 1920s and the Hughes Labor government of the 1930s viewed Italian fascism favourably. They suppressed anti-fascist activities by Italian migrants far more strenuously than pro-fascist ones because the former were organised by anarchists, communists and socialists, who were considered to pose a greater threat to society.

Even during the war period, as the story above indicates, well-known and dangerous fascists were given privileges and entrusted with leadership responsibilities in the internment camps. Although they witnessed the spectacle of violent political struggle in the camps, the authorities consistently chose not to protect the anti-fascists and to leave their tormentors in positions of power.

Internment policy and racism

The internment practices should be understood as an extension of Australia's traditional defence policies and security concerns. As we noted in Chapter 1, from the earliest days of Federation the question of national security was seen to be inextricably linked to the White Australia policy. Wars were fought to keep Australia British, white and racially pure, and the tendency to define the war in racial terms was exacerbated after Japan entered the war in 1941. Like the Germans during World War I, Italians during World War II provided a local 'other', a concrete representation of the enemy, defined (as usual) in ethnic terms. Thus a key function of the internment policies was to articulate a sense of identity and leadership to the Anglo-Australian population at a time when sacrifices were necessary to support the war effort. They helped to define Australia as part of the British–democratic world by clearly isolating and identifying the 'other'—the Italian/German/Japanese enemy.

Australia's internment policies were not original but rather drafted in accordance with policies developed in Great Britain and used throughout the Commonwealth. From 1940 on, the British Army managed to create a climate of panic about 'the enemy within'—anyone of German or Austrian heritage living in Britain, including many who had sought refuge there from Nazi terror (see Pearl, 1983: Chapter 1). Similarly in Australia, Military Intelligence insisted that simply being Italian was sufficient reason for internment, and that any differences among Italians—particularly with respect to the war—were irrelevant. This should be understood as an ideological weapon aimed at the promotion of national cohesion on the grounds of ethnic solidarity. The liberal judgments of the Aliens' Appeals Tribunals contradicted the government's overall strategy to build morale among the mainstream Australian population.

Despite censorship in other areas, the racist press was given a free hand to incite racial hatred and it seems that the media was particularly important in promoting and popularising a chauvinistic view of 'us' against 'them'. The old fear of 'foreigners' taking 'Australian' jobs was brought out again to deny Italians employment during the war. Any attempt by a person of Italian background to speak as an Australian was swiftly disallowed. Bonutto describes how he once wrote to a Sunday newspaper emphasising the detrimental effects of internment from Australia's point of view, and in particular stressing that migrants' labour was necessary for Allied success in the war. The letter was published under the caption: 'Impertinent Internee Writes a Letter. No. 7015 Tells Australia What To Do' (Bonutto, 1963: 104). The message was clear: Bonutto, though an established farmer and a British subject who had emigrated from Italy more than fifteen years before the war began, should not pretend to be part of Australia.

Although there has been little research on the experiences of Italian women during the war years, it seems that the authorities rarely, if ever, considered that Italian women could be a security risk. In fact, women (as mothers and wives) had an important role within fascist ideology as the promoters of patriotism, love for the leader and other moral ideals, and active women's sections of the Fascist Party existed in Melbourne and Sydney in the 1930s. Even more in line with the type of 'evidence' favoured by Military Intelligence was the response of thousands of Italian–Australian women to Mussolini's appeal for gold to fund the African campaign in 1935–36 (Diana, 1988: 77). However, the military's patriarchal assumptions outweighed their suspicion of 'enemy aliens' and only a few were interned along with their husbands. Most remained at home to carry on the economic activities of the household and to bear the brunt of the hostility towards Italians so often expressed in the wider community. Many women remember the war years as times of great hardship (Diana, 1988) and there are accounts of internees' wives suffering from malnutrition and sickness (see Chapter 10 below). However, it is likely that for some Italian women, as for women generally, the war provided the opportunity for involvement in non-traditional spheres of work and for a more powerful role in the family.

Prisoners of war

As the war progressed, and the Japanese moved further south down the Malay peninsula, the government became increasingly concerned about Australia's ability to protect itself. In an attempt to increase Australia's industrial self-reliance and boost production, it placed new emphasis on mobilising all available labour power and introduced a form of industrial conscription (Crowley, 1973: 56). This economic situation provided the backdrop to a singular episode in Australian history: that of the Italian prisoners of war.

Nearly 18 500 Italian POWs were confined in Australia between 1941 and 1947 (Fitzgerald, 1981: 1), representing a (temporary) 50 per cent increase in the Italian-born population of the country. With the exception of those captured in territorial waters, most were brought from the Middle East and India and their importation to Australia proved to be the largest exercise in mass labour migration yet undertaken by an Australian government. Naturally all were men, and it appears that most were fit and in good health which was maintained by fair treatment through their confinement: only 101 (0.5 per cent) of the 18 432 POWs died in Australia, compared with nearly one-third of the 22 516 Australian POWs held by the Japanese in the same period (Fitzgerald, 1981: 116).

The POWs were imprisoned in approximately 30 purpose-built camps across Australia, always physically separate from the internees. Moreover, the treatment of the two groups was consistently motivated by a separate logic. From 1943 on, POW labour was not only used on camp or government work projects but was made available for private use by Anglo-Australian farmers. In a scheme somewhat reminiscent of the colonial system for the assignment of convicts to pastoralists, volunteer prisoners of war were allocated to farms within a 40-mile radius of scattered rural 'control centres'. Employers were responsible for housing and feeding the POWs but were not required to pay award wages: instead, they were levied one pound a week by the Commonwealth, from which the POW received 15 shillings. Trade unions protested against this use of cheap foreign labour, and threatened industrial action in rural industries. However, employer opposition to paying more than the Commonwealth minimum POW wage was sufficiently strong to prevent any change to it.

Indeed, in some instances it seems that not only were the POWs used as cheap labour, but, in a forerunner to the practice of the 1950s and 1960s, were given unpleasant and dangerous jobs in the manufacturing industry for which indigenous workers could not be recruited. The labour of Italian POWs made a significant contribution toward the Australian economy during the war years. Not only did they provide labour to keep farms running while Australian workers were at war, they were also used as a seasonal workforce, transported to meet urgent fruit and vegetable harvesting needs around the country. They also worked on public projects of national importance, such as the transcontinental railway. Italian POWs were valued by the Australian government over and above German POWs precisely because it was felt that the former made better workers. Hence, in 1944 the War Cabinet dropped its earlier acceptance of German POWs and from then on accepted only Italians (Fitzgerald, 1981: 58).

It appears that most Italian POWs enjoyed adequate work and living conditions whilst on the farms. However, their apparent contentment and enthusiasm for farm work needs to be understood in the context of their only other alternative: the prison camp, described by one prisoner as 'an asylum of non-violent lunatics . . . [where] there is a continuous struggle of the nervous system against the fence' (Fitzgerald, 1981: 126). The fifteen suicides known to have occurred in the camps were only the tip of the iceberg: depression, loneliness and boredom with the dull routine of confinement, plus anxiety about the fate of friends and relatives in Italy, were commonly reported conditions.

As Australian soldiers returned to their farms after 1945 there was pressure for the repatriation of Italian POWS. The Australian Workers' Union and the Returned Soldiers' League argued that Australian men should not have to work beside the enemy against which they had fought a few years ago. Understandably, most POWs were also eager to return home, although some escaped in an attempt to remain in Australia, and many made application for emigration after their return to Italy. The terms of the Geneva Convention made it obligatory to repatriate all POWs even if they wanted to stay. Eventually, as ships became available in 1946 and 1947, Italian POWs were shipped back to Italy to reconstruct their disrupted lives.

As can be seen from the above account, several aspects of the prisoner of war episode indicate continuities with the Italian migrant experience both before and after World War II. The most obvious of these is the function of Italian migrants as cheap and expendable labour at times of labour shortage. Perhaps one of the most significant novelties of the period, however, was the formation of close personal relationships between the predominantly Anglo-Australian rural communities and the Italian POWS. Australia in the 1940s saw itself as a straightforwardly British nation and the ethnic homogeneity of its population was indeed greater than at most times before or after. Not only did Australian employers of POWs have to overcome this generally xenophobic rural culture, but they had also to contend with obvious communication difficulties. An additional complication was the fact that most of those who employed the POWs and had face-to-face contact with them were women who were in charge of farms while male relatives were at war.

However, despite these inauspicious conditions, it seems that generally the relationships between the two groups were friendly and often warm. The Italians were typically treated in an egalitarian manner, and often almost like family members. Foreshadowing 1970s multiculturalism, food became a symbol of Anglo-Australians' accommodation to cultural difference, as some farmers cooked and even learned to eat macaroni with tomato sauce! (Fitzgerald, 1981: Chapter 8).

Conclusion

It could be said that World War II had contradictory effects on the relationship between Italian immigrants and their host society. On the one hand, the positioning of Australia and Italy as enemies in the war created a climate in which anti-Italian racism could flourish, and was indeed encouraged by the government. The Australian government implemented a racist policy of surveillance and internment towards the local Italian population which caused considerable individual hardship and suffering. On the other, the large-scale deployment of Italian POW labour had the unintended consequence of fostering attitudes of friendship and trust towards Italians among Australia's predominantly British background and ethnocentric rural population.

In the long term, the structural processes of social and economic change the war catalysed proved to be more significant than the effects of government policies. A larger population was considered necessary to bring security from further aggression, as well as to boost the small economy, and a mass immigration program was introduced. The POW episode had demonstrated how useful Italian labour could be, setting the scene for large postwar intakes from Italy. The surplus peasants of postwar Italy found in Australia a more receptive destination than ever before.

3 Italian migration and settlement since 1945

Stephen Castles

After 1945, Australia embarked on a mass immigration program which was to change not only the country's demographic and economic structures, but also its ethnic composition and national identity. By the 1950s, Italians became the largest immigrant group of non-English speaking background. Mass immigration from 1945 to 1970 laid the groundwork for Italo-Australian communities, which helped to give a new character to Australian urban space in the 1970s and 1980s. Cultural maintenance and community formation played a part in overcoming assimilationist attitudes towards immigrants, and in eroding Anglo-Australian insularity. Italo-Australians have thus contributed to Australa's shift towards a more cosmopolitan society and world-view. This chapter will describe Italian migration and settlement, starting with a brief look at the intolerable conditions which made millions of people leave Italy after 1945. The account will show how Italian migrants came to Australia in the 1950s and 1960s, and stopped coming in the 1970s—a development linked to dramatic demographic and economic changes in Italy. Then patterns of Italian settlement in Australia will be examined, and some statistical and other background information on today's Italo-Australians will be presented. The chapter will begin to link Italian settlement with the changes in Australian policies and attitudes towards immigrants, epitomised in the shift from assimilationism to multiculturalism.

Underdevelopment and emigration

Italy was a country of mass emigration from the time of the *Risorgimento* (unification) in 1860, until about 1970. Some 25 million Italians emigrated between 1876 and 1965—which is roughly equivalent to the whole Italian population of 1861! Patterns of chain migration developed, with whole families or even villages going to certain areas in the USA or western Europe. Northern Italians went both to the Americas and to western Europe, while most southern Italians crossed the Atlantic. Some came back, often in their old age, while others remained to found the 'Little Italies' of New York or Buenos Aires.

Most of those who came to Australia after World War II were from the *Mezzogiorno*—the poor South. At the time of Italian unification in 1860 the south was hardly more backward than the north. But modernisation of agriculture in the north-west (Piedmont and Lombardy) paved the way for commercial farming and industrialisation, while in the *Mezzogiorno* agriculture remained backward due to the semi-feudal system of land ownership. This kept peasants in a state of subservience to the *baroni,* causing rural poverty, low productivity, and stagnation (Palanca, n.d.: 134). As the industries of the north developed, their competition destroyed traditional metal and textile industries in the south (Cinanni, n.d.: 84). The fascist regime which seized power in 1922 perpetuated underdevelopment and regional imbalances (Davidson, 1988: 607–8). Militarism and foreign adventures were designed to divert attention from continuing backwardness, while Mussolini's Urbanisation Law attempted to prevent rural–urban immigration. The peasants were forced to stay on the land, emigration was restricted, and subsidies were provided to prevent the collapse of unproductive agriculture. Despite these policies, and the difficulty in finding work in other countries during the Depression, 3.7 million people emigrated between 1921 and 1945 (Cinanni, n.d.: 51).

In World War II, Italy became a battlefield. Both rural and urban areas were devastated. Postwar leaders decided on a reconstruction strategy based on the industrial resources of the north (Palanca, n.d.: 134). Again, the *Mezzogiorno* was neglected. The result was a continued process of underdevelopment: heavy industry, engineering, textiles and clothing factories took on a modern and centralised character in the north-western 'Industrial Triangle' (between Turin, Milan and Genoa), while the south continued to be characterised by backward agriculture, poverty and demographic pressure. Italy's first Prime Minister, Alcide De Gasperi, advocated emigration as a necessary 'safetyvalve', saying that Italians should 'learn some languages and go abroad'. The General Directorate for Emigration estimated that there were four million persons too many, who could not be supported by the impoverished national economy. Emigration would benefit the country in two ways: firstly, by dispelling social instability and economic malaise, and secondly, by reducing Italy's current account deficit through migrants' remittances from overseas (Rosoli, 1978: 260–1). In the immediate postwar years, there was large-scale emigration from all parts of Italy, but as the north and centre recovered, it became clear that the real problems were still in the south.

Neither the peasant movements of the 1940s, nor the Christian Democratic government's attempts at land reform and industrialisation from the 1950s, did much to break through the age-old cycle of exploitation, poverty, corruption and hopelessness. Emigration was the only way out for the displaced and impoverished farmers of the *Mezzogiorno.* Nearly six million Italians emigrated between 1946 and 1965; four million went to other European countries, while nearly two million moved overseas—mainly to Australia and Canada. At the same time around 200 000 people per year were moving from the south to the labour-hungry new factories of the north (Cinanni, n.d.: 49–65). The internal migrants often experienced cultural dislocation and racism just as severe as that encountered by those who went to other countries.

By the 1960s, the establishment of the European Economic Community and the industrial boom in northern Italy were making overseas emigration less attractive. In the south both agriculture and industrial employment remained low, but the growing network of government services led to increased public employment. Tertiary employment in the private sector, for instance in tourism, also grew. A sub-proletariat developed, which was partly dependent on the state, and partly on the 'grey economy' (or informal sector) which provided casual, undocumented (and sometimes illegal) work. The beginning of the world recession in the early 1970s virtually stopped emigration, and led to considerable return migration from western Europe. Since then, the Italian economy has experienced considerable restructuring. Manufacturing has been marked by rationalisation at home, and the establishment of plants in third-world countries. New industrial development in Italy has shifted from large-scale industry, to decentralised medium and small-scale production, causing the emergence of new regional industrial centres, particularly in the north-eastern and central regions. Thus the old 'bipolar' structure of Italy, dominated by the north–south divide, has been replaced by a 'multipolar' pattern (Palanca, n.d.). Italy is now Europe's third-largest economy, after the Federal Republic of Germany (FRG) and France (Ermini and Halevi, 1989: 16–17).

Devastated by a century of underdevelopment and emigration, the south remains poor: the GDP per head in 1986 was over 20 million lire in Lombardy, but only 10.3 million in Sicily and 8.8 million in Calabria. Unemployment was 7.4 per cent of the labour force in Lombardy and 9.2 per cent in Piedmont, but 16.2 per cent in Sicily and 17.9 per cent in Calabria (Gastaldo, n.d.: 61). Yet emigration no longer appears to be a viable option. Even in the *Mezzogiorno* living standards have improved; indeed they are often better than in possible countries of emigration, such as Australia.

Birthrates are falling fast, so that Italy now has a fairly stable population of about 57 million, and will soon enter the stage of negative demographic growth and an ageing population (Gastaldo, n.d.). Indeed, after one hundred years of mass emigration, Italy has now become a country of immigration. In the 1970s and 1980s large numbers of immigrants from North Africa, sub-Saharan Africa, the Philippines and other Asian countries, and eastern Europe have entered, usually on tourist documents. They have found employment as unskilled factory workers, seasonal agricultural labourers and domestic servants. Others do casual work in the informal sector, or try to make a living as street vendors. Italy was not prepared for the influx, lacking appropriate laws, policies and institutions. With growing demographic pressure in the North African countries, and a long coastline that cannot be effectively policed, some Italians fear the prospect of uncontrolled immigration, with unpredictable social and economic consequences (Fondazione Giovanni Agnelli, 1989). However, amnesties for illegal migrants in 1988 and 1990, and new legislation on migration in 1988 are beginning to provide the basis for settlement policies (SOPEMI, 1990: 44–5, 65–86). Perhaps Italy can now learn from Australia's experience of multiculturalism!

Large-scale migration 1951–70

The Japanese victories in the Pacific War in 1941–42 had convinced Australia's leaders that the country could no longer rely on Britain for its security, and that a larger population and a strong economy with a modern manufactuing sector were essential. In 1945, the Australian Labor government abandoned its traditional hostility towards foreign labour, and set up a Department of Immigration. The first Minister of Immigration, Arthur Calwell, called for 2 per cent population growth per year, of which half was to come through immigration. Calwell used the slogan of 'populate or perish' to help overcome working-class suspicion of immigration, telling the public that 'we must fill the country or lose it' (Collins, 1988: 21). New entrants were to be directed into jobs unwanted by Australians, in infrastructure projects like the Snowy Mountains Hydro-Electric Scheme, in heavy industry such as the steelworks of Newcastle and Wollongong, or in the new engineering and textile factories of Sydney and Melbourne. Moreover, the public was told that eventually the migrants would be fully assimilated as 'New Australians'.

In the early years, the aim was to attract migrants from Britain. The target was 70 000 migrants per year, and a ratio of ten British migrants to every 'foreigner'. However, not enough British people wanted to come, and the Department of Immigration began recruiting in European Displaced Persons Camps, giving preference to refugees from the Baltic and Slavonic countries, who were perceived as both 'racially acceptable' and anti-communist. Australia developed a system of preference for 'desirable types' of immigrants. Non-Europeans—particularly Asians—were to be completely excluded. Holt, who succeeded Calwell as Immigration Minister, argued for British and European immigration to hold Australia against the 'hungry millions of people in the resurgent continent of Asia' (House of Representatives, *Hansard* 6 December 1950: 3794). 'Desirable types' formed a hierarchy, with the British at the top, followed by northern Europeans, eastern Europeans and finally southern Europeans. It was believed that northern Europeans would be better educated, adapt more quickly to the 'Australian way of life', be more conformist in political terms, and would be of greater economic value (Vasta, 1990b).

There was great resistance to recruitment of southem Europeans, and only limited quotas were admitted in the late 1940s. A distinction was made between northern and southern Italians. The *Sydney Morning Herald* (SMH) declared: 'Italians, particularly from the north, made good settlers before the war, though some undesirable types got in. As people they are industrious . . . One complaint against them is that they are not easily assimilable and tend to form foreign colonies' (5 February 1948). Ten years later a member of parliament said:

> I think we should concentrate on the northern Europeans because they can be assimilated more easily than southern Europeans . . . The northern Italians, for instance, can be be assimilated very easily . . . I believe they are very attractive people, highly skilled and with a fine cultural history. . . The Sicilians . . . have had no law but that of the tooth and the knife. . . We are not getting a good, average cross-section of people among our Italian migrants (House of Representatives, 16 September 1958: 1253–5).

Despite all this, southern Europe became the main source of migrants in the 1950s, and Italy the largest single country of origin after Britain. Capital in search of scarce labour could not afford to exclude 'less desirable types', but a hierarchy of entrenched prejudice had been established to meet the newcomers (Vasta, 1990b).

Immigration Offices were set up in several European countries. Assisted passages (at a fare of £10) were offered to selected British migrants, as well as to ex-servicemen from the British Empire, the USA and other wartime allies (as long as they were white). Migration agreements were concluded with the UK, Malta, the Netherlands, West Germany, Italy, Greece and several other European countries (CAAIP, 1987: 4). The result was a two-class system of immigration: British migrants and, later, those from northern European countries were frequently given assisted passages, and had full labour-market and civil rights upon arrival. Those from eastern and southern Europe were less likely to get assisted passages, were frequently directed into undesirable jobs, and were generally treated as inferior (Collins, 1988: 23–4).

As Chapter 1 showed, Italian migration to Australia before World War II was small in scale. After 1945, spontaneous movements soon started, and 33 000 Italians came by 1950. In the late 1940s, the Australian government began considering recruitment of northern Italians. The USA was willing to provide loans to help ship out the 'surplus' population, in order to reduce the 'communist threat', but would not take the migrants herself, instead putting pressure on Australia to do so (Bosworth, 1988: 614). In March 1951 a bilateral accord between Italy and Australia came into effect: 20 000 migrants per year were to be admitted for five years. They were to be provided with financial assistance by both governments, and with loans from Italian charitable organisations. The first batch were to be young men, though later family reunion was offered. Medical checks were to ensure that only healthy men were selected, while criminals, communists and fascists were to be excluded. Those who came on assisted passages had to work where directed by the Australian authorities for two years. Temporary accommodation was to be provided in camps and hostels.

However, initial migration did not proceed smoothly. Australian authorities were afraid of public opposition, and were so selective that only 62 out of the original 8191 applicants were accepted (Bosworth, 1988: 614). Moreover, 1952 was a year of recession in Australia, and many of the newly-arrived Italians could not obtain work. Finding themselves almost penniless in isolated camps, like Bonegilla in northern Victoria, they started to complain about the food, the hostility of the local population, and the failure to provide employment. The Australian authorities feared unrest and communist agitation. Matters came to a head with riots at Bonegilla in July 1952. Australian troops with armoured cars were sent to quell the

Migrants from Italy on their way to the Bonegilla Reception Centre in 1956 get their first taste of Australian sliced bread. (*Don Edwards, Department of Immigration*)

disturbances (Dugan and Szwarc, 1984: 154). Demonstrations by unemployed Italian workers took place in Sydney, Melbourne and Brisbane (Bosworth, 1988: 614). As a result, assisted passages were suspended and immigration levels drastically cut.

As economic conditions improved in 1954, the accord with Italy was renewed. Many of the Italian workers were directed into hard manual jobs in industry or on large-scale construction projects. Others were sent to Queensland to cut sugar cane. In 1961, after further troubles and protests at Bonegilla, the accord was suspended again and later renegotiated. Overall, assisted migration accounted for only 20 per cent of total migration from Italy. Up until 1969, Italians, unlike northern European and British migrants, had no right to assistance to bring their families with them (Bosworth, 1988: 613–4; Cresciani, 1985a: 95). Nonetheless family reunion did take place, since all permanent immigrants had the right to bring in their spouse and children, and to sponsor other relatives.

As Table 3.1 shows, the 1950s and 1960s were the main period of migration from Italy to Australia. Over 360 000 Italians came

The Bonegilla Reception Centre was the first stop for many Italian migrants arriving in Australia after World War II. (*Department of Immigration*)

between 1947 and 1976, but about 90 000 departed, making a net migration of about 270 000. During the period 1951–60, 6.5 per cent of total emigration from Italy was directed to Australia, with an average of 17 000 entrants per year. After 1961 the proportion began to decrease as migration to other western European countries, or from the south to the north, became more attractive. Only 4.5 per cent of Italian emigrants went to Australia from 1961 to 1970 (Bosworth, 1988: 616), 7200 people per year. By the early 1970s, as a result of recession in Australia and growing prosperity in Italy, more Italian-born people were leaving Australia than entering (Price, 1979: A21).

The Italian-born population of Australia increased from 120 000 in 1954 to 290 000 in 1971. Then it started declining, reaching 262 000 in 1986. Italians were the largest immigrant group after the British, making up over 12 per cent of the overseas-born population in the 1960s. Table 3.2 gives the figures at various censuses. Italian-born people made up 2.3 per cent of the total population of Australia in 1966, a figure which fell to 1.7 per cent by 1986.

Most migrants came from Calabria, Sicily, Abruzzi and Campania, although there were some from the north, particularly the Veneto and Friuli Venezia Giulia. The majority were from rural areas,

Table 3.1 Italian migration to Australia 1947–76

	1947–51	1951–61	1961–71	1971–76	Total 1947–76
Total net migration	33 280	179 420	72 333	–4 463	280 570
Annual average	8 320	17 942	7 233	–892	9 675

Note: Figures are for financial years from 1 July to 30 June. Net migration is the number of arrivals minus the number of departures. A negative figure means that more people departed than entered.
Source: Calculations from Table 2.2 of Price, 1979.

particularly from small towns, yet they soon concentrated in Australia's growing industrial cities. Most migrants were aged between 20 and 40 when they left Italy. They were usually impoverished, and came in order to obtain the means for family survival, or to earn the money needed to buy land or pay debts at home. Often their education was limited to primary school level, and most had not received any vocational training beyond the most basic level. Although there have always been some better-educated migrants, the failure to recognise their qualifications in Australia has often made it hard for them to pursue their professions: many skilledd workers and professionals have been forced into unskilled manual work.

Most Italians migrated not as individuals, but as participants in migratory chains: the first migrant from a certain Italian village, usually male, established a bridgehead, finding somewhere to live

Table 3.2 Italian-born persons in Australia

Census year	Italian-born population	Percent of overseas born population	Percent of total population
1881	1 880	*	0.1
1891	3 890	*	0.1
1901	5 678	0.7	0.2
1911	6 798	*	0.2
1921	8 135	0.9	0.2
1933	26 756	3.0	0.4
1947	33 632	4.5	0.4
1954	119 897	9.3	1.3
1961	228 296	12.8	2.2
1966	267 325	12.5	2.3
1971	289 476	11.2	2.3
1976	280 154	10.3	2.1
1981	275 883	9.2	1.9
1986	262 435	8.1	1.7

Note: * figure not available.
Sources: Australian censuses as reported by Borrie, 1954; Price, 1979; Price and Martin, 1975; Jupp, 1988; DIEA, 1983.

and a livelihood. Then he was joined by his wife, children, relatives and *paesani* (friends and neighbours from the native village). This pattern was unintentionally reinforced by Australian immigration policy: under sponsorship arrangements, Italians already in the country could help their relatives get visas by undertaking to provide accommodation and work for them on arrival (Burnley, 1988: 626). Thus colonies were established—a whole group would move from a village in Italy to a certain area of an industrial town or a farming district in Australia. This made it possible to keep links with the community of origin, and to maintain specific dialects and cultural practices in Australia.

Patterns of settlement

Italian settlement is closely interwoven with the evolution of Australia's economic and regional structure. Before 1945, the greatest concentration of Italians (one-third) was in Queensland, and most of them worked on the land. The introduction of cane-cutting machines in the 1960s drastically reduced the need for rural labour (Menghetti, 1988). Today, less than 7 per cent of the Italian-born live in Queensland, and many of these are in Brisbane. Similarly, in Western Australia many Italians settled initially in the gold mining areas in the 1920s and in the agricultural areas in the 1940s and 1950s. By the 1960s they were moving into the Perth metropolitan area, where the great majority live today (Stransky, 1988: 605). Ware describes how Italian chain migration has responded to shifts in Australia's political economy.

> The first 1920s migrants from Lettopalena in the Abruzzi went to Proserpine in north Queensland as cane farmers and cane cutters. By 1947 the first of them had moved to Newcastle [in NSW], where by the 1970s there was a community of some 150 families who had moved from Lettopalena to Proserpine to Newcastle. In Newcastle the older men tended to work for the BHP [steel] company, whilst the younger men were concentrated in the concreting business, which had come to be regarded as an Italian speciality in Australia (1988: 618).

Before World War II about 40 per cent of Italians in Victoria lived in country areas such as Shepparton, Wangaratta, Myrtleford, Mildura and Swan Hill. Italians in Melbourne were mainly in central areas, like Carlton, where many were shopkeepers. After 1945, the rapid expansion of manufacturing in Melbourne (and to a lesser extent in Geelong) attracted most of the new migrants. By 1981, almost 90 per cent of Italians in Victoria lived in Melbourne. Initially most lived in central areas: Sicilians in Brunswick, *pugliesi* in Fitzroy and *viggianesi* in Carlton. Within a few years, many moved out, mainly to the northern suburbs, in search of better housing (Bertelli, 1988: 630–1).

Italian chain migration to Sydney started in the 1920s. By 1933 there were 400 Italians in the inner-city area of Leichhardt (Burnley, 1988: 627), as well as groups of fishermen in Balmain and market gardeners on the western outskirts. The settlers in Leichhardt came mainly from the Lipari Islands, Sicily, Vicenza and Udine (Ware, 1988: 618), while the market gardeners were mainly Calabrians. Postwar migratory chains strengthened these communities; for instance Leichhardt had 6000 Italian-born residents by 1961 (Burnley, 1988: 627). Italian settlement also increased in the west and south of Sydney, with employment shifting from the primary sector to manufacturing, construction and transport. Many market gardens became residential areas, as land values increased. Calabrians and Sicilians (some of whom had moved from north Queensland) settled in Fairfield in the west of Sydney, making it the largest single Italian community in New South Wales (10 747 Italian speakers in 1986).

Patterns of return to Italy also influenced community formation: as shown in Table 3.1, return migration exceeded new entries by the 1970s (although the number of Italo-Australians continued to grow through births in Australia). Rates of return varied, since development in certain Italian regions offered better employment prospects than in others. Return was greatest to northern Italy, and lowest to Calabria. This affected the size and structure of Italian settlements in Australia, contributing for instance to the decline of the Italian communities of Leichhardt, Petersham and Five Dock in the inner city of Sydney (Burnley, 1988: 627).

Italo-Australians today: an overview

One aim of the postwar immigration program was to rapidly increase the population. It has indeed more than doubled from about 7.5 million in 1945 to about 17 million in 1990. Table 3.3 shows that the overseas-born population grew far more rapidly than the total population between 1947 and 1971. By 1971, immigrants made up one in five of the total population, a share which has since remained constant, reflecting the relative decline in immigration in the 1970s.

Nearly five million people migrated to Australia and settled permanently between 1945 and 1989 (BIR, 1990: 32), with the Italians (8.5 per cent of total intake) making up the second-largest group after the British (41 per cent of intake). Immigrants have come from an ever-wider range of countries. Although the British Isles played a major part throughout the postwar period, immigration from Europe declined dramatically from the 1960s, while immigration

Table 3.3 Australian populaton 1947–86

Census year	Overseas-born	Total population	Overseas-born per cent of total
1947	744 187	7 579 358	9.8
1954	1 286 466	8 986 530	4.3
1961	1 778 780	10 508 186	16.9
1971	2 579 318	12 755 638	20.2
1976	2 718 318	13 548 448	20.1
1981	3 003 834	14 576 330	20.6
1986	3 247 301	15 602 163	20.8

Sources: DILGEA 1988a: Table A3; Census, 1986.

from New Zealand, Asia and Latin America increased. As a result, the ethnic composition of the population has shifted considerably. In 1947, nearly 90 per cent of the population were Australian-born, and most of the rest were from the UK. In 1986, 79 per cent of the population were Australian-born and 21 per cent were overseas-born. Twenty per cent of the Australian born were children of immigrants. In other words, over two-fifths of the Australian population were immigrants or children of immigrants.

According to the 1986 census, 7.2 per cent of the Australian population were born in the UK and Ireland, a further 7.2 per cent in other European countries, 1 per cent in the Middle East, and 2.6 per cent in Asia. Two per cent of the Australian-born were Aborigines. Figure 3.1 shows how the composition of the immigrant population has changed since 1901.

In 1986, the 262 000 Italian-born were the second largest overseas-born group in the population, following the UK- and Ireland-born.

During the period of mass migration in the 1950s and 1960s, there were far more Italian-born men than women in Australia. Subsequent family reunion reduced the imbalance, but, as the 1986 census showed, there is still a slight male surplus: 141 400 men compared with 120 500 women (a ratio of 1173 men for every 1000 women).

Because Italian migration virtually ceased 20 years ago, there are very few young Italian-born people: only 0. 8 per cent are aged under 15 years (compared with 27.9 per cent of the total population), and 4.4 per cent are aged 15–24 (compared with 17.9 per cent of the total population). Most Italians are concentrated in the higher age groups, with 14.2 per cent aged over 64 (compared with 9.8 per cent of the total population) (ABS, 1989). Such figures have some value in planning for future aged-care needs, but tell us little about the demographic structure of the Italo-Australian community, because they exclude children born to Italian parents in Australia.

Figure 3.1 Australia: per cent of overseas-born population by continent of origin

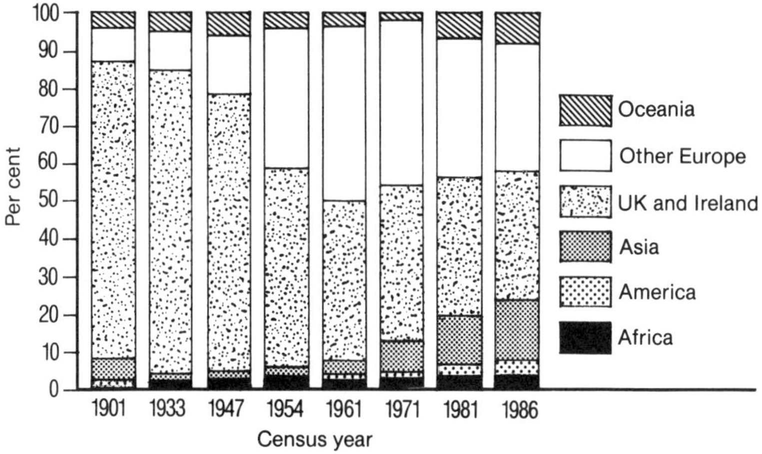

Source: BIR 1989: Table A3.

Citizenship and the second generation

Australia regards all immigrants as potential citizens. Citizenship can be obtained after two years of residence in Australia. The 1986 census showed that 59 per cent of overseas-born persons have become Australian citizens. There are substantial variations for different countries of origin. Only 47 per cent of persons from the UK and Ireland and 24 per cent of persons from New Zealand had taken up citizenship. This compared with 76 per cent of Italian-born persons, 91 per cent of the Greek-born, 95 per cent of those born in the USSR and 63 per cent of persons born in Asia.

Table 3.4 The ten largest immigrant groups in Australia, 1986

Country of origin	Number	Per cent of overseas-born population
UK and Ireland	1 127 000	34.7
Italy	262 000	8.1
New Zealand	212 000	6.5
Yugoslavia	150 000	4.6
Greece	138 000	4.2
Germany	115 000	3.5
Netherlands	95 000	2.9
Vietnam	83 000	2.6
Poland	68 000	2.1
Lebanon	56 000	1.7

Source: DILGEA, 1987b.

Anyone born in Australia who has at least one parent who is either a citizen or a permanent resident, is automatically a citizen. Australian-born children of Italians are therefore Australians, even though they may still speak Italian and identify with their Italian heritage. In 1986, there were 300 997 persons who had been born in Australia with at least one Italian-born parent. Of these, 190 878 (63.7 per cent) had both parents born in Italy, while 12 853 (4.3 per cent) had an Italian-born mother only, 66 992 (22.3 per cent) had an Italian-born father only, and 29 024 (9.7 per cent) had one Italian-born parent and one born elsewhere but not in Australia (DILGEA, 1988b: 82). Thus the Italo-Australian first and second generation[1] together made up 563 000 people, or 3.6 per cent, of the total population of Australia.

Second-generation Italo-Australians are sill overwhelmingly concentrated in the younger age groups: in 1986, 37 per cent were aged under 15, 35 per cent from 15 to 24, 19 per cent from 25 to 34, and only 9 per cent over 35 (DILGEA, 1988b: 84). The Australian-born second generation of Italo-Australians started entering the labour market in the 1970s and 1980s. The new generation is far better educated than their parents, and has different perspectives and aspirations. Now that the migrant generation is reaching retiring age, the full impact of the new generation on Australian society and culture is beginning to be felt (see Chapter 11).

Intermarriage

Italians (like other southern Europeans) have tended to intermarry much less with Australian-born people or other migrant groups than have north-western and eastern European immigrants. However intermarriage is on the increase: in 1961 only 21 per cent of Italian-born men who got married in Australia had Australian-born brides; by 1976 the figure had risen to 51 per cent and by 1986 to 64 per cent. As for Italian-born brides, in 1961 only 3 per cent married Australian-born men; a figure which rose to 23 per cent in 1976 and 49 per cent in 1986 (ABS, 1989: 59). These figures show that women are less likely to marry outside the Italian community than men, but that the propensity is increasing for both sexes. However, a proportion of the Australian-born brides and bridegrooms are undoubtedly second- (or third-) generation Italo-Australians, so that precise data on intermarriage with other ethnic groups cannot be given.

Family and household

The family and home ownership are high priorities for Italian migrants. Over 90 per cent of their households in 1986 were family units without non-family members living in them. The figure was similar to that for other southern Europeans (Greeks, Maltese, Yugoslavs), but much higher than for eastern or western Europeans (70–80 per cent), Asians (77 per cent) or the Australian-born (74 per cent). Altogether there were 161 600 households with Italian-born heads, with an average size of 3.6 persons (ABS, 1989: 64).

No less than 70 per cent of Italian households owned their own dwellings outright in 1986, while a further 19 per cent were still paying off housing loans. This is the highest rate of home ownership of any ethnic group in Australia. By comparison 36 per cent of all overseas-born residents and 35 per cent of the Australian-born owned their dwellings outright and 34 per cent of all overseas-born and 38 per cent of the Australian-born were purchasing dwellings. Italian migrants have always been eager to own houses, and have been willing to make great sacrifices to do so. It is generally believed that this is connected with their peasant origins: lack of land ownership put southerners at the mercy of the *baroni,* so that owning land and house was always a priority. Owning a house also provides security for old age.

Italian speakers

The 1986 census indicated that over two million people spoke languages other than English at home, the most common being Italian (416 000 people), Greek (267 000) and Chinese (131 000). One way of getting an idea of the size of the Italian community is to compare the number of Italian-born persons with the total number who said they spoke Italian at home, in answer to the census question on language use. The Italian-language speakers include the majority of the first generation, plus those members of the second and third generations who regularly use the Italian language, and is a very rough indicator of maintenance of Italian culture. Table 3.5 shows the distribution of Italian speakers by state. The largest number were in Victoria, followed by New South Wales, South Australia, Western Australia and Queensland. Most Italo-Australians are bilingual, speaking Italian at home, and English at work or school. Often the language spoken at home is a distinct dialect such as *calabrese*, Sicilian or *furlan* (see Chapter 12).

Italian neighbourhoods

Chain migration combined with the availability of jobs and cheap housing led to the concentration of Italian settlements in specific areas. Some Italian farming communities still exist—most notably

Table 3.5 Italian-born people and Italian speakers, 1986

State/Territory	Italian-born	Italian-speakers	Italian-speakers (per cent)
Victoria	109 204	178 097	42.8
New South Wales	73 174	113 203	27.2
Queensland	17 418	26 115	6.3
South Australia	29 607	48 179	11.6
Westem Australia	27 751	43 590	10.5
Tasmania	1 259	1 590	0.4
Nonhem Territory	1 301	1 040	0.3
Aust. Capital Territory	2 721	3 951	0.9
AUSTRALIA	262 435	415 765	100.0

Source: Jupp, 1988:969–71.

Mildura in Victoria, Griffith in New South Wales and Mareeba in north Queensland. But the major focuses of Italian communities are the big cities: in 1986 three quarters of Italian-born people lived in Melbourne, Sydney, Adelaide and Perth, and only 16 per cent lived outside the 12 major urban centres (Ware, 1988: 617–18). There are no exclusively or even predominantly Italian areas—nowhere do Italian speakers make up more than 22 per cent of the population. However the concentrations are large enough to give certain neighbourhoods a typically Italian character, especially in view of the large number of Italian shops, cafés and restaurants. Such concentrations provide the basis for Italian clubs, churches, welfare organisations and facilities for the elderly.

Victoria has the greatest absolute number of Italians, with over 100 000 in Melbourne alone. All the main Italian areas are parts of Melbourne, either in the centre or the north. The earliest concentration was in the central area of Carlton, which is today an up-market neighbourhood, near Melbourne University, with high-class Italian restaurants, cafés and shops. Migrants moved out of this original 'Little Italy', buying houses in the surrounding suburbs. Further north, Broadmeadows is the home of the huge Ford motor works, where many Italians work.

The main Italian areas of Sydney are in the industrial inner-west and outer-west. One of the earliest areas of settlement, Leichhardt, has maintained its Italian flavour, although many Italians have moved out to surrounding areas, or to the sprawling western suburbs. Fairfield has the largest Italian-born population in absolute numbers. Outside Sydney, there are two major concentrations: the steel city of Wollongong, which has also had an Italian fishing community for many years, and the agricultural area of Griffith, which actually has the largest Italian percentage of population of any area in NSW. This area will be discussed in Chapters 4 and 7.

Adelaide has Italian neighbourhoods in several central districts, with Italian-born people making up over one-fifth of the population in some cases. There are relatively few Italians in non-metropolitan areas of South Australia. Western Australia has concentrations of Italians in its capital city, Perth, particularly in the centre and north of the city. However there is also a large and long-established community in the harbour and fishing town of Fremantle. The number of Italians in Brisbane is fairly small, about 10 000 in the central district, making up 1.5 per cent of the population.

From assimilation to multiculturalism

Italo-Australians are the largest group of non-English speaking background in Australia. Together with over one hundred other immigrant groups of varied ethnic and cultural background, they have helped to change Australia's culture and national identity. This was never envisaged by the architects of the postwar immigration program. At first the aim was predominantly British immigration. When this proved unattainable, policies were designed to bring about complete social and cultural assimilation, so that immigrants would become indistinguishable from the Anglo-Australian population. Once admitted, immigrants were treated as future citizens: naturalisation could be obtained easily after five years.[2] Government policies included the provision of initial accommodation, generally in hostels or camps, as well as help in finding work. Good Neighbour Councils were set up to create goodwill between migrants and Australians at the local level. There were no guestworkers: permanent family settlement was seen as the key to assimilation. This is not to say there was no discrimination: non-British migrants had to register their addresses with the police, efforts were made to exclude Italian communists, and a number of political activists were deported (Vasta, 1990b).

Many politicians and social scientists believed that any special measures for migrants would hinder assimilation. It was best to totally immerse the newcomers in Australian society. Pamphlets for 'New Australians' were written in English, even though the recipients could not understand them (Collins, 1988: 238–9). There was public discrimination against people speaking other languages, who were often told to shut up or speak English. Psychologists devised 'scales of Australianism' to allow individual measurement of the process of absorption (Wilton and Bosworth, 1984: 21–4). Migrants were to work and live among Australians, to avoid the formation of ethnic enclaves. The school was to have a key role in making the children of migrants into Australians; there were no special courses for migrant children, and they were forced to speak English from the outset (IAC, 1960).

By the 1960s, the basic contradiction of assimilationism was becoming obvious: 'New Australians' were meant to speak English, behave like Australians, and to be absorbed into the population. At the same time they were needed as manual workers in factories and construction, to replace Anglo-Australians who were moving into white-collar jobs. Institutional barriers often kept migrants in low-paid jobs, while welfare services were sometimes inaccessible to migrants, and did not meet their special needs (Martin, 1978). Not only closeness to the factory, but also experience of racism in Anglo-Australian neighbourhoods, caused migrants to cluster together. In the inner-city areas, migrants could create their own communities, with shops, cafés, doctors, lawyers, schools, churches, social and welfare associations and newspapers. The reconstitution of the ethnic group in the new country provided support networks and a sense of belonging.

Assimilationism was based on the idea that only Anglo-Australian culture was legitimate, and that other cultures would have to disappear. It fitted in with other racist elements in Australian identity, in particular the oppression of Aboriginal people, and the exclusion of Asians through the White Australia policy. But by the 1960s, world-wide decolonisation and anti-racist movements in other countries were leading to a questioning of Australian racism. In 1967 a referendum decided overwhelmingly that Aborigines should be granted full citizenship. Australia's international relations were changing too: by 1966, Japan was Australia's biggest export customer, and trade with south-east Asia was growing rapidly. The White Australia policy was a serious embarrassment. Both major parties decided to abandon it in the mid-1960s, although only a small number of middle-class Asians were to be let in each year.

The reforms introduced by the 1972–75 Whitlam Labor government included new policies towards migrants. Non-discriminatory immigration rules were at last introduced. Immigration Minister Al Grassby enunciated the doctrine of multiculturalism in his famous speech on 'The Family of the Nation'. The Australian Assistance Plan—designed to improve and restructure welfare services—took account of needs of NESB migrants, such as invalid and widows pensions, migrant housing and low-interest loans, family health insurance, and work-based childcare (Jakubowicz et al. 1984: 60–1). The Whitlam government was not primarily concerned with cultural pluralism but rather with the improvement of welfare and educational systems, and their adaptation to a multi-ethnic society. Nonetheless, the involvement of spokespersons and organisations of migrant groups did encourage the formal constitution of ethnic community organisations, such as the Italian welfare agencies COASIT and FILEF. An ethnic rights movement, embracing community organisations of all kinds led to the formation of Ethnic Communities Councils in the states (DIEA, 1986: 31–4).

The 1975–82 Fraser government retained multiculturalism, but redefined the policy in cultural pluralist terms. Multiculturalism was now said to mean that Australian institutions should adapt to the diverse composition of the population, while ethnic groups should be allowed to retain their languages, traditions and cultural identity, as long as they were loyal to the 'overarching' values of Australian society. Until mainstream services could be made culturally appropriate for diverse ethnic groups, social services were to be provided through ethnic community organisations, supported by the Department of Immigration and Ethnic Affairs (DIEA) (Galbally, 1978). Other special institutions and services included the Australian Institute of Multicultural Affairs, the Multicultural Education Program, the Adult Migrant Education Service and the Special Broadcasting Service (SBS) (Castles et al., 1988: 66–7).

This approach fitted well with the neo-liberal agenda: the problems encountered by migrants were defined as individual deficiencies, resulting from poor English, lack of knowledge of Australian institutions, or failure to adapt to an industrial society. 'The structural marginalisation of migrant workers through labour market segmentation was ignored. Migrant welfare was removed from the mainstream social system, and delegated to the ethnic group. The condition for employment as a 'migrant welfare worker' was knowledge of the language concerned, rather than professional qualification. This provided welfare on the cheap, since pay, staffing levels and conditions could be far lower than in government agencies (Jakubowicz et al. 1984: 81).

When the ALP returned to power in 1983, the cultural pluralist policies of the previous government were initially continued. However, the non-discriminatory immigration policy and multiculturalism were rapidly becoming controversial. The 'Great Immigration Debate' started in 1984, when the historian Geoffrey Blainey called for restrictions on immigration and warned of a threat to identity and social cohesion through what he called the 'Asianisation of Australia'. Politicians of both the right and left began to feel that there was widespread opposition to multiculturalism, and that cuts in the area would meet with little opposition. In the 1986 budget, the Australian Institute of Multicultural Affairs was abolished, funding for English as a Second Language (ESL) teaching was cut, and plans were made to merge the SBS with the Australian Broadcasting Corporation (ABC). But the cuts led to protests, demonstrations and strong public statements by leaders of migrant organisations. This ethnic mobilisation threatened the Labor hold on marginal seats in Sydney and Melbourne. In an amazingly rapid about-turn, many of the cuts were reversed in early 1987. The new direction was signalled by the establishment of an Office of Multicultural Affairs (OMA), with wide powers to monitor government policy; the setting up of an Advisory Council on Multicultural Affairs (ACMA), to advise the Prime Minister, and the dropping of the proposed ABC–SBS merger.

But the debate was soon to break out again: in 1988 the Report of the Committee to Advise on Australia's Immigration Policies (CAAIP, 1988) asserted that many Australians did not understand multiculturalism, and were worried that it was leading to a division of the nation into separatist minorities. The debate was taken up by then Opposition Leader, John Howard, who attacked multiculturalism, and stated that a future Liberal–National government would reserve the right to restrict Asian immigration to safeguard 'social cohesion'. Although Howard got considerable popular backing, there was little elite support. Employers emphasised the economic merits of immigration, while the unions and the ALP attacked Howard's proposed 'one Australia' policy as a veiled return to the White Australia policy. Liberal leaders in states with large migrant populations—Greiner in New South Wales and Kennett in Victoria—refused to support their federal leader. Howard lost his leadership of the party soon afterwards, and it is widely believed that his policies on immigration and multiculturalism were a contributory factor. Subsequent Liberal leaders have expressed support for non-discriminatory entry policies and multiculturalism.

Since 1988, the ALP government has attempted to reshape multiculturalism. It argues that an ethnically diverse population is better placed to respond to the challenges of increased international trade and communication, and above all to provide the opening to Asia which is seen as crucial to Australia's future. The most significant statement of the new approach is contained in the *National Agenda for a Multicultural Australia* (OMA, 1989), which identifies 'three dimensions of multicultural policy'—cultural identity, social justice and economic efficiency. Multiculturalism is not defined in terms of cultural pluralism, but as a system of rights of all citizens in a democratic state. These rights, however, are limited by an overriding commitment to the nation, a duty to accept the Constitution and the rule of law, and the acceptance of basic principles such as tolerance and equality, English as the national language and equality of the sexes. The program contained in the document is based on the recognition that some groups are disadvantaged by lack of language proficiency and education, as well as by discrimination based on factors such as race, ethnicity, gender or culture.

Conclusion

Italian migration to Australia before 1945 was small in scale, but it did help to establish migratory chains and to lay the foundation for Italo-Australian communities in both rural and urban areas. In 1947, Italian-born people were only 0.4 per cent of the total population of Australia and 4.5 per cent of the overseas-born population. By 1971 they were 2.3 per cent of the total population and 11 per cent of the overseas-born population. Today, there are over 400 000 Italian-speaking people in Australia—the largest group of non-British background. The mass movement of the 1950s and the 1960s was the product of a unique constellation of factors, which are never likely to be repeated: economic and social development have removed the need for emigration from Italy, while Australia is undergoing economic difficulties, which make it an unattractive destination for prospective Italian migrants.

The migrant generation were mainly of peasant origin, from Sicily, Calabria, Veneto, Abruzzi, and Campania. In Australia the overwhelming majority became industrial workers. This was not a matter of choice: urbanisation and the development of manufacturing in Australia made it inevitable. For these people migration meant not only the move half way across the world, but also the leap from rural to industrial society. The data on chain migration and settlement, on family structures and residential concentration presented in this chapter describe the migratory process. But they do not help us to understand its individual dimensions. What does it mean to be forced to leave one's home by oppression and poverty, to carve out a livelihood in the harsh bush country of Queensland, and then to be forced to move yet again, because technological progress makes cane cutters superfluous? What does it mean to be among the first Italian settlers in an Australian city, and to try to build a community in a strange environment?

The rest of the book will try to answer these questions, by looking at the many-faceted development of Italo-Australian communities. This will lead on to another major theme: the role of Italian migrants in the emergence of a multicultural society, and the consequences of this new approach to national identity both for Italo-Australians and for Australian society and culture in general.

4 Italians help build Australia
Frank Panucci, Bernadette Kelly and Stephen Castles

Italian migrant workers helped to develop Australia after World War II. Without them and the other immigrant workers, the country would be a very different place today. In this chapter, Frank Panucci describes some of the experiences of Italian men and women in construction and manufacturing, while Bernadette Kelly looks at Italian farmers. The chapter also provides some statistical information on Italians in the Australian labour market.

Construction and factory workers

The postwar immigration program led to a labour market segmented by ethnic background and gender. Italian and other southern European migrants were often scathingly referred to as 'factory fodder'. The Australian authorities recruited mainly unskilled people; while in Italy, it was the unskilled, unemployed men in the southern regions who were the focus of De Gasperi's policy encouraging emigration. In any case, the occupational status of the migrants was not simply a reflection of their skill level; given the structural barriers placed in the way of recognition of immigrants' qualifications, it was not unusual to find people with skills and qualifications doing unskilled work. Moreover, many migrant workers were recruited on the condition that they take jobs assigned to them by the Australian government for at least two years.

Recruitment of predominantly unskilled workers, refusal to accept the qualifications of those who were skilled, assignment of workers

Italian engineering workers are shown here celebrating the completion of the first boiler at the Loy Yang Power Station, La Trobe Valley, Victoria. *Left to right* D. Di Fabrizio, A. Barbieri, D. Calabrese, C. del Buso, N. der Horst and P. Rosato. (*Italian Historical Society, Melbourne*)

to heavy manual jobs, often in remote areas, and lack of language courses, educational and training opportunities—all these factors led to the development of what Lever-Tracy and Quinlan have called the 'southern European occupational ghetto' (1988: 82). Segmentation was often largely predetermined by entering the labour market at the lowest point and in industries which tended to be labour-intensive or required very limited formal skills, which made subsequent upward mobility very difficult. Employers were clear about the advantages of recruiting migrant workers:

> . . . in 1953 McLennan of BHP described Italians as 'a hardworking race, especially those in the unskilled category' . . . BHP records in fact show a strong predilection for southem European immigrants, based on the view that they were readily available, eager to migrate and less reluctant to undertake hazardous, dirty and enervating jobs. As a result of the language and recognition difficulties and limited job market knowledge of recent non-British immigrants, the company anticipated greater stability from such workers. This in fact proved to be the case (Lever-Tracy and Quinlan, 1988: 47–8).

Statistics demonstrate that the Italian-born in Australia have, on the whole, done well in econonomic terms: high rates of home ownership, lower than average unemployment and higher rates in the self-employed and employer categories. However, these figures say nothing about the experience of Italians working in hard, dirty

Enzo Nogoretto came to Australia from Italy in 1951 to work on a Bundaberg cane farm. He subsequently bought an 83-hectare property, where he grows 1500 tons of cane each year. (*Australian Official Photograph*)

and dangerous jobs, doing a lot of overtime or more than one job, as well as having all adult members of the family in paid employment. The following case studies will provide a more qualitative understanding of the conditions faced by Italian workers in Australia.

Italian men in construction: the Snowy Mountains scheme

One of the key requirements for postwar economic expansion was the availability of cheap and abundant energy. The Snowy Mountains provided the perfect natural conditions for the development of a hydroelectric system which could provide vast quantities of power. The massive size of the project and its labour-intensive nature provide the classical setting to look at the role of immigrant workers in postwar Australia's development.

A massive army of workers was required, for a project in which '16 large dams, one of them capable of holding nine and a half times the amount of water in Sydney Harbour, eight power stations with a total capacity of nearly 4 million kilowatts and 90 miles of tunnels were constructed in less than 25 years . . .' (Kobal, 1982: 15). The workforce was made up of immigrants from over 26 countries as well as Australian-born workers. Many Italian workers were employed in this workforce as tunnel diggers and other types of labourers. In fact many of the Italians who took up work at the Snowy were among those earlier involved in demonstrations at Bonegilla and Sydney (see Chapter 3 and Cresciani, 1988a: 253), when they asked to be given jobs as laid down in their immigration contracts, or to be returned to Italy.

The conditions at the Snowy were difficult, arduous and isolated. Wage levels were higher than for jobs in the cities, and there were large amounts of overtime to boost the pay packet. The almost exclusively male workforce were stationed in camps on the work-sites, allowing workers to save a fairly high proportion of their wages. This was an important factor for the Italian men, as many of them had come to Australia by themselves, leaving their wives and families at home. Work on projects such as the Snowy allowed them to save up to bring their families out to Australia. For those who were unattached, the money allowed them to undertake a quick return to their country to marry, or in some cases to take proxy brides (see Chapter 10). Others used the funds to assist the passage of members of their extended family or people from their villages.

Similar conditions existed in the construction of railways, power and communication links which would traverse the desolate centre of this great continent. The other aspect that must be remembered is that these jobs did not offer long-term employment, but rather served as a starting point from which to enter more permanent employment, usually in the large urban centres or to venture into small business.

Most of the work on the Snowy scheme was contracted out by a principal contractor to numerous subcontractors, who employed the majority of labourers and tradesmen (Snowy Mountain Authority, 1961: 20). A number of workers were able to put together work gangs, and establish their own small subcontracting firms. Thus some subcontractors were migrants who recruited employees from their own country of origin by offering positions to family and friends. Chain migration also had its effects on the work experience of migrants. The first reference point for *many* migrants was their community and family contacts, so there was a tendency for people to congregate in similar work places. Working for a fellow national in an unfamiliar country led to an expectation of shared cultural norms and a sense of solidarity in a new environment. However, in practice the pressures of competition often meant that national and cultural ties succumbed to monetary considerations. The negative side was that smaller subcontractors, the majority of whom were migrants, were identified by unions as employers who were likely not to abide by award conditions and pay rates.

The Italians in the Snowy became concentrated in particular occupations, for example in masonry, particularly in tunnelling and building retaining walls (McHugh, 1989: 39). Some observers present the view that Italians became concentrated in such jobs because they had pre-migration experience in marble quarries and sulphur mines. However, this does not explain all occupational concentrations, as most Italian men who arrived in the 1950s were rural workers. McHugh explains the concentration in masonry work by the fact that the majority of Italians arrived at the time when tunnelling was commencing, while the existing workforce had already become established in other occupations.

In view of discriminatory attitudes amongst employers it is not by chance that Anglo-Australians in the Snowy were very rarely found in dangerous occupations underground or on the towers. One attraction of the high-risk occupations to migrants was the 'monetarisation' of health and safety conditions: rather than attempting to make the workplace safer or to stop work in hazardous conditions, extra payments were made for dangerous work. Since many Italians came from an experience of chronic unemployment, they were prepared to work under adverse conditions in order to earn as much as possible while employed, to provide for future economic security.

Employment based on ethnic ties was manifested in large firms in the construction and engineering sector. One example was the Italian-based Electric Power Transmissions (EPT), the company which was responsible for constructing the pylons and laying the high tension electricity lines. Its workforce consisted of large numbers of Italian and Spanish workers. Chain migration also provided a pool of workers for an Italian construction firm, Legnami Pasotti, which was engaged to build accommodation in the Snowy area for construction workers. 'Pasotti came from Brescia, near Milan, and most of the three hundred tradesmen he brought out were from northern Italy' (McHugh, 1989: 51). Italian companies and managers suffered from lack of local industrial knowledge and experience, and in some cases from lack of acceptance by the local business community. Shared industrial relations and human resource practices led to a measure of security in a foreign environment for employers as well as for employees.

On the Snowy, 27 Italians were killed in accidents, nearly 20 of them underground (McHugh, 1989: 248). These figures do not include people who contracted diseases which only manifested themselves many years after they had completed their work. Miners and tunnellers are two groups who frequently suffer from respiratory and auditory problems as a result of their work conditions. The following story reminds us of the human realities of hazardous work.

> The worst multiple fatality of the Scheme occurred when four young Italians plunged to their deaths down a lift shaft . . . On 16 April 1958, Benito Fizzol, Antonio Guseli, Giuseppe Rugolo and Michele Di Salvio stepped onto a platform at the top of the shaft and started to fix heavy concrete pipes into position to be lowered. At over three hundred metres, it was claimed to be the longest single stage lift in the world . . .
>
> The men called out to the hoist operator to lower the platform a little so that they could secure the pipes to the guide rails. As he started to do so, a gear wheel on the hoist broke, and the cable suddenly ran free, dropping the four men, four tonnes of pipes, and the platform, down the shaft and slamming them onto a set of pipes nearly a hundred metres below. The operator only heard the crash—they didn't even have time to scream (McHugh, 1989: 236).

Migrant workers of non-English speaking background were and are concentrated in industries and occupations which have higher than average accident rates and also pose a greater threat to health. Perhaps when we examine the economic development of a nation we should pay more attention to the people who risk their lives, and not only to those who risk their capital.

Italian women in manufacturing

In the early years of settlement, most Italian women joined the workforce as wage earners in the manufacturing sector.[2] The 1971 census showed that 64 per cent of Italian women in the workforce who had immigrated in the preceding five years were employed in manufacturing (Alcorso, 1991). A factory job was usually the first experience of work in Australia, and some women were later able to move into other jobs, for instance as employees in hospitals, shops and offices, or as proprietors or helpers in family businesses. Italian women's employment patterns reflect those of their male counterparts, but the women suffer from the added disadvantage of a discriminatory Australian labour market which is heavily segmented on gender lines. Typically men and women do different types of work, and the former are better paid. For instance in 1985, the average weekly income for Italian men working full-time was $363; the average for Italian women working full-time was $265 (73 per cent of the male figure) (Castles et al. 1986: Table 6.1).

Italian women's child-bearing and rearing roles led many of them to interrupt their employment, or to take up paid work in their homes. The growth of outwork was due both to inadequate child-care facilities and changing production processes in the clothing trade. Italian women were forced to do without the informal child-care arrangements, provided by the extended family and the village structures in their country of birth. Provision of child-care outside the family is relatively underdeveloped in Australia, compared with most European countries. This problem affects the Australian-born population too, but is more serious for women of non-English speaking background because of their unfamiliarity with local structures, and because the services are often culturally and linguistically inappropriate.

The double contribution given by Italian women is highlighted in recent research by Caroline Alcorso (1991). Here are extracts from two of her case studies.

> Natalia migrated with her family to Australia in 1952; she is now 52 years old and has three children . . . She came from a small northern village, and while she never had a paid job before coming to Australia, she had the characteristic training of a young peasant girl in the 1950s; she was apprenticed to a village dress maker for three years, and had one year of training (unpaid) at a Singer sewing factory. On coming to Australia it was natural that she should seek work in the clothing industry, and she never had trouble in finding work as a machinist in clothing factories where many women she knew worked. Natalia worked in a pyjama factory until the birth of her first child in 1967; three years later, after her second child, she began working in a shirt factory until 1976 when she had her third child. After that she decided to stay at home, and obtain sewing outwork through her cousin, which she continued until recently . . . she preferred the factory work to outwork: the former had better wages and conditions. Working as an outworker eight to ten hours a days, five days a week, usually brought around $200, though the amount, based on piece rates varied; and she received no sick pay, holiday pay or other award entitlements. Although she belonged to the clothing trade union . . . she feels the union has little power to achieve much for clothing workers. If it was not for the money, Natalia is definite that she would not have continued to work; her husband, a formwork carpenter, didn't like her to work . . . Overall she feels that the pay has been poor for her years of effort . . .
>
> Rosa grew up . . . in a southern Italian village. After arriving in Australia, Rosa took the first job she could get working as a factory hand in a clothing factory . . . [As] she was being underpaid in that factory, she began looking for work elsewhere and eventually got a job in the clothing factory where her sister worked . . . [S]he then arranged with the factory to employ her as an outworker . . . She has repetition strain injury from the work . . . [and] has had two operations over the last fifteen years; she has never received workers' compensation. Although it suits her to work at home, she finds outwork tiring, boring and isolating; for a change, she began working casually in a clothing factory in 1987. However, conditions in the small factory were very bad; she 'worked like a slave' . . . So after three months, Rosa decided to return to outwork . . .

> Rosa said she was not satisfied with her current domestic or working life—she would have liked to do the Higher School Certificate and eventually to have gone to university. She comments: 'Once I was clever, and I had a good brain—now, after years of sitting in front of a machine, it is not working well—I get confused. If it was not for the money, she would not want to work (Alcorso, 1991).

These accounts exemplify the work and life experiences of many Italian women who, out of economic necessity, had to enter into paid employment while being forced to continue all the homemaker duties. The labour market experience of the vast majority of women is one of being employed in relatively low-status jobs. They have little possibility of career mobility, since they usually have interrupted employment experiences, and their occupations do not have any career structures.

Farmers

Italian involvement in Australian agriculture has a long history. An important factor influencing the migrants choice of occupation and place of settlement was their social and geographical background. Price (1963: 30) noted that the majority of southern European settlers came from relatively small villages and towns and that cultivation of the land was an important part of life in these villages. Italians arrived in Australia with a strong desire for self-sufficiency as independent landholders.

A system of mutual support, with labour and equipment being shared, assisted in the process of getting established. Peasant skills, ingenuity and resourcefulness aided Italians as pioneers in new enterprises and enabled them to maximise existing resources. These factors plus their willingness to work long hours and sometimes do two jobs, sometimes gave Italians an advantage over their Australian counterparts. In several areas Italians were able to withstand crises in particular industries and to use these periods to buy out Australians who were ready to leave farming (Burnley, 1976: 82–9; Borrie, 1954: 56–7).

Areas of Italian settlement

There were Italian settlements in several parts of Australia well before the turn of the century. In the Daylesford area of Victoria, Italians were amongst the pioneers who turned to agriculture as the gold rush days of the 1860s came to an end. They settled as potato growers, wine growers and mixed farmers (Pascoe, 1987: 133–5).

Bernadette Collura from Sicily drives the tractor on her family's fruit farm near Perth, WA. (*Australian Official Photograph*)

In New South Wales there was also a substantial number of Italian settlers in rural areas before the turn of the century. One significant settlement was 'New Italy' on the Richmond River. In Western Australia, Italians took up agricultural land in areas surrounding Perth and were also very active in fishing. Gamba's 1952 study of the Italian fishermen of Fremantle documents how Italians were instrumental in establishing the fishing industry. Italian involvement in the industry commenced around 1881 and by the turn of the century the majority of licensed fishermen were of Italian origin—mainly from the regions of Sicily and Puglia (Gamba, 1952: 5).

The inflow of Italians into rural areas, particularly in Queensland, increased after the turn of the century. The 1933 census showed that one-third of all Italians born in Australia resided in that state. Many were attracted by the opportunities for agricultural work and by the possibility of eventual land ownership. Most became orchardists or tobacco growers in the south of the state or sugar-cane farmers in the northern region. In the sugar-cane area many started out as cane cutters and progressed to own their own farms. A drastic fall in the price of sugar in the 1930s resulted in many Australians leaving the industry and Italians took advantage of this situation to buy farms (Burnley, 1976: 82–5).

Italians in the Murrumbidgee Irrigation Area

The contribution of Italians to the success of a rural project has been widely acclaimed in the Murrumbidgee Irrigation Area surrounding the city of Griffith in the south-west of New South Wales. Today Italians can be found in all areas of trade and commerce. Most noticeable however is their presence in the farming sector, where they hold the majority of the small- to medium-size horticultural farms and some of the large-area rice, wheat and sheep farms. Italians and their descendants are now estimated to number around 12 000–13 000, or 60 per cent of the 21 000 people in the Griffith area.

The first Italians arrived as the government-sponsored project was being established in 1911. They worked on the construction of the irrigation canals. The inflow of Italians continued as the farms were established and work became available. The earliest arrivals were from the province of Treviso in the Veneto and these numbered 33 by the 1921 census. Amongst the new arrivals were a few *calabresi*, *abruzzesi* and Sicilians. By the end of the decade there were 197 Italians of whom 33 were women. The total doubled by the end of the 1930s and many spouses and families arrived, which evened up the ratio between the sexes.

Upon arrival some Italians found work as building and construction workers, but the great majority became agricultural labourers on Australian-owned farms. Gradually Italians were able to gain sufficient means to lease and eventually buy their own farms. By 1933 over 10 per cent of the 600 horticultural farms in Griffith were Italian-owned (Price, 1955: 8). By 1947 Italian ownership had increased to 27 per cent. One factor which enhanced Italian chances for farm ownership was the high failure rate amongst Australians who had taken up the farms as part of the World War I soldier resettlement scheme. Many of them lacked the necessary skills and tenacity to cope with the harsh conditions. As Australians forfeited their farms, Italians were able to buy them for relatively low prices. Through hard work Italians were able to repair farms which were often damaged through waterlogging or salting, and bring them back to full productivity. The Italians' ability to call on extended family networks for support, and also their peasant skills and ingenuity, allowed them to succeed where others failed.

The gradual takeover of farms by Italians often led to hostility on the part of Anglo-Australians. As early as 1927, attempts were made to prevent any more Italians from settling in the area or having the same rights as Anglo-Australians to buy farms. During World War II the sale of farms to Italians was prohibited. In 1947 there were further attempts to restrict the sale of farms to Italians on the basis of claims that they did not make good farmers. Langford-Smith, a geographer, argues that the assertions about Italian farmers were quite unjustified. While some Italian vegetable growers had caused waterlogging and salting through lack of knowledge of the hazards, Italian horticulturalists had in fact repaired and improved many previously damaged blocks (Langford-Smith and Rutherford, 1966: 99).

Immigration stopped during the war years but picked up rapidly afterwards, and by 1954 the Italian-born population numbered 2280. The proportion of northerners was 75 per cent in 1947 but in the postwar years the proportion of southerners increased. By 1970 it was estimated that approximately 50 per cent originated from the north of Italy, mainly from the Veneto, whilst 40 per cent were from the south —Calabria and Sicily—and 10 per cent from Abruzzi. The Italian purchase of farms continued: by 1970, Italians or their descendants held 56.5 per cent of all farms in the area and 80 per cent of horticultural farms between 8 and 27 hectares. Italians had begun to move into large area farming with production of rice, sheep and wheat (Huber, 1977: 68–72). Department of Agriculture estimates in the early 1980s showed that Italians owned around 10 per cent of large-area farms and 13 per cent of rice farms (Kelly, 1983: 155).

There was still envy of the Italians' success and this led to tension, mistrust and a distinct social distance between the groups. This made it difficult to involve Italian farmers in Agricultural Extension programs and to pass on advice and information vital for the treatment of trees and vines. In the early 1950s an effort was made to provide a channel of communication between the Italian and Anglo-Australian communities. Al Grassby, then an extension officer with the local agricultural authority, set up a continental music club which was a venue for interaction and also a means to promote further Italian participation in other community organisations (see Chapter 7). This activity was successful in drawing Italian men into Anglo-Australian organisations but only a few Italian women were drawn into the Anglo-Australian women's organisations (Tully, 1962: 15–20).

The present situation

Italian migration to Griffith has been minimal in recent years, thus the resident Italian families are very well established. Italians play a major part in the farming and business sector, and second-generation Italians are well represented in most professions, with the exception of the medical profession. There has been increasing Italian representation on decision-making bodies and in the various trades and farming associations such as the Growers' Association (Kelly, 1985). In the last 27 years there has always been some representation of Italians in local government (Kelly, 1984: 131). In 1990 four of the twelve elected councillors were of Italian origin and these included for the first time an Italian-born woman, Nives Piccoli. The president of the Shire, John Dal Broi, was an Australian-born son of Italian parents, who had held this position for six years.

One example of the increasing recognition of the Italian presence was the twinning of the city of Griffith with Treviso and several surrounding villages in the Veneto region. This led to visits of Italian officials to Griffith in 1983, and a return visit of Griffith people to complete the process in 1984. During these celebrations, gifts were exchanged between local governments and reunions were held, which allowed branches of families to meet, sometimes for the first time. During the Griffith Italians' return visit to Italy, recognition was given to their hard work and achievements in their new land.

Another indication of Italian initiative is the construction of a Scalabrini Home for the Aged. This project was commenced by people from the Veneto region but quickly won the support of Italians from all the regions. Fundraising functions, such as *festa* days, dinners featuring regional cuisine and ladies' luncheons, were held. The activities surrounding the fundraising were important in bringing together the separate regional groups. They were also effective in involving some Italian women in community activity where previously they had remained within family structures (Kelly, 1985; 1989).

There has been an increase in participation in social organisations (Kelly, 1983: 150–1). This is more evident amongst Italian men and for second-generation Italians generally. Several large social clubs play an important role, by providing sporting facilities, a place for men to meet for a drink or a game of cards after work, and are used as venues for weddings and other social occasions.

The labour market position of Italo-Australians

The economic goal of Australian immigration policy until the 1970s was to provide unskilled labour for infrastructure projects, mining and manufacturing. There were always exceptions: some Italian peasants became self-employed farmers, others became entrepreneurs (see Chapter 5). But the general picture was international rural-urban migration in the form of a shift from agricultural work to low-skilled industrial work. Is this still the case today? Do Italian-born Australians remain concentrated in low-skilled manual work? And are second-generation Italo-Australians still concentrated in the type of jobs their fathers and mothers did? This section will present some statistical evidence on the first issue, while the position of the second generation will be examined in Chapter 11.

There are four tendencies which we might expect to change the initial low socio-economic status of Italian migrants. The first is connected with economic restructuring. As industrial and technological developments reduce the number of unskilled jobs, it is obvious that workers will move out of them. The shift may be to unemployment, out of the workforce (for instance through early retirement), to self-employment or into more skilled jobs.

The second tendency is connected with the migratory process: new migrants often take jobs which local people do not want—low-skilled jobs with poor pay and conditions. As Italian workers gained knowledge of the labour market, and developed informal networks, they had some chance of getting better jobs. On the other hand, many workers got 'locked into' low-status jobs: the pressure of work and lack of schooling prevented them from learning English and gaining further training; discrimination by employers sometimes closed off entry into better jobs; and unused skills became obsolete. The question is whether the positive trends outweighed the disadvantageous ones.

The third tendency is demographic: as the migrant generation ages, some leave the workforce, while others become more firmly established in their jobs. In industrial countries, young workers generally have higher unemployment rates than older ones. The unemployment rate of the Italian-born was the lowest of all birthplace groups in 1989: 3 per cent, compared with 6 per cent for all Australian-born people in the labour force (ABS, 1990: 92), mainly due to the high age-profile of the Italian-born (see Chapter 3). One cause for departure from the workforce is poor health: many Italian workers in industry have retired early due to industrial illnesses or accidents (Alcorso, 1988).

The fourth tendency is social mobility in the real sense: that is movement from low-skilled to higher-skilled employment. There is no precise way of measuring this. Obviously, most social mobility is intergenerational: second-generation Italo-Australians have generally been able to get much higher standards of schooling and tertiary education than their parents. Six per cent of Italian-born people in Australia in 1986 had not been to school at all, while 30 per cent had left school at the age of 12 or younger. Only 1.4 per cent had tertiary qualifications (BIR, 1990b: 12–15). We lack comparable figures for second-generation Italo-Australians, but it can be assumed that virtually all stay on at school until the age of 16, with many going on to gain tertiary qualifications. On the other

Figure 4.1 Italian-born men by labour force status, per cent

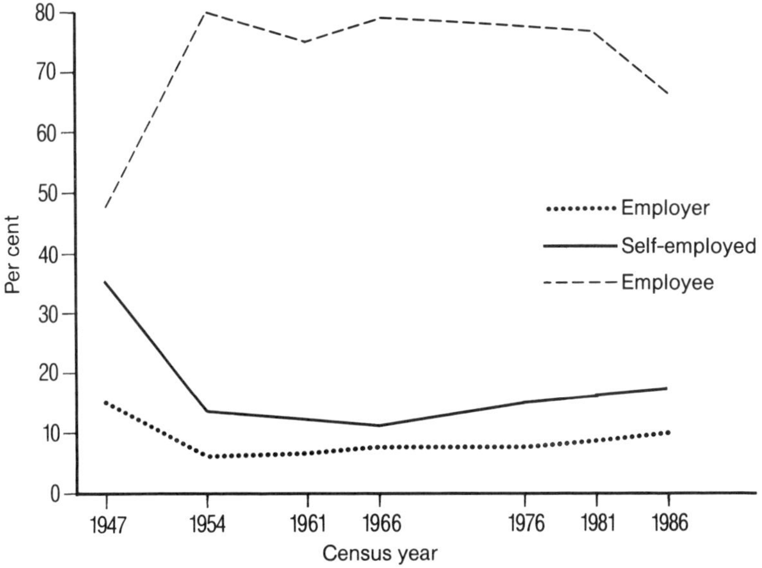

Note: Family helpers and unemployed are left out.
Source: Censuses of the various years.

Figure 4.2 Italian-born women by labour force status, per cent

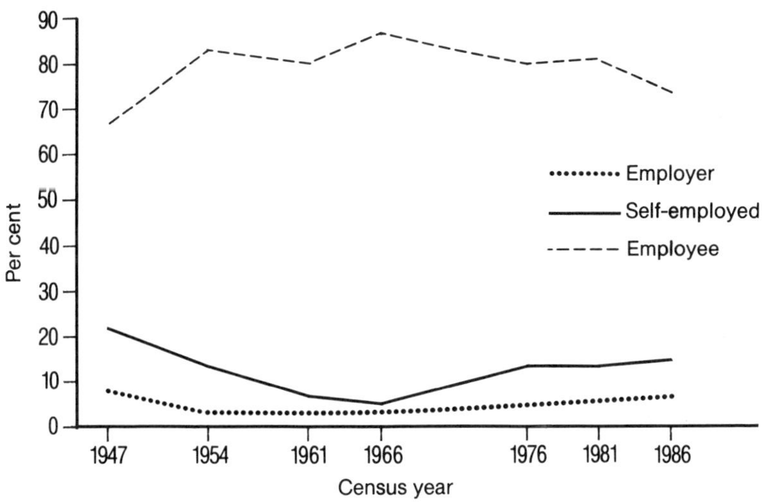

Note: Family helpers and the unemployed are left out.
Source: Censuses of the various years.

Figure 4.3 Italian men compared with all men in the workforce by occupation, 1986

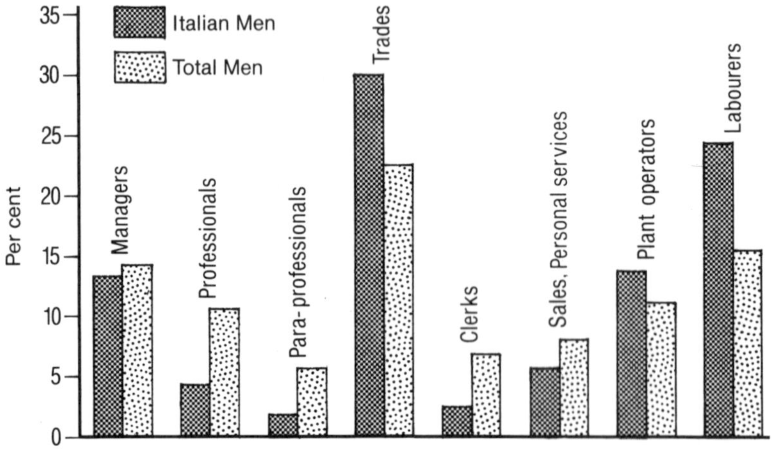

Source: Census 1986.

hand, many first-generation Italian workers have trade qualifications—11 per cent in 1986, which was higher than the rate for the Australian-born population (BIR, 1990b: 14–15).

The total Italian-born workforce increased from a total of 95 074 persons in 1954 to 170 207 in 1971, after which it declined, reaching a figure of 138 805 by the 1986 census, of whom 97 335 were men and 41 470 were women (BIR, 1990b: 22–3). The decline is due to the ageing of the Italian-born population, at a time when there was little new immigration from Italy. Figures 4.1 and 4.2 examine the employment status of Italian men and women.

The charts show that high proportions of both Italian men and women were employers in 1947. This was because many of the prewar immigrants were small farmers or shopkeepers. Nearly all postwar migrants became wage earners, so that the rate for employees rose to over 80 per cent for Italian women and nearly 80 per cent for Italian men. By 1966, only 8 per cent of Italian men were employers and 11 per cent were self-employed. For women the rates in 1966 were 4 per cent employers and 6 per cent self-employed. However, the trend became reversed, as Italian-born people left the factories and set up businesses. By 1986, only 67 per cent of Italian men were employees, while 10 per cent were employers and 17 per cent were self-employed. For women, the figures were 72 per cent employees, 7 per cent employers and 13 per cent self-employed.

It is impossible to present accurate time series on occupational status, because statistical categories have changed over the years. In 1966, only 4.2 per cent of Italian-born men were managers and administrators and 1. 1 per cent were professionals; 67.6 per cent were labourers and related workers. By 1981, the figures had risen to 5.5 per cent managers and administrators and 3.7 per cent professionals, while the proportion of labourers and related workers had fallen to 59.4 per cent. The proportion of Italian women who were managers and administrators only rose from 1 to 1.3 per cent in the same period, while the proportion of professionals increased from 1.4 to 3.5 per cent. The share of labourers and related workers fell from 53.9 per cent in 1966 to 32.7 per cent in 1981. Figures 4.3 and 4.4 show the occupational patterns for Italian-born men and women in 1986, in comparison with the total workforce of Australia.

Figure 4.3 shows that Italian-born men still have an occupational distribution which differs markedly from the overall Australian pattern: they are overrepresented in the manual categories of trades, plant operators and labourers, and underrepresented in the white-collar categories of managers, professionals, para-professionals, clerks and sales and services. The manager category needs some interpretation, since it is generally seen as a high-status area. In fact it includes small shopkeepers and farmers, so that the fairly high representation of Italians does not necessarily indicate upward

Figure 4.4 Italian women compared with all women in the workforce by occupation, 1986

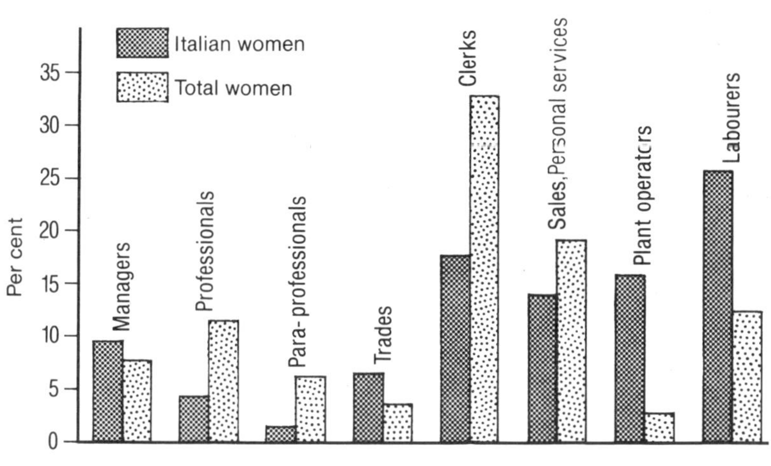

Source: Census 1986.

mobility. For women, Figure 4.4 shows a somewhat similar picture. However the overrepresentation in the manual categories of plant operators and labourers is even more marked, and the underrepresentation as clerks is also dramatic.

It is also useful to look at the distribution by industry. In 1966, 39 per cent of Italian men were employed in manufacturing and 23 per cent in construction. By 1986, the proportion in manufacturing had fallen to 24 per cent and that in construction to 18 per cent. The decline in these sectors was matched by a shift into the service sectors, such as wholesale and retail trade, finance, property and business services, and community services. As for women, the peak figure for manufacturing was 62 per cent in 1954, declining to 55 per cent in 1966 and 26 per cent in 1986 (few women are employed in construction). Again, there was a marked shift into the services.

In 1986 there was a continued concentration of Italian men and women in manufacturing and, to a lesser extent, in wholesale and retail trade. Italian men were highly concentrated in construction, while women were concentrated in community services. The comparison with the rest of the population at this time shows a slight overrepresentation of the Italian-born in agriculture, forestry, fishing and hunting, and a marked overrepresentation in manufacturing and construction. The Italian-born were underrepresented in finance, property and business, public administration and defence and community services (BIR, 1990b).

The overall conclusions of the analysis of the labour market position of Italian migrants are clear. In the postwar period, most Italian immigrants became manual wage earners in manufacturing and construction. As the structure of the economy has changed, and the Italian immigrants have become both more integrated and older, the employment situation has changed for some. They have become employers or self-employed, while others have moved into non-manual jobs in the service sectors. Nonetheless, Italian-born men and women still remain substantially overrepresented in relatively low-status manual jobs in the construction and manufacturing sectors, and underrepresented in higher-status white-collar jobs in other parts of the economy.

5 Cappuccino capitalism: Italian immigrants and Australian business

Jock Collins

Most studies of Italian immigration have focused on the working class and their role as 'factory fodder' for Australian industry. The contribution of Italian migrants in small and large businesses is, to a large extent, a forgotten story. This chapter tells that story: it deals with the experience of Italian immigrants and their children who became independent producers, small businesspeople, or even—in a few cases—captains of industry. The businesses that Italians first entered were in areas related to farming and fishing. Other areas of Italian business were in 'traditional' specialisations of food, clothing and footwear, often initially serving the Italian 'enclave'. But as new opportunities arose and Australians gradually accepted Italian food and other products, Italian businesspeople gradually broke away from an ethnic enclave.

The dream of independence

Most Italian migrants who arrived before 1947 were of peasant background. The traditional desire for peasant independence became, in Australia, a 'craving for an independent small business' (Price, 1963: 142). Their skills in agriculture, fishing and traditional crafts such as carpentry, terrazzo-work and shoemaking, led them to seek to establish businesses in these areas, although they often had to work for a time as labourers to build up sufficient capital. Similarly, Pascoe points out that 'the dream of land ownership is intrinsic to peasant culture . . . The history of Italian cultivation in

Australian soil is a long one, and, together with fishing, has profoundly shaped Italo-Australian culture' (1987: 131). Overall, Pascoe describes the history of Italian cultivation as 'one of great success' allowing Italians to achieve 'land ownership on the same small scale basis that they had expected in Italy' (1987: 132). A key to this success was the co-operative method of farming and finance, peasant farming skills and the 'involvement of compatriots in other parts of the food-processing chain, especially as fruiterers, restaurant owners and cooks, and as small goods manufacturers' (1987: 133).

In the inner metropolitan areas before 1945 about one-fifth of Italians and other southern Europeans were employed as unskilled labourers, another one-fifth as skilled tradesmen and only 'a minute fraction' in the professions or in commerce. About half of all southern Europeans were employed in the 'catering business' as 'wine saloon-keepers, oyster-bar proprietors, fishmongers, restaurant-keepers, fruiterers, confectioners, ice-cream vendors, florists, hotel proprietors, cooks, waiters, barmen or shop-assistants' (Price, 1963: 156). Why did Italians and other southern Europeans in cities move into catering? Price argues that small catering businesses were 'ideally suited' for southern Europeans who were seeking rapid independence. These businesses required little capital to start, allowed a number of men or family groups to live cheaply on the shop premises, and were less subject to trade union and other restrictions on long hours of work. Moreover, they 'fitted in well with the peasant tradition of family labour—the wife and children could help in the kitchen or behind the counter, thereby reducing labour costs substantially' (Price, 1963: 156). In addition, little English was required other than for the person in charge. As Price comments, '[f]ishing, commerce and some of the skilled trades—tailoring, cabinet-making, shoemaking, hairdressing, terrazzo-paving—offered similar opportunities' (Price, 1963: 156).

Price and Pascoe stress the importance of 'cultural continuity', but underplay the role of social relations between Italians and Australian employers, bosses and the community. An important reason for Italian migrants moving into small businesses was that the relations between them and the established British-Australian community were characterised by friction and distrust. Independent small businesses allowed migrants to escape this hostility, or at least confront it on their own terms. Although Italians and other southern Europeans escaped the colour bar, introduced in 1901 through the White Australia policy, hostility to non-British migrants was caused by economic competition with the Australian and British-born working class. Employers were eager to use Italian labour to undermine wages and conditions. The resulting conflict between Italian and Australian workers was examined by several official inquiries. The

1904 Royal Commission found that Italians worked for lower wages, were viewed as less militant by employers, and that 'some employers tended to use Italian labour to split the solidarity of the Australian unions' (Borrie, 1954: 143). The 1925 Ferry Report recorded the fear and suspicion between Australian and Italian workers in Queensland which arose out of the low wages and poor conditions that Italian workers accepted. In the 1930s, there were riots as Italians were used as strike-breakers on the Melbourne wharfs.

In this way, Italians became the object of Australian racism and prejudice. This limited their opportunities in wage labour. The 'independence' of small and large business was attractive, because it provided an escape from the racism of other workers and of employers, particularly when Italians were limited by and large to labouring on farms or, in later years, to dangerous and dirty jobs in factories, whatever their skills or qualifications.

Most Italians in the prewar period came to Australia through chain migration, which is linked closely to the role of the Italian petit bourgeoisie in Australia. Chain migration meant that new arrivals would be sponsored by a relative who often owned a farm, restaurant or shop. In return for the money advanced to pay the fare to Australia, the new arrivals would work long hours for low pay in the business. The sponsors would give advice and guidance to the newcomer, and often were a source of finance as the newcomer himself eventually moved into an independent business and sponsored, in turn, other relatives and friends to Australia.

Italians and small business in the postwar period

By 1947, a surprisingly large proportion of Italians had moved from wage labour to small business. The 1947 census recorded that half of all Italian males in the workforce were either self-employed (36.8 per cent) or employers (15 per cent). In contrast, less than a quarter of Australian-born males in the workforce were either self-employed (14.1 per cent) or employers (7.9 per cent). Similarly, while nearly one-third of Italian-born females in the workforce were self-employed (21.9 per cent) or employers (8.1 per cent), less than 10 per cent of Australian-born women were self-employed (5.9 per cent) or employers (3.2 per cent) (Colas, 1988: 89–90).

After World War II agriculture continued to be an important site of Italian small business (see Chapter 4). But during the post-1947 immigration program, most Italians entered the workforce as 'blue-collar' workers in manufacturing and construction. Migrants moved into the big cities such as Sydney and Melbourne, where they settled in old working-class suburbs close to the centre. This concentration provided the opportunity for a further extension of small-business activities. At first, most centred on the culinary, cultural and service needs of the Italian community: delicatessens, cafés, restaurants and other services. Italians also moved into the building industry, refurbishing houses in the Italian tradition. In areas of major Italian settlement like Carlton in Melbourne, Italian small businesses took on a dominant role in the local economy. A similar situation occurred in Sydney's 'Little Italy' in Leichhardt, where there were 175 Italian businesses by 1976.

By 1981, 24 per cent of Italian-born males in the Australian workforce were categorised as employers or self-employed while only 16.4 per cent of Australian-born men were in these categories. Similarly, 17 per cent of Italian-born women were either employers or self-employed, compared to 12.1 per cent of Australian-born women in the workforce. Some migrant groups, such as Greek and Dutch males, and Greek, Dutch and Lebanese women, had an even higher representation in these categories than Italians (Collins, 1988: 89–90). Italians were overrepresented among the self-employed in all industries other than fisheries, while Italian employers were overrepresented in all industries other than wholesale trade and the agricultural, fisheries and textiles industries. The second generation are excluded from this calculation.

One interesting feature is that the industries into which Italian small businesses were concentrated in 1947—agriculture and fisheries—were the very industries in which they were underrepresented in 1981. This suggests that while cultural explanations—which emphasise the continuity of small-business activities in Australia with pre-migration activities—were very useful to explain the movement of Italians into small business in the prewar and immediate postwar period, they are of much less use today. In 1981 Italians had a relatively large presence in industries such as food and beverage manufacturing, clothing and footwear manufacturing, general construction, retail trade and personal services. The 1986 census showed little change in these patterns.

However, industry aggregates hide the detail of Italian concentration in specific niches. More detailed data show that there is a relatively high Italian presence in the following areas within the retail industry: clothing fabric and furniture stores; men's clothing; shoe repairers; grocers, confectioners and tobacconists; fruit and vegetable stores; liquor stores; bread and cake stores; fish shops, take-away food shops and milk bars. Fruit and vegetable stores are by far the greatest area of Italian concentration in the retail industry, with Italians accounting for nearly one-third of all self-employed and employers in this sector of Australian retailing (Collins, 1989: 14).

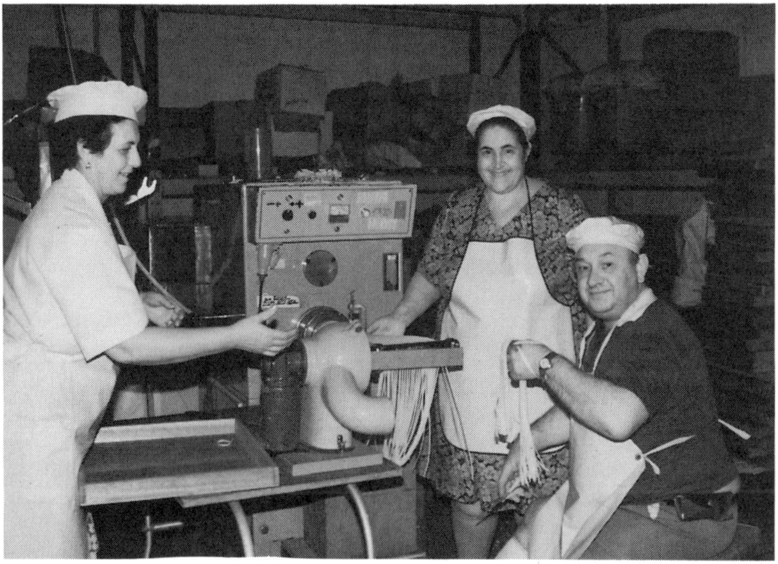

Flaminio and Filomena Fina operate Pasta Fina in Wollongong, New South Wales. They are among many Italian who have set up their own small businesses. (*Turo Chiodo*)

Italians and small business: survey results

There have been only two surveys of Italian small business in Australia, both conducted in the late 1980s. Lampugnani and Holton (1989) surveyed 98 Italian small businesses in South Australia across the broad span of industry types, while Castles et al. (1991) surveyed 45 Italian small businesses in Sydney, mostly retail businesses in the Leichhardt area. Both surveys had to abandon random sampling because of the high rejection rate. In the Lampugnani and Holton study, small business was defined as employing less than 50 workers, while the Castles et al. study used the Australian Bureau of Statistics definition of a small business as one employing less than 20 workers.

One of the key questions in the international literature relates to the reasons why migrants go into small business. Some theories suggest that certain ethnic groups have a cultural affinity to small business; a sort of 'natural' business acumen, such as has been suggested for the Jews (Waldinger, 1986: 6). The Lampugnani and Holton survey pointed to the 'strong ideology of independence characteristic of Italian–Australian business operators' with independence and autonomy mentioned by half the sample as the main attraction to business ownership (Lampugnani and Holton, 1989: 13–14). The problem with such approaches is that they do not allow for the influence of the circumstances that new migrants face in different countries at different times. An alternative approach suggests that blocked mobility in waged or salaried employment often motivates migrants to move into small business (Collins and Castles, 1989).

The Sydney study found that for some Italians, a move into small business simply continued what they did in Italy. For others, it was a response to conditions in Australia. Of the 45 Italian businesses interviewed in the Sydney study, the most frequent response (twelve) to the question '[w]hy did you go into business for yourself?' was that they were following in the family business tradition. As a shoe-shop proprietor put it, 'my father already had his own shop, so it seemed natural'. The remaining responses fell almost evenly into four groups. Many (seven) stated that they moved into business because of their experience in the Australian workforce, which was often characterised by downward occupational mobility and racist antagonism from bosses and fellow workers (Collins, 1988). One bistro owner stated that there was a 'lack of other type of work that I could do', while the owner of a construction business said that he moved into his current business 'because I was tired of seeing my labour go to nothing'. However, unlike the experience of other migrants, unemployment was generally not a factor in the Italians' move into small business. While 40 per cent of the Lebanese and 26 per cent of the Vietnamese surveyed had experienced unemployment, only 2 per cent of the Italians had.

The other two themes evident in the responses were that small business would allow them to make more money (seven) and gain independence (seven). Others valued the independence that 'being your own boss' gave them. As one hairdresser put it, his own business gave him 'freedom: the ability to decide on my own'. The accountant agreed, saying 'that was my ambition: to work for myself'. It is possible that many who answered about valuing independence do so because of their experiences as 'dependents' in the workforce, and may also be evidence for the 'blocked mobility' hypothesis.

The question of the success of ethnic small business is important, given the rate of failure of small business in general. According to one report, 40 per cent of small businesses in Australia fail in the first two years, while 85 per cent fail in five years (Neals, 1989: 67). Since both the Sydney and South Australian studies interviewed only current businesses, the samples are biased towards the successful: only thirteen out of the 45 Italian businesses in Sydney had set up in the last five years. The majority had survived much longer than the average life of small businesses in Australia. More than half of the sample claimed that the business was profitable. These findings seem to support the finding that migrant small businesses have a greater success rate than Australian-born businesses (Strahan and Williams, 1988: 80). Only four of the Sydney sample had 'gone broke' previously, while nine reported that they had friends whose business had failed.

Another important aspect relates to the method of finance. Most of the small businesses surveyed relied on banks to finance their business, a finding supported by the South Australian study (Lampugnani and Holton, 1989: 14). This contrasts with the experience of Vietnamese and Greek small businesses in Sydney, who tend to rely more on savings and family sources for finance (Castles et al., 1991: 132). This suggests that Italians have established themselves in the Australian community to the extent to which they can get access to major institutions such as the banks.

Some overseas literature on migrant small business stresses the importance of members of the same ethnic group as customers (Wilson and Martin, 1982), while others argue the opposite: that it is only when ethnic businesses transcend the 'ethnic enclave' that they become successful (Waldinger, 1986). The Sydney study found that Italians still formed an important part of custom. Nearly half reported that more than 70 per cent of their customers were Italian, while another seventeen reported that Italians made up 50–70 per cent of total custom. Moreover, nearly half of the businesses reported that they bought their present business from an Italian, indicating ethnic continuity in the business. A similar finding, 'that a certain enclave sector still exists' among the customers of Italian small businesses, was reported in South Australia, although the study found that 'Italian ethnic businesses did not stay in the enclave or ghetto, but moved beyond it' (Lampugnani and Holton, 1989: 17, 19). The differences in the importance of the 'ethnic enclave' in the Sydney and South Australian studies could be explained by the fact that the Sydney study concentrated on retail businesses in Leichhardt, Sydney's 'Little Italy', while in South Australia the Italian businesses surveyed came also from the primary, manufacturing, and building and construction industries where customers are less localised.

If Italian small businesses are relatively successful in Sydney, it may be due to the role of the family rather than any innate business acumen. Both Australian studies strongly supported the importance of the family to Italian small business. In the South Australian study, the family was considered 'the major cultural resource for the business', providing business partners and labour in the majority of businesses studied. The study stressed that the family was more important than 'ethnic networks'—such as 'co-ethnic' suppliers, business links and employees (Lampugnani and Holton, 1989: 14). In the Sydney study, most businesses were operated by both husband and wife. In all but one of the businesses, children worked: three-quarters reported that two or more children worked in the business. They were paid in two out of three cases, although their actual rate of pay is not known.

One explanation for the survival of Italian small businesses is that while hourly rates of return are small, long hours of work permit a sufficient weekly profit. Only five businesses surveyed in Sydney were open less than 40 hours per week. About one-third (fifteen) were open between 40 and 50 hours per week, while the majority were open for more than 50 hours per week: fourteen between 50 and 60 hours, three between 60 and 70 hours, while seven reported that they were open more than 70 hours per week. Indeed, three Italian businesses (a fruit and vegetable shop and two restaurants) reported that they were open for 84 hours per week!

A corollary of the long hours demanded by small business is that most business owners complained of the lack of adequate time for the family and for leisure. When asked about the frequency of holidays, the wife of a small supermarket owner said that she had a holiday 'only when giving birth'! A fruit and vegetable shop owner, who arrived in Australia in 1956, said that he has never had a holiday in Australia, while a café owner said that he had only one holiday, and that was twelve years ago. Others replied that they had holidays 'only on weekends'. Only half of the sample replied that they had regular holidays: seventeen had yearly holidays, while another six had regular holidays, but not each year.

Many Italians moved into small business to provide a better life for their family, particularly the children. It is ironical that the long hours of work meant that they did not have enough time for the family. For example, the shoe-shop proprietor complained that running a business left 'very little time for personal life', while a bathroom sales business owner mentioned that the business 'interferes very much with family life'. Nevertheless, the majority surveyed (28) responded in the affirmative to the question '[d]o you want your kids to go into business?' Less than a quarter (ten) replied in the negative. When asked a more general question about the aspirations they held for their children, most (eighteen) answered that 'it's up to them' or 'whatever makes them happy'. Twelve hoped that their children would move into university and professional jobs.

The picture that emerges from the Sydney and South Australian studies is one of success through hard work over long hours. It is hard to provide accurate information about finances, since small businesses are notorious for their guarded stance on such matters. Many often survive by keeping two sets of books, one for the tax man and a 'real' one for themselves. The impression, though, is that many of these businesses were marginal in the sense that the average hourly rate of return was very low. Only by using unpaid family labour did many businesses survive. This view is supported by the finding that only one-half of businesses surveyed reported that they were profitable. For many Italians in small businesses, it appears that they have moved from marginal worker to marginal entrepreneur.

Small business is described in the literature of class analysis as a 'contradictory class location' (Wright, 1985). The self-employed and small employers have the 'freedom' to determine the pattern of their labour day, but they take the responsibilities of the business home with them since they do not have a bundy clock marking the end of the working day. These independent businesses are dependent on the supplies, pricing policies and practices of the large corporations that dominate the wholesale side of retailing. The small entrepreneurs work hard for their children and families but have little time left to spend with them other than in the shop itself. The 'business' dominates social life for these people who moved into small business to be free and independent. Their desire is to make money, yet many work for years struggling to make ends meet.

The role of women in these small businesses is crucial, but is also often neglected. In most Italian small businesses in Sydney, women are responsible for many business tasks, work very long hours in the shops and then have the traditional family responsibilities as mother and houseworker when they return home. They emerge as the backbone of the success of Italian small businesses in Sydney. These Italian women faced the intergenerational, cultural conflict that other Italian women face in Australia, yet the freedom of running their own businesses often leaves them with less time and energy to deal with family and household matters. Yet without their input, the businesses would surely fail.

Similarly, the children are a critical source of labour in Italian small businesses in Australia. Work is expected of them, often unpaid, since the rationale for moving to Australia and into business is to provide educational and employment opportunities for the children which the parents so often lacked. The Sydney study did not conduct detailed interviews with second-generation Italians. However, the impression was that their experience in their parents' business was generally sufficient to turn them against aspirations of moving into small business themselves.

Italians who move into small business, particularly in the retail sector, have a much greater incidence of dealing with the Australian public than their working-class compatriots. They are the 'public face' of the Australian Italian community. Australian attitudes to Italians are often formed on this basis, with resulting stereotypes emerging that 'all Italians seem to own fruit shops, restaurants or cafés'. As a result, they also confront attitudes of racism and prejudice. Many of those surveyed in Sydney reported incidents of racial antagonism, particularly in the early days of settlement. This reveals another contradiction. Small business is seen as a way of avoiding racism and prejudice in the workplace, yet Italians in small business are more exposed to the racism and prejudice of the Australian public. Perhaps the persistence of the 'ethnic enclave' for many Italian small retail businesses is a response not only to economic advantages, but also a means of minimising exposure to racism and prejudice.

The Italian bourgeoisie in Australia

While most Italians have been employees or small businesspeople, a few have risen from relatively humble beginnings to the status of scions of the Australian ruling class. The names Sir Tristan Antico, Franco Belgiorno-Nettis and Bruno Luigi Grollo are well known in Australia. They are part of what Ruth Ostrow (1987) called 'the new boy network', the newcomers who have made their names in corporate Australia. Each year the magazine *Business Review Weekly* (BRW) lists the wealthiest 200 Australians. Surprisingly, about one in four of these wealthiest Australians are migrants from non-English speaking countries who usually arrived penniless. For them Australia truly is the 'lucky country'.

Sir Tristan Antico was born in Piovene, 150 kilometres north of Venice. He arrived in Australia at the age of seven. After leaving school, Antico worked as an office boy while he studied accountancy at night. In 1949, Antico and a partner started A&C Concrete Services, which was so successful that the company took over Pioneer Ready Mixed Concrete in 1954 (Ostrow, 1987). Success followed, so that by 1962 Pioneer expanded its operations overseas. Today Sir Tristan is head of Pioneer Concrete, with a minimum net fortune estimated by BRW to be $44 million. He has extensive interests in the horse-racing and stud industry, owning the stud Baramul (BRW, 1990: 95).

Franco Belgiorno-Nettis lived in Puglia in southern Italy before being drafted into the army. After the war, Belgiorno-Nettis completed his study in electronics and engineering and then decided to emigrate to Australia in 1951. As he tells it, 'I decided to go somewhere and thought of Australia—a young country with plenty of engineering projects. Also my wife, then my fiancée, Amina, wanted to come. She knew a bit of English. Australia was far away, and we could start from scratch. After five years helping to set up a division of an Italian power company in Australia, Belgiorno-Nettis and his Italian-born friend, Carlo Salteri—an engineering graduate from Milan University—decided to establish their own business. They started Transfield Pty Ltd, a company specialising in heavy engineering (Ostrow, 1987). Today Transfield has 25 hectares of workshop facilities producing 80 000 tonnes of steelwork annually for such projects as the Perisher Ski Tube and the Sydney Harbour Tunnel. Transfield is now a multinational corporation with plans for offshore operations to earn half of the revenue. BRW estimates the minimum net worth of Belgiorno-Nettis and Salteri at $270 million (BRW, 1990: 60). Belgiorno-Nettis has been an important influence on the arts in Australia. In 1973 he founded the Australian Biennale and the Transfield art prize, which have now been incorporated into the mainstream of Australian arts events (Ostrow, 1987: 48–52).

Bruno Grollo and his brother, Rino, are famous as the builders and half-owners of the landmark Melbourne office tower, the Rialto, and owners of the recently completed Shell headquarters, also in Melbourne. The Grollo brothers followed in the footsteps of their father, Luigi, who settled in Australia in 1928. Luigi Grollo started as a farmer in norhern Italy, and then worked as a labourer in Australia before setting up as a builder (Ostrow, 1987: 40–7). In the 1970s the brothers Grollo took over their father's concrete business and expanded into property development. They have a reputation of very good relations with their workers, enabling them to complete buildings in minimum time. The Grollo brothers had, in 1990, an estimated net worth of $550 million (BRW, 1990:62).

Italians have therefore made inroads into the Australian ruling class. They initially took advantage of 'niches' that became available with the expansion of Australian capitalism in the 1950s and 1960s. Today they have moved into the centres of corporate capitalism in Australia. While few in number, they provide an important 'demonstration effect' of the extent to which Italian migrants have penetrated all social classes in Australia, with some able to make it to the top. To some, these Italian millionaires are the symbol of the success of Italian migration to Australia. However, while Italians in big business often favoured Italian and other migrant labour, providing employment opportunities, these were generally limited to traditional labouring and building trades. It is difficult to see how the majority of Italo-Australians have gained in other ways from the success of the rich few. Their experiences are the exception, not the norm, for Australia's postwar Italian migrants.

Conclusion

Italians, like many other postwar migrants, have a disproportionate presence in the small business sector of the Australian economy. The picture that emerges is one of success through hard work and family labour. Some Italian experiences lend weight to the notion of 'blocked mobility': Italians move into small business because of discrimination, downward social mobility or unacceptable experiences in the Australian labour market as wage labourers. Others had a family history of small business, so that a move into small business in Australia represents a continuity of family tradition. While many Italian businesses still serve mainly Italian customers, others have spread throughout the Australian economy. For a few, small business has been a stepping stone to large-scale enterprise and great wealth.

It is clear that the contribution of Italians to Australian business is critical to an understanding of the Italo-Australian community today. The initial movement into small business was in areas related to traditional Italian products. The Italian delicatessen, fruit shop, café and restaurant have changed the culinary habits of Australians: pasta and cappuccino have become part of contemporary Australian culture. Similarly, the Italian barber and shoe repairer became familiar sights in many of Australia's suburbs. These Italians contributed to the process of change of Australian society from a predominantly monocultural, Anglo-Celtic society to a multicultural one. They became the public face of the Italian community in the minds of Australians. They simultaneously created and helped break down stereotypes of Italian migrants.

6 Place and community: the construction of an Italo-Australian space

Robert Pascoe

By the year 1960, some historians argue, the various groups of Italian immigrants had coalesced into something called 'the Italo-Australian community' (Bosworth, 1988: 615). This notion of 'community' gained wide general usage, described in Italian language newspapers as the *comunità,* and recurring in the speeches of political leaders, and in the discourse of popular speech. The term referred to all people of Italian descent living in Australia. It implied that they had more in common with each other than with other Australians; that the differences within this 'community' (Sicilians versus *veneti* in Australia, for instance) were weaker than the differences outside the collectivity. Such a 'community' has been bonded by certain historical processes, both in the act of migration and through the effects of settlement, has developed a language and set of rituals of its own, demonstrates a reasonably uniform political outlook, and occupies a geographically defined 'place' in Australian cities and towns. This is the basis upon which an Italo-Australian 'community' is deemed to exist. To the extent that this historical judgment is accurate, several questions arise. What were the processes by which this sense of 'community' developed? What is the sense of itself held by this community? In this context we will pay most attention to the non-linguistic manifestations of this identity, especially issues of territory, ritual and the like, as these define its 'social' rather than 'interpersonal' quality. Finally, we need at least to speculate on the impossibly difficult question of whether this Italo-Australian identity has helped redefine the dominant culture in

Australia. The chapter is organised around these three central questions.

The processes

Italian settlement in Australia may be understood in three overlapping stages: the *scouts,* the *farmers,* and the *builders.* Each stage was associated with a new and bigger wave of immigrants, in the 1850s, the 1920s, and the 1950s. In the 19th century hundreds of young Italian men, many of whom were attracted by the gold discoveries of the 1850s, came to the Australian colonies as manual labourers. Very few of the young men who arrived in the 19th century married Italian women and settled down in Australia, or acquired land and other businesses. We term them 'scouts' to capture this sense of their pioneering role. This was the experience of some of the group who landed in the 1920s as well, but they advanced further into the core of Australian life and culture. This second wave learned from the experience of the first, knew their way around Australia, began to devise strategies to set themselves up as farmers, as fisherfolk, and in small urban businesses. By the time of the third wave, these earlier migrations had provided a stock of knowledge and understanding which could be drawn upon in the construction of a recognisable 'community' (Pascoe, 1987).

Some criteria for determining the extent to which a sense of 'community' was established can be suggested. By 1910, before the second wave of immigrants, the hybrid language 'Australian' already existed in its fully developed form. By 1950, in advance of the third (and major) immigration, rituals and ceremonies of a distinctly Italo-Australian kind already existed. But it was not until 1960 that a third criterion was satisfied—that of an inviolable sense of Italian 'space' in the midst of an Australian city. The markers of 'community'—a popular language, shared public ceremonies, and a recognised territory—developed across all three waves of immigration. Italian migration to Australia is unique among all the non-British streams of migration for three reasons: Italian migration to Australia has been large in proportional terms; it was a multiple event, not a single act of immigration; and it permeated every colony (state) of the continent. These three features meant the Italians were different from other immigrants. The Chinese came in much larger numbers in the 1850s, but only to two colonies, and not again in significant numbers until the 1970s. The Germans, the Greeks, the Lebanese and any other groups one could care to mention, came in smaller numbers, or only to one part of Australia, or in only one or two waves.

The multiplicity of waves is important because each wave reinvigorates the sense of 'otherness' of the ethnic minority. A minority regards itself as 'other' to the dominant sense of 'self' characteristic of the majority. Each new wave also provides a creative interchange between the older immigrants and the younger. When the waves are spaced no more than 30 years apart, the older immigrants provide a model for the next generation. Melbourne builder Luigi Grollo, who arrived in 1928, employed many fellow Trevisans in the 1950s who went on to set up their own firms (Pascoe, 1988). The relative numerical size of the Italian population in each state has also been a crucial factor in explaining the timing and sequence of each stage in the coalescence of an Italo-Australian 'community'. Queensland and Western Australia were the most popular destinations for the 1920s wave: this fact helps explain the numerous and significant Italian farming and fishing localities in those states. Since World War II, however, Victoria's Italians have taken a clear lead in numerical terms: roughly 42 per cent of Italo-Australians now reside in that state. The political experiences of Melbourne's Italians are often indicative of trends in ethnic politics generally. Strategies developed in Melbourne around multicultural issues often find their way into arenas in other parts of Australia's federal political structure. The development of Italian-speaking branches of the Australian Labor Party and the political interventions by Italo-Australian welfare agencies are cases in point (see Chapters 8 and 9).

The scouts

The early influx of labourers was the first stage in the development of an Italo-Australian 'community'. They were reconnaissance scouts, itinerant male workers who entered the colonies through all the available ports and tried all avenues of manual and professional employment. There were far more of these immigrants than is generally recognised. The shipping lists for the port of Melbourne for 1860, to take a random year, indicate 100 arrivals with Italian surnames. Yet very few of these immigrants appear in the city directories of subsequent years, indicating that the great majority were highly mobile and transient, perhaps working briefly in one location before moving on.

A key theme that emerges from the documentation available from this period is that of a collectivist, spontaneous culture. As they were 'men without women' to recall a phrase used in Canada (Harney, 1984), their relationships with other men were intense and focused on the workplace. They moved in small groups, often twos and threes, and came together in bigger crowds on special occasions, public holidays and on major construction sites. They were timber cutters, fossickers, labourers on railway construction sites, charcoal burners, farm labourers, cane cutters, and combinations of such workers. The building of the Cairns Railway, in the 1880s, the dredging of the dam at Healesville, Victoria, in the 1920s, or quarrying stone for the Great Ocean Road, in Victoria in the 1930s: these were examples of large projects, each involving dozens of Italian (and other) itinerant male labourers.

The political outlook of such men was radical democratic in the 19th century and communist or anarchist in the early 20th. They were influenced by Italo-Australians with strong political leanings such as Raffaello Carboni, Francesco Sceusa, Quinto Ercole, Francesco Carmagnola (Bentivoglio and Di Leonardo, 1984). Very few of these men were labourers themselves, but their ideas appealed to itinerant workers who had very little opportunity of achieving reform in the traditional political structures of the new country. This group of men had a well-defined political consciousness, but, paradoxically, no strong sense of community. This apparent contradiction arose out of their social situation. There was simply not a large enough pool of eligible marriage partners until the 1950s (except for those men who chose to remain within the tight circumscription of the Italo-Australian country towns) and few Italian-language institutions.

Most men in fact returned home to Italy in their middle or older age, even some like Carboni whose political and material success might otherwise have induced them to remain in Australia. When those who stayed in Australia did marry, the usual choice was an Irish-Australian woman, often an older widow with children. Their Australian-born children rarely learnt Italian, and any distinctive identity which might properly be termed Italo-Australian gradually dissolved. This was particularly true until the 1920s, even in those localities (Daylesford, Victoria; the Richmond River area of New South Wales) where Italians clustered in the late 19th century. The unmarried labourers often returned to Italy late in life, after years in Australia. An inquiry into lung diseases among Kalgoorlie goldminers in 1911 found that dozens of northern Italian men had gone home, often to die soon after (Pascoe, 1987: Chapter 5).

These Italian 'scouts' were highly mobile, much like their Anglo-Australian contemporaries, traversing whole regions and crossing colonial lines in search of work. Information on jobs, wage levels and working conditions passed through their networks. Indeed, just as in the USA before 1870, before 1920 Italo-Australians were more widely dispersed than they would be at any moment after. In other words, their thin dispersal across the continent amounted to a kind of reconnaissance, a buzz of gossip about economic opportunities throughout Australia. Such labour market intelligence helped inform the pattern of seasonal migration followed by Italo-Australian labourers. One of the most travelled paths, for much of the 1920–40 period, was the inland corridor from northern Queensland sugar farms to the citrus areas of south Queensland and New South Wales. Word of mouth was sufficient to keep these labourers informed, and friendships struck up in one cane-cutting season could lead to co-operation in succeeding years. One's first friendships here, and at Kalgoorlie or in Gippsland, arose out of *paesani* linkages, but quickly extended to 'friends of friends' in similar occupations.

The first stage in the history and culture of Italian people in Australia may thus be thought of as lacking a centre, or centres. Any notion of 'community' that may have been embryonic failed to find ritual or territorial expression.

The farmers

The second stage in the development of an Italo-Australian community came logically out of the first. To some extent it was the result of Australian government policy from the 1920s (MacDonald and MacDonald, 1970), favouring chain settlement. But in another way it arose out of the earlier 'scouting' phase. Groups of labourers co-operated in the purchase of sugar farms, fishing boats and other capital investments. The classic form this took was on the north Queensland cane fields: the oldest member of each cutting gang was supported in getting his own farm, and then the others in turn were supported. This co-operation distinguished them fundamentally from the local Australian cane cutters, who worked for individual gain, and, as a consequence, were steadily outnumbered in winning farm ownership. At Fremantle, the fisherfolk maintained a similar level of co-operation at each stage in the evolution of their industry: from the early days on Rockingham Beach, to the Depression years at Fremantle, through to the 1948 establishment of a Fishermen's Co-operative, and to the sophisticated crayfishing operation at Geraldton in later years (Bosworth and Bosworth, 1990).

The 'farming' stage represented a qualitatively different phase in the evolution of 'community'. Appearing on the scene were wives and children who were linked economically and culturally to the lives of men. Often the same property was shared by two or three farming families such as the Zanattas of Stanthorpe, Queensland (Pascoe, 1990: Chapter 2), whose Australian settlement commenced in 1923. Just as unpaid family labour was fundamental to *la cultura contadina* (Italian peasant culture), so too, in Australia, women's and children's contribution to the domestic economy was vital to material success. In a sense, however, the significant and interesting feature of this stage was its cultural expression, for it was in this phase that the Italo-Australian *festa* first made its appearance. The *festa* can be seen as an 'imaginary' solution to the problem of reconciling the cultural conflict between the old country and the new. It provided the immigrant generation with a statement of their identity in the country town and helped explain to their children the source of their ethnicity. The street festivals of north Queensland and Gippsland country towns in Victoria, and the fishing festivals of Fremantle in Westem Australia and Port Pirie in South Australia had their origins in the period from about 1930 to 1950. (Their US counterparts started in the 1890–1910 era—a similar period of cultural anxiety.)

The cultural anxieties in the immigrant experience arose out of the demands placed on the second generation by their Australian contemporaries, and the growing sense of distance from the traditional life of an Italy fast receding from view. The 'imaginary' solution involved the re-enactment of the *festa* from the old town—not as they might have experienced it, but as it was remembered and reconstructed in popular memory. The *festa* was therefore changed: it ceased to be a magical ritual, a fertility rite tied to the seasons of the agricultural year, and instead became a statement of identity among Italo-Australians. The first *festa* to be reconstructed in this way were associated with rural settlements, and only later did these festivals develop in the urban Italo-Australian settlements. As we shall see, this ritualisation of their experience was part of the process of Italo-Australian placemaking.

The builders

The third stage is arguably the most interesting and distinctive, but could not occur except as a consequence of the other two. The rural primary settlements typical of the 'farming' stage did not grow—they lacked the institutions necessary for differentiation, complexity and development. Even the largest and most continuous settlements, such as north Queensland, failed to develop Italian-language newspapers, political networks, or other evidence of this third stage. The urban settlements were a different story. In localities such as Carlton, Leichhardt, North Perth and Fremantle, a variety of Italian institutions (cafés, restaurants, shops, churches, newspaper offices, building companies) provided an alternative society, with its own opportunities and contacts (Valente, 1977; Pascoe, 1987; Bosworth and Bosworth, 1990). Indeed, not only could immigrants find all their needs met, these enclaves grew and developed as some of the pioneering entrepreneurs made good. These primary urban settlements were the crucible of the Italo-Australian identity, in a far more confident way than had been true of the relatively circumscribed world of the rural settlements. We have termed this period the phase of the *builders* in an effort to denote this active sense of constructing a community in these inner-city localities.

Community leaders of the 1990s could often trace their personal ancestry to these localities: although few Italo-Australians live in the inner suburbs today, most of the Italo-Australian businesses and shops established there 30 or 40 years ago are still prominent and visible parts of the urban landscape. Declamations in neon lights or signpainting announce to all the world an Italian identity: BORSARI'S CORNER (Carlton), GINO'S BAKERY (Leichhardt) or PAPA LUIGI'S (Fremantle) are loud statements indeed. These and other symbols tell visitors to the area, even those who cannot read Italian, of the area's cultural property. This partly explains the enduring symbolic power of such localities. The secondary settlements, those suburbs to which Italo-Australians later moved, or where their children reside, do not usually claim the same intensity of identification: these localities carry their signs of Italo-Australian presence rather less flamboyantly. Knowledgeable observers can recognise the characteristic Italo-Australian ornamentations in the housing stock (Rimondini, 1982), but the visual evidence is demonstrably more subtle. The visual cues are there for the Italo-Australians themselves, not for the casual observers. Melbourne's Trevisans, for example, like to plant a fir or two in their front yard: this (unwittingly) becomes one of the features which links place and community.

The process underlying these connections between place and community has its echoes in the migration and settlement experiences of all Australians, since four-tenths of the nation's growth since 1788 is attributable to immigration. Indeed, the lyrical cynicism of the old Italian peasantry and the irreverential radicalism of the Australian working class have some obvious points of similarity, and these became evident at specific junctures—on the Victorian goldfields in the 1850s, among quarriers and coalminers in Gippsland and northern Victoria, or in the postwar building industry, to cite some examples. Yet animosity or indifference can equally be instanced—on the north Queensland cane fields, in the mines and on the woodline at Kalgoorlie (Pascoe and Bertola, 1985), or on the Melbourne waterfront in the 1928 strike. The two nomadic tribes—the Italo-Australian labourers and their Anglo-Australian counterparts—did not coalesce, at least not to the same extent as Irish immigrants eventually found (or demanded) acceptance by Protestant Australian workers. An Italo-Australian identity developed out of these specific historical circumstances.

Identity

The Italo-Australian 'community' finds its identity in the social relationships of the workplace, the country town or fishing village, the urban neighbourhood, and the public ceremonies of these places. It relies considerably on verbal means of communicating, as it is a highly articulated oral culture. In the first stage, the 'scouts' had a sense of themselves which was strongly regional, and they represented all Italian regions. The supra-regionalism which emerged in Australia was patently not a transplanted Italian nationalism because the symbols and meanings of the Italian State were not universally accessible to them. Instead, the Italo-Australians were bonded by the processes of interaction with the dominant culture of Australia, processes which varied according to each of the three stages. The 'scouts' had a sense of being Italian which recognised that the catastrophic events which shaped their being (the uprisings of 1848, the *Risorgimento,* the 1898 food riots, 'the mutilated victory' of the First World War and so on) had few parallels in the Australian experience.

The identity of the Italo-Australian farmers and fishing families was more stable and secure; the second stage in the evolution of an Italo-Australia 'community' is noteworthy for the first successful lodgement of a specifically distinct ethnic identity. At Daylesford and on the Richmond River some separate sense of identity can first be detected. These immigrant communities did not (or would not) use their own language freely in the streets of the towns (nor even in the 'New Italy' classroom), but they were expressing themselves in other ways. The northern Italian peasant farmhouses of the Yandoit Valley (near Daylesford) still stand as a testament of this group. A butcher in nearby Newstead still sells the 'bull-boar' sausage introduced by the newcomers of the 1850s. Examples of this rural folk culture abound throughout country Australia, to be found in this distinctive old gravestone here or that abandoned vineyard there. The examples turn up in the oddest of places: at Cobar in outback New South Wales are farmhouses built by a *veneto* named Tozzi (Boughen, 1986); on Tasmania's Maria Island a former convict settlement was transformed into an Italian agricultural colony.

The values of this group may be summarised in terms of the old peasant triangle of family, work and land. The resources of the entire household were directed to squeezing a living out of a new and forbidding environment, calling upon ancient skills and abilities in intensive agriculture. Economy, resilience and ingenuity were some of the personal attributes prized in this group. Men's and women's labour were equally valued, but there were few opportunities for individualism or for careers which led out of the farming or fishing life. Their identity was a group identity. The Italo-Australian men of Koo-wee-rup could pride themselves on their physical strength, as evidenced each year in the tug-of-war contest at the town fair. The women of Fremantle drew pride from the homemade banners held high in the Blessing of the Fleet procession. The International Club at Stanthorpe, in Queensland's Granite Belt, is a monument to the sense of group solidarity shared by local Trevisans and Sicilians. Each of these examples of rural Italo-Australian culture illuminates a local pride, a sense of measurable 'otherness' from the neighbours, and a comparatively static identity. Its children have bitter-sweet memories of remaining loyal to a culture which was ostracised by many around them (Baggio, 1989).

In the third stage the Italo-Australian identity is more complex, more secure and more influential. Important aspects of the earlier phases are still evident. The political orientation of the 'scouts' finds its urban translation in firm support for the ALP and the failure of certain Italo-Australian parvenus to attract compatriots across to the conservative side of national politics. The old habits of the traditional Italian peasantry find expression in the backyard vines and annual salami rituals of Italo-Australian suburbia. But there is a much more public face to this identity in Australia's main cities. Fremantle's Blessing of the Fleet has graduated from a quaint folk festival to one of the major cultural events of the Perth metropolitan area: political and civic leaders jostle for a part in the proceedings. Bus-loads of rural and urban Italo-Australians congregate at the San Carlo (formerly Vaccari) Home for the Aged in Melbourne's northern outskirts each Italian National Day to hear speeches from the local consul and other dignitaries. The Lygon Street Festa (whose name has also changed) is an interesting mix of secular and religious themes in the old immigrant locality of Carlton, now spruced up and elegant. New buildings in and around Lygon Street are self-conscious imitations of traditional Italian streetscapes.

Placemaking

The ethnic neighbourhood is, above all, a place where the two key distributive markets (labour and housing) are gradually taken over and owned by Italo-Australians. This assists the rate of home ownership and access to local employment—vital aspects of the multiplier process, giving the newcomers some leverage in the new country. In cultural terms, the neighbourhood is a point of orientation. Each immigrant culture divides up its urban space according to various but consistent criteria, and embeds certain cultural values in the new environment.

International emigration and settlement in the new country involve a substantial challenge to the individuals concerned. Their sense of distance, of territory, and of the social uses of spaces, are all threatened in the new environment. Whereas they might have once understood life as organised around the *cortile* (courtyard), the new reality of Manhattan or Manchester tenements imposed a different set of environmental restraints on their behaviour (Gabaccia, 1984; see also Cavallaro, 1981: Chapter 4).

Italy's stubborn regionalism is everywhere evident in immigrant neighbourhoods. The regional Italian distinctions within Boston's 'Little Italy' operate from literally one tenement block to the next (De Marco, 1981). These regional distinctions (Sicilians in one set of apartments, *abruzzesi* in the next) reveal the maintenance of characteristic urban forms—nucleated, dispersed or multiply-nucleated—among the regional groupings of Italians in San Francisco (Cinel, 1982). There is no reason to suppose the Australian experience would have been vastly different, and close scrutiny of *Sands and MacDougall's* directories indeed reveals that such discriminations of urban morphology can also be found in Australian cities. Distances among *paesani* are re-established in the host society, and unconscious patternings of residential choice formed. In Carlton, the *viggianesi* clustered around Argyle Square, while the *trevisani* and *furlani* scattered themselves across the suburb. This would not be a sufficient description of the immigrant sense of place, however, because the residential patterns—powerfully evocative of ancestral arrangements though they are—are merely the outward expression of the underlying dynamic of the immigration process, that is, of the immigrant's sense of identity.

Placemaking is a more general quality of this immigration, and it is necessary to understand the placemaking strategies set in motion. In contemporary Australia these can be analysed in all their ethnographic richness, and they take us back to a general approach which favours a linguistic rather than urbanistic style. There are three conceptually distinct aspects to placemaking. Naming is one obvious strategy. Anglo-Australian immigrants usurped Aboriginal nomenclature, often transferring indigenous significations from one geographical feature to another (wrong) one. Similarly, Italians will speak of 'Brunswick' or 'Coburg', not as they are in conventional cartographic terms, but as emblems of a new Italo-Australian identity. Ritualisation is a second strategy, the making over of a territory for the regular celebration of a *festa* or some such. Institutionalisation is a clumsy but necessary term for a third strategy, the creation of all those institutions needed to make the area 'complete', that is, without which it could not fully function as a 'Little Italy'. In Melbourne's Carlton, for example, the Jews had established a Kadimah, a library, which they saw as indispensable—when the suburb became Italianised, this building was transformed into something more valuable in the Italian community's estimation, a hall for a mutual aid society. We will now examine these three strategies in more detail.

Naming is the affixation of imported signifiers to local landmarks. It corresponds roughly to the first three defining features of territoriality in Sack (1986): by this means the newcomers classify, communicate and (linguistically) control. Despite the cultural influence of Italy and Italian on colonial Australia, no Italian words entered the local vocabulary, and there are surprisingly few Italian placenames. Even some which appear to be Italian in origin (such as Roma, Queensland) turn out on closer inspection to have different roots (a Governor's wife). The postwar immigrants had some, but little, impact in this sense. 'The most important naming strategies have involved the corruption of Australian place names (Coburgo) or of Australian proper nouns (*la fensa, la farma*) rather than actual renamings. Boston's *prada* or Columbus Park do not have their Australian equivalents. Italian builders and town councillors, however, have in the 1970s and 1980s begun to be honoured with streets and parks. Sydney's Bossley Park has its Dalpra Street; a Matisi is recognised in Perth's northern suburbs; and so on.

Rituals are different, though linked, to naming. Rituals include any event which occurs in public view on a regular basis and has a defined set of participants. The motions and behaviours which take place in a successful ritual are strongly cathartic, and help shape or reinforce the identity of those participants. Celebration is a distinctive feature of Italo-Australian life—it is something which was easily transported from one country to another and is characteristic of an emigrant group which is still close to its peasant ancestry. In Sack's terms (1986), ritual reifies power (by occupying space), displaces attention (its participants temporarily become someone else), is impersonal (collectively) and neutral (they set aside political or ideological differences). A successful ritual welds together a group of people who were feeling alienated, divided, powerless and homeless. Within the context of rituals the participants are given permission to use traditional gestures, postures and movements, and to re-establish preferred distances amongst each other. Rituals such as the Italo-Australian *festa* indeed sacralise the new urban environment—often in contest with the host culture. By their collective action, the immigrants propose a new and different relationship between the inhabitants of a space and the territory itself. This of course is extremely threatening to the older residents

Gaetano 'Vince' Mazziotta who arrived from Viggiano in 1937, photographed outside his shoe repair shop in Northcote, Melbourne. (*State Library of Victoria*)

of that town or suburb. When the first Blessing of the Fleet procession made its way along Fremantle's main street in 1948, the local Anglican minister stood on the footpath, his arms akimbo, laughing out loud. *His* Fremantle was disappearing, whether he knew it or not.

The institutions created within the neighbourhood provide its cultural structures. They are containers in the placemaking process, giving a sense of identity more durable than one ritual event, and also, in Sack's typology (1986), create emptiable space (space which otherwise remains empty), and which engenders more space. Institutions carry out all these functions, quite apart from their economic benefit. The mutual aid societies were the earliest institutions—notably the Eolian Clubs in Sydney and Melbourne. They replaced the informal gatherings of itinerant workers in people's houses. The clubs multiplied, as did the shops and local businesses. Newspaper offices, Italian-language churches and other institutions made up the full range of services. By 1960 the sense of an Italo-Australian 'community' was complete.

The dominant culture

It is no exaggeration to say that Italo-Australian life and values have influenced the direction and focus of Australian culture generally. The Irish were not formally and finally assimilated into Australian life until the 1950s—their separate identity, especially in the 1880–1940 period, provided a powerful antidote to the smug provincialism of Protestant middle-class Australia. The Italians succeeded the Irish as the main cultural alternative in Australia: throughout the 1950–80 era, urban Italo-Australians offered a style of living which was visibly distinct. They blazed the trail for 'multicultural' Australia. Most of the experiences of other postwar newcomers (Greeks, Maltese, Lebanese, Turks, Arabs generally) were variations on an Italo-Australian theme: prejudice against children in the schoolyard, stereotypical reporting in the mass media, unfair treatment in the workplace. Older and wiser Italo-Australians nod their heads as they recognise these familiar incidents in modern life: they underwent these same rites of passage a generation ago.

The Italo-Australians were not assimilated by the dominant culture of postwar Australia, and instead had three major effects on Australian life. The first is symbolised by food, but amounts to much more: they demonstrated that just as eating can be an occasion rather than a tiresome routine, ceremonies are vital to human societies, providing flash, colour and meaning. Australians looked with new understanding at their indigenous rituals (such as the Melbourne Cup, Sydney's Easter Show, or the Australian Football Grand Final at the Melbourne Cricket Ground) and embraced enthusiastically many new immigrant rituals. Second, the Italo-Australians transformed and animated the built environment in ways which became broadly endorsed by the population at large: there was a recovery of public spaces which went well beyond the boundaries of the immigrant enclaves. Finally, the most ineffable, but most significant, contribution of the Italo-Australians was the challenge they provided to the set ways of conventional Australia. The accommodation of the Italo-Australians required other Australians to value diversity above conformity: as will be discussed in Chapter 15, the failure of the anti-Asian pressure group in the 1980s was a testament to the success of this new enthusiasm for cultural diversity. Often without being aware of it, the Italo-Australians' sense of place and community was an important part of the new cultural identity of Australia.

7 Community leaders in rural Australia and the construction of 'the Godfather'

Al Grassby

The Murrumbidgee Irrigation Area (MIA) is a specialised farming zone where water provided by large-scale irrigation schemes allows the intensive production of fodder and cereal crops, fruit, vines and vegetables. Now comprising 182 000 hectares, it was founded in 1906 in order to increase agricultural output by exploiting the land of dry southern New South Wales. British immigrants and later, returned World War I soldiers, were given small plots of land. However, the soldier settlers' inexperience with irrigation farming and the lack of expertise of the New South Wales Department of Agriculture created considerable problems with salinity and soil damage in the 1930s, and hundreds of amateur farmers fled back to the coastal cities from whence they had originally come. The Rural Bank of New South Wales, which had been financing the projects, found itself saddled with farms, bankruptcies and no farmers. That is, until the Italians began to arrive.

Despite the fact that government bodies such as the Water Conservation and Irrigation Commission were opposed to Italian settlement, many Italian migrants came to the region after World War II. Thev were experienced farmers, they had the tradition of generations, and they worked together. Often a group of brothers shared a single bank account and chequebook. They were a godsend to the banks, and they brought prosperity to a depressed area. The young men were products of World War II which had disrupted lives and education. Most did not have more than two years' schooling and many had less. They typically began by leasing a few acres of salt-damaged land from Anglo-Australian farmers. A horse and single furrow plough would represent their biggest investment, and stoop labour marked the cultivation of crops such as carrots. Although trevisani *and* calabresi *were the largest groups to settle in the area, smaller numbers of migrants came from Abruzzi, Piemonte, Friuli and Sicily. Italian settlement concentrated around the town of Griffith, half of whose population today is made up of Italians and their children (see Chapter 4 for more detail).*

In recent years, national attention has been focused on Griffith, and the area generally, in the context of concern about the expansion of organised criminal activities linked to drug growing and trafficking. Italians have been the subject of considerable suspicion on the grounds of alleged 'Mafia' connections. Below is the story of one Italian-born Australian who became the subject of such allegations. It is told by Al Grassby, whose connections to Griffith started during his years as a government agricultural officer and continued after he became the member for the Riverina in the federal parliament, Minister for Immigration in the 1972 Whitlam Labor government, and Commissioner for Community Relations in 1975.

Pietro Callipari: a 'Godfather'?

'Godfather' is defined by the *Macquarie Dictionary* as a 'man who stands sponsor for a child at baptism or confirmation' and also 'one who exercises power and dispenses protection while keeping in the background, grey eminences'.

The many godfathers from Italy who have lived and served in Australia were indeed 'grey eminences' who dispensed the protection of advice, guidance and leadership against the exactions of an often cruel and bigoted society. They were unsung and unrecognised (by Anglo Australians) and were never honoured or even recorded in local histories. They were men of high and gentle integrity who did not seek pre-eminence, and when they attained it within their own community were careful not to exploit it for personal gain nor aggrandisement nor permit others to do so.

My awareness of their existence came from my work in agricultural extension. An assessment by the Bureau of Agricultural Economics in 1952 found that extension services had failed to communicate adequately with Italian-speaking farmers in the Murrumbidgee Irrigation Area. A trio of agricultural extension pioneers (Reginald Richard Pennefather, David Vogel Walters and Joan Hearman Tully) led a campaign to correct this deficiency. I was appointed to devise and carry out extension campaigns for Italian-speaking farmers who comprised more than half of the total farming popula-

Al Grassby at the 1973 Griffith Wine Festival when he was Minister for immigration. In 1975 he became Commissioner of Community Relations. (*Australian Official Photograph*)

tion of the area. They supported my initiatives in launching bilingual radio programs and publications and pushing for interpreters, but they wisely ordained that there had to be grass-roots participation by the farmers themselves.

Faced with the same problem in Anglo-Australian society it would have been possible to have called upon dozens of leaders such as councillors, alderpeople, shire presidents, local members of parliament and the officers of the established farming organisations. But the Italian half of the population of the area had no formal leaders at all. The 'British settlers', as they called themselves in those days, had the monopoly of all public positions in councils, co-operatives, hospitals, and community organisations.

We therefore determined to seek out the informal leaders who had migrated from Italy, and worked successfully to establish themselves. They were looked up to for their ability, and their advice and help were sought by their friends and neighbours. They were never known as 'godfathers' and would have laughed if anyone had said this. The term[1] came into prominence in the 1970s and it was applied to one Pietro Callipari, who embodied the concept of unsung community service.

One incident serves to epitomise the mixture of ignorance and prejudice which dominates so many people in Australia when they try to relate to the million people of eight generations with an Italian connection. The individual at its core was a young police constable posted to Griffith, New South Wales. He was Anglo-Saxon, monolingual and monocultural and found himself sent to a town with people of more than 30 different backgrounds but falling into two main divisions, those who were English-speaking and those who were Italian-speaking. As was natural for a man of his background, he gravitated to the company of people like himself, and it was from them that he heard the gossip about the disappearance of the local Liberal Party candidate, Donald Mackay. Among the theories was that the ubiquitous 'Mafia' had been involved.

On one occasion, while off duty, the constable was spending a convivial evening at the Yoogali Club, the largest social club of its kind in the Riverina, taking its name from the little township of Yoogali which means 'to exalt' or 'make merry', a particularly appropriate name for a place with three clubs with a combined membership many times the population of the village itself. The club was founded by five Italian migrants in the 1930s and has always been multilingual and multicultural both in its management and its membership.

During the course of that evening I arrived from Canberra in the company of a local alderman. Before long a group of old friends had gathered and it was decided to have dinner. Among the guests was a man whom the constable recognised; he immediately set out to officially observe this very public dinner, took a careful note of the names of everyone present and later sought their addresses. Within a few days he had compiled a report on this gathering which he had determined was suspicious because it was attended by the man known locally as 'the Godfather', though Pietro Callipari was never given this name by any of his family, friends or *paesani.*

Callipari was born in Plati, Calabria, in February 1924. The population of Plati at the time was around 6000 and the little town totally depended on the network of farms of which Plati was the centre. The Callipari family was comfortably off by the standards of the time, and Peter (as he was to be known in Australia) was directed towards a seminary to study for the priesthood. It was an old adage that every family should aim to have a lawyer to protect them in the present and a priest to ensure protection in the hereafter. Peter did not complete his studies and he was never ordained but his education was comprehensive and his orientation to service was strong. Like so many of his *paesani,* the call of migration captured him and he joined the exodus which saw half the town leave and settle in Australia. The great majority headed for Griffith where chain migration ensured settlement without tears. The first to arrive would call relatives and friends and it was not long before a great human bridge linked the two towns.

Peter Callipari arrived in Australia on 8 August 1949 at the age of 25; he was the trailblazer of his family in coming to Australia. Arriving in Sydney, he was given his first job in Australia by a *paesano* who wanted to build a bus line.[3] Peter worked loyally and well, but it was not long before his own quest for independence took him to Griffith, where he established a boot and shoe repairing business on the main street, Banna Avenue. His arrival in a struggling community was hailed as a blessing. Here was a man who was well educated, one who had trained for the priesthood and who quickly grasped the fundamentals of the English language. Before long his little shop became a centre for the struggling farmers to come in, to talk and informally seek advice from young Peter. As the years went by his advice was more and more sought after and he became a bridge between his *paesani* and the puzzling and inscrutable bureaucracies that served this small Australian community.

At that time the entire structure of society was against recognising Italians as equals. The Griffith Producers' Co-operative relied on Italian settlers for their turnover but none was employed there or was part of the directorate or the management. The Shire Council was dominated by large-area farmers who were exclusively Anglo-Australian. The same applied to the Hospital Board, all the professions, and all business activity. The only exception to the Anglo hegemony was the Greek community, which wisely invested in property, shops and cafés, and served both Anglo and Italian with complete evenhandedness while recognising that Italians mostly paid their debts while many others often did not.

It was this complete absence of any kind of professional elite which created so much dependence upon young Peter Callipari. His *paesani* were certainly not going to place themselves in the hands of foreign lawyers, accountants and water bailiffs if they could avoid it. It was not only a matter of language but of understanding the system and coming to grips with it. It had not been too many years before that no Italians ventured to stay in Griffith after dark unless prepared for street battles with the 'British' push. The curfew was lifted to go to the hospital or the cemetery but it was wise to leave at dusk. The schools also played their part in regimenting assimilation. Italian was banned in the classroom and playground. Italian was also banned on the local radio station and Italian films were simply ignored. The pretence was that Griffith was exclusively 'British'.

As the community prospered so did Peter Callipari, and his little shop expanded into a retail store with shoes for all. Peter found his language and negotiating skills in daily demand and as the operations became more sophisticated so did the problems. A farmer seeking a bank loan would go to Peter to take him to the bank manager and then recommend him. It was said that he was the only man in Australia who received daily phone calls from the State Bank manager's office to make sure he was well. The legal profession came to depend not only on his interpreting skills but his understanding of the people and their problems. From the bank to the lawyers to the powerful Water Conservation and Irrigation Commission, and then in later years to the elected representatives, he was on constant call, day and night, seven days a week.

In the 1960s the political parties became more responsive to the non-British population, and particularly to their potential electoral power. Again it was Peter Callipari who led the deputations to the members and ministers, and in turn it was Peter who was being more and more consulted by the flag-bearers of the various parties.

He performed yet another public service when it came to weddings, wakes and baptisms. He had built up a complete filing system covering all the families who had settled in Griffith from Plati. So when a wedding was planned it was he who organised the invitations which went to every *platiota* even if in other states or cities. It was also Peter who was asked to invite the local dignitaries.

As the community grew so did his guest list until it peaked at 2000 at the wedding of Peter's last daughter. In the case of a death it was Peter who made the arrangements for the burial and the dispatch of wreaths, and the turning out of the mourners. And his list not only extended to everyone from Plati in Australia, but reached back home so that there were always telegrams and messages from overseas to be read, particularly at weddings.

Such was his status that in campaign times no minister or member ever came to Griffith without dropping in at the little shop and paying their respects to Peter. As he gradually became involved in my campaigns and political successes, his allegiance was recognised but he was nevertheless consulted by all.

His family comprised Teresa, Lina, only son Tony, Mary, Sue and Lilly. They had all worked in Peter's shop; they had all helped with his countless requests and cases. They were all happily married and made Peter a grandfather several times over. Family life kept Peter in Griffith without even a visit to his native town for more than twenty years. However, he went in 1973 to welcome me, when during an official visit to Italy, I travelled to both Cavaso del Tomba and Plati. As Minister for Immigration I wanted to acknowledge the great contribution the towns had made to Australian settlement.

His community work continued on his return to Griffith; his shoe shop became bigger and he built a modest travel agency. But times had changed and he was no longer the only point of literate reference in Griffith. There were Italian doctors, accountants and lawyers, many of them *calabresi,* the parish priest at Griffith was Italian, there were shops, businesses and restaurants; most of the fruit farms were now Italo-Australian and many of the large-area farms were also becoming Italo-Australian owned. The mayor of the city was Italian; so were members of the Hospital Board, the co-operatives. The old dream of integration had become a reality and the burden once shouldered exclusively by Peter Callipari was shared among scores of literate professionals.

Worn out by his ceaseless labours he retired in 1985. The Italian families he had served for more than 30 years joined together to build his new home. For most of his life he had lived in a modest bungalow with his wife and six children and many a visiting relative. But the time came for him to have his typical Italian dream house, a *piccolo palazzo* on which one friend would work on the concrete, another on the brickwork, another the plastering, and yet another on the roof, until by a wonderful demonstration of voluntary labour it was complete. To the Anglo-Australian, however, despite all the improvements in community relationships, it was a symbol of his status as 'the Godfather'.

It was recalled how, in the 1960s, he had been charged with possessing an unlicensed pistol. All that was involved was that some family friend passing through had left a dismantled pistol in Peter's glove box. Someone reported he had a gun. Technically the bits and pieces constituted a gun and so he had his day in court. The list of testimonials would have been enough to make him at least Blessed, but years later when Griffith was caught up in the artificially fed mass hysteria about the so-called Mafia, the ignorant and bigoted pointed to Peter. Those same people went on to criticise his dream house and in latter days the title 'Godfather', once bestowed in affection by Anglo-Australians, became more a term of accusation and abuse.

The man who had served thousands of people, who had set so many on the road to success, who had battled the uncaring bureaucracy, even had to front up to unsympathetic priests who wanted to deny the sacraments to someone they held not to be in good standing: Peter Callipari, at 63 years of age, was old beyond his years and a sick man.

There was to be no Order of Australia for this fine servant of the people; not for him a seat in parliament or even on the local council. He died on 16 September 1987, and when I drove from Canberra to Griffith for his funeral the Parish Priest, Reverend Father Peter Beltrame said, 'we shall not see his like again'. Not only his family but his legions of friends and admirers once again combined to do him honour and interred him in the first traditional family tomb ever built in Griffith cemetery.

The weekend after his burial, curious Anglos were making the pilgrimage to see the tomb of 'the Godfather' just as a few years before they had driven out on Sunday afternoons to see the house of 'the Godfather'.

8 Community networks and institutions

Caroline Alcorso, Cesare Giulio Popoli and Gaetano Rando

Chapter 6 has reviewed the factors involved in the emergence and growth of Italian communities in Australia: the nature and chronology of the migration process, the class background and gender roles of the migrants themselves, and the characteristics of the receiving society. These factors shaped the emergence of Italo-Australian communities, discernible by the use of an Italian language, identifiable neighbourhoods, public ceremonies and communal institutions. Such community life developed first in certain prewar farming areas and fishing villages but flourished later in the inner suburbs of Melbourne, Sydney and other Australian cities.

This chapter will discuss the public institutions which both stimulated the development of communities and which have provided visible indicators of their emergence. The most important of these have been the Italian-language media and the recreational, welfare, cultural and sporting associations. Some of these, like COASIT and the APIA Club, have developed into large-scale organisations whose voice is heard within Australian politics. The chapter will also examine the role of the Catholic Church. While the Church was historically (and remains) a predominantly Irish institution, some sections of it have been sensitive to the culture and needs of its multi-ethnic congregation and indeed have been central to Italian community life. However, it is necessary to stress that the dividing lines between what are considered public and what private (and between organised and informal) institutions in the Italian community are somewhat arbitrary. The espresso bars of Leichhardt and Carlton have played a role in providing a sympathetic meeting place for Italian migrants and reinforcing a sense of Italian identity commensurate with that of the clubs which are formal institutions established to foster these goals. However, it is with the latter—the public institutional life of the Italian community—that this chapter is primarily concerned.

Italians and the Catholic Church in Australia

The role of the Catholic Church in migrant settlement and community formation in Australia is a neglected topic in academic works on immigration and ethnic affairs. Yet an understanding of the religious life and practices of immigrant groups can shed considerable light on the migrant experience in Australia as a whole. Existing studies suggest that, for a significant part of the Italian immigrant cohort who arrived in the 1950s and 1960s, the Catholic Church was enormously important. Despite the differences between the style of worship practised in Italy and that of Irish Catholics in Australia, the Catholic religion nevertheless provided a familiar place for Italian migrants, and institutions where assistance could be sought during the settlement process. In the words of Father Adrian Pittarello, the Church was something with which Italian migrants could identify because they felt it to be 'part of themselves' (1980: 83). Thus the observance and celebration of religion continued to play an important role in the lives of many Italian migrants, although it seems that most experienced a more ambiguous and problematic relationship with the Church and its institutions in Australia than they had in Italy (see Pittarello, 1980; Lewins, 1978: Chapter 5). In the discussion that follows we trace first the contours of Catholicism as practised by Italian priests in Australia and then examine the relationship between Italian migrants and the mainstream Catholic Church, which by the 20th century had become thoroughly Irish in personnel and culture.

Italo-Australian priests and monks

Missionary priests from various Italian orders have been involved in the white settlement of Australia since the 1840s, when three Italian Passionist fathers were brought to Australia to assist in the conversion of Aborigines (Bosi, 1989: 29). Other 19th-century priests continued in the tradition of this first endeavour, undertaking heroic expeditions to remote and little-populated regions where they founded tiny, marginal settlements, held masses and ministered to reluctant Aborigines and white settlers of various national backgrounds. Conflict between Italian and Irish priests erupted sporadically, with Italian priests and bishops tending to be associated politically with the conservative English orders against which Irish Catholicism was in revolt. It is clear that although the 19th-century Italian priests did not see their role as ministering primarily to other Italians, conflicts were often played out in nationalistic terms and in some cases (such as those of Bishops Cani and Torreggiani, respectively of Rockhampton and Armidale) were associated with an escalation of anti-Italian racism (Bosi, 1989: 79 ff).

In the 20th century, Italian priests from certain orders began to play a role more specifically targeted to the growing numbers of Italian migrants in Australia. One of the earliest to be noted for this practice was the Franciscan Father Mambrini, whose arrival appears to have been of considerable importance to the culturally isolated Italian cane cutters of north Queensland. An Italian-background woman who grew up in Innisfail remembers the periodic visits of Father Mambrini, commenting that:

> . . . since there were no Italian priests, many families didn't christen their children until he arrived. When he did, people would travel over a hundred miles . . . for the occasion . . . You would have a dozen or more children of all ages being baptised and it was followed by a lively and happy reunion of families coming together after a long time (Bosi, 1989: 95).

Both the pastoral function played by Italian priests for Italian migrants in Australia and the role of religious occasions in providing opportunities for social networking were aspects of Catholic religious life which became more important in the following decades.

As the urban concentrations of Italians (and particularly Melbourne's Italian population) grew after the 1920s certain figures stood out in this development. Father Modotti, for example, a Jesuit priest, started a religious/community paper *(L'Angelo della Famiglia)* and attempted to develop certain suburban centres as the basis of a strong Italian Church, with the object of overcoming the scattered nature of Melbourne's Italian population at the time (Bosi, 1989: 96–7).

Priests of other orders were also important. The Salesians, for example, continued the early pioneering work of Italian priests by establishing missions in Broome and in the Kimberleys (Western Australia) in the interwar years and also attempted to promote the development of Italian community life through the funding of mutual aid societies and schools.

But the most important relationships between Italian priests and Italian migrants at the community level have been those developed by the Capuchin and Scalabrinian orders in postwar Australia. These two orders have tended to take responsibility for the bulk of Italian

The Scalabrians operate a number of homes for the Italian aged throughout Australia. At the Vaccari village, opened in 1979 in South Morang, near Melbourne, the Claretiane nuns assist in providing a happy environment for 85 of the elderly. (*Il Globo*)

pastoral care carried out by the Catholic Church and there has been a considerable amount of institutional development associated with their activities. Hostels, kindergartens, orphanages, newspapers, recreational, welfare and social centres and, most recently, homes for the aged have been developed through initiatives of these two orders.

While the first *Scalabriniani* arrived in Australia in 1872, the postwar founders of the Scalabrinian order arrived in 1952, foisting their enthusiastic plans for ministry in areas of high Italian (and migrant) density upon a reluctant Australian Catholic Church. Welcome initially only in north Queensland and the Illawarra region of New South Wales, Scalabrinian priests quickly became associated with notable community institutions in each place. In Silkwood (Queensland) Father Orsi's intervention finally convinced the local bishop to permit the celebration of the *Festa dei Tre Santi,* a religious feast day of enormous cultural significance to the local Sicilian migrants. The significance of this defence of their traditional celebrations against the bans imposed by the unsympathetic Irish-

Australian Bishop who viewed them as primitive and superstitious was great for north Queensland's Sicilians, whether religious or not.

Another famous Scalabrinian initiative was the founding, in 1955, of the Italian (now International) Centre in Wollongong, which was conceived as a meeting place for those activities, reunions and events in the Italian community that it was inappropriate to hold inside the church (Bosi, 1989: 161). Educational and recreational activities were provided at the centre, which has been heralded as an early example of multiculturalism in the sense that it provided a space for freer cultural and linguistic expression than was normally encouraged in 1950s Australia.

The *Cappuccini,* on the other hand, centred their pastoral work more around spiritual activities such as the mass and missionary work. They became established as an order in Australia in the late 1940s and early 1950s, slightly before the *Scalabriniani.* However, *Cappuccini* were also associated with many significant welfare and other institutions in the Italian community in the 1950s and 1960s including newspapers (see below), the Italo-Australian Welfare Centre and a soccer team that eventually developed into Australia's largest Italian club—the APIA (short for *Associazione Polisportiva Italo-Australiana*—Italian–Australian Sporting Association, see pp.112, 123) (Bosi, 1989: 123).

As well as playing a role in community development in particular localities, both the *Cappuccini* and the *Scalabriniani* in the postwar period founded interstate religious organisations that aimed at incorporating Italian migrants into communal structures at the parish level. The Capuchins' Catholic Action (ACI), founded in 1954, was an attempt to transplant an Italian institution onto Australian soil, as well as to mobilise Italian migrants politically against what was seen as the communist menace. Six years later, the *Scalabriniani* responded by initiating another parish-centred organisation (this time based on a US model) that was more politically progressive and had an egalitarian, rather than paternalistic philosophy, the Italian Catholic Federation (FCI). The extent of involvement of Italo-Australians in these organisations is not clear but it would not seem to be great. For example, at the end of the 1980s, after a period of expansion, there were 34 branches of the FCI across Australia with 1500 active members (many of whom were second-generation Italians—see Bosi, 1989: 187).

Italians and the Australian Catholic Church

While the work of the Italian priests and monks described above has been important in terms of the development of communal Italian institutions in Australia, by far the predominant religious experience that Italian migrants have had in Australia has been in Irish Catholic parishes where they found the practice of religion, as well as the social life surrounding it, to be culturally alien and unattractive—'soup without salt', in the words of a respondent to a recent survey conducted by Father Pittarello. In stark contrast to the role played by the Church in Italy and to that of the missionary Italian priests described above, it does not seem that this mainstream Australian Church had a significant integrative effect on Italians in Australia—indeed the opposite may be true.

In a study of Italian settlement in Queensland conducted in 1951, W. D. Borrie concluded 'that the Roman Catholic Church had not formed a focal point for strengthening community ties among Italians' (1954: 119) and went on to point out that many Italian settlers were politically anti-clerical. Since then there has been some debate about the degree of Italian migrants' involvement in organised religion in Australia. The traditional view put by Anglo-Australian writers such as Lewins (1978) and Kelly (1979) is that Italian migrants become progressively less religiously observant after their arrival in Australia for reasons ranging from the inferior quality of their faith and simple laziness (Kelly, 1979) to the 'insensitivity towards, and disregard of, Italians' sub-cultural identity and the avoidance of special structures for Italians' pastoral care characteristic of the Australian Church' (Lewins, 1978: 108). Pittarello has challenged this view, arguing that 'moralising scholars' have misunderstood the nature of Italian migrants' religiosity. Nevertheless, he too argues 'that perhaps, Italian migrants cared more for the Catholic Church in Australia than the Australian Catholic Church, at least initially, cared for them' (1980: 89). It seems that there is consensus on the verdict recently passed by another Scalabrinian, Father Visentin, that 'despite the various modifications to traditional practices,[1] the Catholic Church in Australia did not successfully cope with the cultural and linguistic diversity of people within its parishes. Migrant Catholics found themselves to be disadvantaged' (Visentin, 1980: 2).

Indeed, in Pittarello's study, one of the most disappointing aspects of the Australian Church from the point of view of Italian migrants was precisely the narrowness with which it defined its role, its bureaucratic nature and the private, rather than social, form that religious observance took. As one respondent commented 'here, after one has been to mass, it's all dead' (Pittarello, 1980: 46). Other testimonies have confirmed these findings, and have revealed also the level of racism directed towards Italian migrants by some Irish Catholic priests, officials and congregations. One Italian woman, whose experiences were recorded in an oral history project, describes the discriminatory practices prevalent in her Catholic school. Italian students were systematically ignored in class and marginalised in school life generally. Any girl of Italian origin, for example, was excluded from the Eucharistic Congress in which all the other students participated: '[we] were not in the school activity at all. We were told that we weren't needed' (Loh, 1980: 21).

Secular Italian associations in Australia

Indeed, it is in the face of the racism perpetuated in most of the mainstream institutions of postwar Australia that the development of ethnic-specific organisations needs to be understood. Italians have established secular associations of mutual support and assistance in Australia for more than 100 years. One of the earliest recorded associations (the Society for Mutual Support) was established in 1881 to assist the victims of the Marquis de Ray's failed scheme (see Chapter 1). Most of the associations which were established after this society had a regional or provincial orientation. In 1903, for example, the Eolian Society was established in Sydney. By the 1930s it was the largest Italian club, drawing on the 8000-strong Italian community, and its activities ranged from football teams to Italian lessons to Italian-language radio programs to a theatre group (Rando, 1987).

However it was in the years of mass migration of the postwar period that we see the growth of several large recreational/sporting/cultural clubs such as the Marconi Club (1958), the APIA (1954) of Sydney and the Fraternity Club in Wollongong (1959) (Pascoe, 1987: 171; Rando, 1987). During the 1960s and early 1970s, many regional associations were also formed. In recent years, the majority of new associations founded have been of a contrasting type again, consisting primarily of cultural associations (for example the Italian Writers' Association, founded in 1986) and religious associations with the extension of the Catholic Federation through Sydney. New pensioners', aged and ex-servicemen's associations have also been formed, while the aged membership of existing clubs has been expanding (Rando, 1987). Today in New South Wales alone there are at least 80 such clubs in metropolitan Sydney and at least 30 others in rural centres of high Italian population (Wollongong, Griffith, Newcastle, Lismore and Queanbeyan).

An important dimension to many clubs' activities (and an important survival skill since the decline of Italian migration to Australia in the early 1970s) has been their ability to attract second-generation Italians as well as their parents. For some Italian parents the club *ambiente* provides a safe place where teenage children can socialise in controlled surroundings. The club remains the centre of social life for many Italians, as well as an institution in which traditional ways continue to be practised, albeit in a somewhat ossified manner. As one Veneto club-goer remarked: 'I think we're preserving the Veneto traditions here much better than they do in Italy . . . I think we're more attached to the old ways than they are . . . I don't know what we would do if the Club wasn't there . . . with the Club . . . there's something for everyone, for ladies, for old people, for children, for families' (Loh, 1980: 96).

COASIT

The impetus to establish the *Comitato Assistenza Italiani* (COASIT), was a 1967 Italian law which gave Italian consuls overseas the power to establish welfare and educational communittees for migrants. While Sydney COASIT was under the aegis of the Italian government, the Melbourne branch was more independent and was quickly successful in attracting Australian government funds. It was the first ethnic welfare organisation in Australia to receive a Grant-in-Aid to employ a qualified social worker. COASIT also relied on the material support of Italian migrants, especially in the early years: in 1969, 50 per cent of its income came from the Italian government, 25 per cent from the Australian government and 25 per cent came (via fundraising activities) from the Italian community.

COASIT's main activities in the early years were case-work-based welfare counselling and assistance, and the teaching of Italian to Italian-background children after school. During the 1970s COASIT expanded into other areas with state and federal government support. In Melbourne, for example, two child-care centres and a women's refuge were established, social research projects were undertaken in the Italian community, a library and information centre set up and additional workers, such as a community health nurse and workers for the ethnic aged, were employed.

Towards the end of the 1970s, COASIT began to formalise links with the Italian Socialist Trade Union Federation (UIL) and with private foundations in Australia from which it received funds. Undoubtedly, however, one of the major catalysts of its continued expansion was the controversial federal (Liberal–Country Party) government decision in 1981 to provide state funding for the privately-run 'ethnic schools', including both the traditional after-hours classes and the so-called 'insertion classes' initiated by COASIT. The latter are community language familiarisation classes primarily aimed at non-Italian children and taught by private teachers in state and Catholic primary schools. COASIT was, and remains, the major beneficiary of this funding and in 1986, 42 000 children in 151 schools in New South Wales alone were learning Italian under the Insertion Class Program.[2] In addition, approximately one thousand New South Wales students of ages 7–15 learnt Italian after hours.

The other main area of expansion for COASIT's activities in the 1980s was in the field of aged services, a direct response to the considerable problems being faced by the growing number of aged Italians living in isolation with inadequate social support. As in the area of education, COASIT has been a major beneficiary of government grants used to employ social workers, and establish daycare centres and home-visit programs in Sydney and Melbourne. COASIT has also established certain semi-autonomous organisations in different cities, such as the Pensioners' Club and the Italian Historical Societies in Victoria, Western Australia, Queensland and New South Wales.

COASIT has traditionally had a conservative perspective on its work, arguing that its activities contribute to greater social cohesion in Australian society, and that pragmatically, it is more cost-effective for the Australian government to fund semi-voluntary organisations than deliver welfare services itself (COASIT, 1988: 2). However, it has always voiced a critique of mainstream services in Australian society, on the basis that they are not accessible or culturally appropriate to NESB migrants, and has consequently warmly embraced multicultural policy, which recognises the role of ethnospecific organisations. In 1988, the Sydney president summed up COASIT's overall approach of the last twenty years in the following words:

> . . . all our efforts have always been directed at ensuring that the well-being, aspirations and rights of the individuals who make up the Italian community are accepted and recognised within the broader framework of Australian society. We [see] our organisation as a legitimate part of a new exciting dynamic Multicultural Australia. This is a vision which must continue to provide a basis for . . . the years to come (COASIT, 1989: 4).

FILEF

The *Federazione Italiana dei lavoratori Emigrati e Famiglie* (FILEF) was founded in Italy in 1967 by Carlo Levi—artist, writer and independent left senator, who became its first president. In Levi's analysis, FILEF was to act as a catalyst of political forces within Italy: migration should be perceived as a national rather than an individual issue. Levi's key idea was that this forced exodus was not a valid means of solving the social and economic problems of the nation, and that FILEF should work towards the elimination of the necessity for emigration. Abroad, FILEF's primary function was to restore a social, collective life for the Italian workers and peasants who, uprooted from their homes, found themselves isolated in a strange country.

Branches of FILEF were soon formed wherever Italian migrant workers were present; Australia was one of the first countries in which FILEF was established—in Melbourne in 1971, and a year later in Sydney. Subsequently FILEF opened in Adelaide, and eventually in Perth. FILEF's activities increased considerably within the progressive environment brought about by the Whitlam government (1972–75). Although FILEF's founding members were almost exclusively migrant workers with basic skills and little education, from the late 1970s onwards the organisation began to attract newly arrived migrants, many with tertiary qualifications, who had come to Australia for reasons no longer exclusively related to economic difficulties. These new members have helped FILEF maintain and expand existing ties with Italy's culture (Halevi, 1989: 225). Today's FILEF is an organisation based on the voluntary work of its members and supporters, with some Australian and Italian government funding. On May Day 1974, FILEF launched a fortnightly newspaper *Nuovo Paese* (New Country), which became a monthly magazine in 1986. It now has a national distribution of over 8000 copies.

In the context of Australian multicultural society, FILEF's political agenda for social welfare is aimed at the promotion and the advancement of the rights of migrant workers and all working people. FILEF acts in support of trade unions, political parties, and other organisations with which it shares similar aims and objectives. These co-ordinated efforts revolve around issues such as the environment, the conservation of natural resources and the management of industrial, human and public resources.

Like COASIT, FILEF provides information to the Italian community through its library and referral service. The latter covers a wide range of areas, including assistance with union, work and housing-related issues, Italian and Australian pensions and workers' compensation. Besides the Italian community, FILEF provides consultation to other groups, organisations and bodies, both government and non-government, on matters regarding the Italian community and culture, both in Italy and Australia. Cultural activities include bilingual theatre productions; audio-visual exhibitions, such as photographic exhibitions on migration and the history of contemporary Italy; production of resource materials for the teaching of Italian in primary schools and a number of books, most of which deal with the usage and teaching of the Italian language in Australia.

One of FILEF's main concerns (and points of contention with

COASIT has been the maintenance of the Italian language among the first generation of migrants, along with the goal of bilingual education for second-generation Italo-Australian youth. The FILEF school committee has, over the years, promoted an active debate on the maintenance of Italian and other community languages, taking a specific interest in state and federal government policies on language education. Amongst educational activities provided by FILEF are courses in Italian for first- and second-generation migrants, English courses for migrant women, and for people with limited English. The educational needs of Italians in Australia have also been met by a number of courses (conducted in Italian) ranging over a variety of topics concerning Italy's culture and civilisation. There are also programs designed to equip migrants with basic skills, such as photography and computer courses.

In the mid-1970s, the FILEF Women's Group was inaugurated in order to deal with migrant women's issues at work and in the community (Vasta, 1990a: 133–4). One project conducted in the early 1980s in Coburg, Melbourne, was concerned with establishing childcare services within a government clothing factory. Over eighteen months of struggle was necessary to secure funding and permission from state and federal governments (Zaccari, 1986: 3).

FILEF also organises activities and recreational events for the Italian community designed to promote participation in Australian society. These include public debates and meetings, film nights, discussion evenings, and celebrations of traditional occasions, such as Italy's Liberation Day, May Day and an annual *festa*, which is held in each city where FILEF is represented.

The Italo-Australian media

Print media

The first known instance of the publication of an Italian-language newspaper in Australia was *L'Italo-Australiano Rivista Mensile Organo degli Italiani Sparsi per le Terre Oceaniche* which appeared in Sydney in 1885. Edited by Francesco Sceusa (see also Chapter 1 and p. 112), the purpose of the paper was to promote the interests of Italian immigrants, keep them informed of events in Australia and Italy, provide a focus of cohesion for the Italian community in Australia and propose reforms for the betterment of conditions for Italian workers.

Indeed, one of the major roles of the Italo-Australian press has remained that of looking inwards towards the Italian community in Australia and debating the social problems present both within the community itself and in its relationship with Australian society. A dominant theme for quite some time was the difficulties faced by Italian workers and their efforts, both collective and individual, to achieve equality of opportunity in employment. Equally important was its function of providing news from Italy, a role which the English-language press has rarely, if ever, fulfilled. *L'Italo-Australiano* ceased publication after six months. It was succeeded by a series of other papers, at first on a sporadic basis, promoted mainly by left-wing intellectuals. As the Italian communities consolidated in the 1920s, production became more consistent and systematic and presented a variety of approaches across the social and political spectrum from *Il Corriere degli Italiani in Australia* (1928), the official organ of the Italian fascist movement in Australia, to relatively short-lived papers of socialist and anarchist inspiration such as *La Riscossa* (1928) and *L'Avanguardia Libertaria* (1932). Italy's entry into World War II brought about the closure of all papers. Most of the staff of the various papers ended up in internment camps, irrespective of their political beliefs, and several hand-written newspapers were produced in the camps.

Revival was brought about by the anti-fascist *Italia Libera* movement which in 1944 commenced publishing *Il Risveglio.* The advocacy of a pro-Labor stance and the protection of Italian workers in Australia in the difficult climate of the closing years of the war were among the objectives of the paper, which ran all major articles in English as well as Italian. The establishment of links with Australian society was also an important aim, and the paper proved a vital focal point for the Australian Relief for Italy appeal. Strongly democratic and progressive, *Il Risveglio* encouraged debate on controversial issues. It met considerable opposition from the hierarchy of the Catholic Church which promoted the publication of its own papers for the Italian community. As the radicalising effects of World War II on Italo-Australians abated in the 1950s, *Il Risveglio* was forced to close.

Instead, two national weeklies of a more traditional nature came to dominate the Italian reading audiences of Australia. Initially, each was associated with a different faction of the Catholic Church—the virulently anti-communist Sydney-based *La Fiamma* with the Capuchins and, after 1959, the more progressive *Il Globo* with the Scalabrinian order (Bosi, 1989: 179). However, neither were religious papers in the sense of the earlier *L'Angelo della Famiglia.* The most successful proved to be *La Fiamma,* now mildly progressive in its stance. Its current print run is 28 000 and it continues to cater for first-generation immigrants, although it is attempting to attract the second generation with a weekly two-page feature in English. Its readers are interested above all in Italian sports, the TV guide, crime reports and death notices, while there is much less interest in Italian and Australian politics and current affairs.[3] Centre-right in Australian politics and somewhat towards right-of-centre in Italian politics, the Melbourne weekly *Il Globo* (current print run approximately 35 000) has a similar type of content and readership as *La Fiamma* but without English-language content. Both papers are now owned by interests claimed to be linked to the Italian Christian Democrat Party. Their conservative tendencies tend to appeal to the bulk of the older first-generation Italian immigrants. Their forays into Australian politics are mainly limited to immigration, welfare and other issues which directly affect the Italian community, while there is sometimes substantial reporting of the Italian centre-right political spectrum, particularly with respect to migration-related issues.

Nuovo Paese (see section on FILEF) can to a certain extent be seen as a successor to *Il Risveglio* and indeed continues some of its basic ideas. It presents an excellent digest of Australian, Italian and other overseas news and is particularly concerned with issues relating to Italian workers in Australia. Unlike other Italo-Australian print media it presents substantial English-language content (approximately 20 per cent compared to 3 per cent of *La Fiamma*). More modern and progressive than *La Fiamma* and *Il Globo, Nuovo Paese* presents a less commercial orientation, stimulates in its readers an interest in current issues and encourages active participation. It can be seen to represent a specific sector of the Italian community in Australia: what Bertelli has described as the *impegnati,* the more socially and politically sensitised, and better-educated immigrants of the late 1960s and 1970s who have brought their Italian experiences to bear through political activity in Australia (Bertelli, 1986: 4).

The above three papers can be said to have an established circulation at a national level but there are others—at least twenty—which circulate in various localities. Of these the longest running has probably been the Sydney weekly *Settegiorni* (1962–86). In other centres Italian-language newspapers have tended to come and go. Perth's *La Rondine,* edited by Alfredo Strano, lasted some three years (1970–73) and previously, *L'Eco Italiano* had survived for only eight months in 1958–59.

Italian-language magazines such as *Esaurito, Tempo Libero, Australia Ieri Oggi Domani,* which have tended to focus on particular aspects of Italian and/or Italo-Australian culture, have also tended to be relatively short-lived. There are few exceptions. One is the Sydney monthly *L'Opinione,* published by Guido Cicinelli but backed by Evasio Costanzo, which provides an often humorous but always satirical and decidedly biased commentary on the Italo-Australian community and those issues which most concern it, as well as copious commentary on the Italian sporting scene. The other notable exception is the 30-year-old *Messaggero* published in Melbourne by the Scalabrinians. It is the most conspicuous example of the Church-sponsored press which has a role of informing, instructing and giving religious news, but also deals widely with social, health and other issues.

Electronic media

Broadcasting in the Italian language on Australian radio stations began in the late 1930s with a fifteen-minute Italian program on 2SM Sydney which ran for a period of approximately three years. Suspended during World War II, Italian-language broadcasting was resumed in the early 1950s on commercial stations in Griffith, Sydney and Melbourne and, some years later, in a number of other centres of Italian settlement. Such programs were severely restricted both in terms of the on-air time made available (closely tied to advertising revenue) and by the provisions of the *Broadcasting and Television Act* (not abolished until 1974), by which non-English speech was limited to a maximum of 2.5 per cent of total weekly transmission time (except for 3XY Melbourne). Any speech of more than 25 words had to be accompanied by a word-for-word English rendition on air. It was not until 1975 with the establishment by the federal government of two multilingual radio stations, 2EA (Sydney) and 3EA (Melbourne), paralleled by the development of community language broadcasting on a number of public (community access) stations, that Italian-language programs experienced a dramatic expansion both in air time and coverage: from less than twenty hours per week in 1973 on some 10 stations to the current total in excess of eighty hours per week on nearly 30 stations.

Today, Italian is the most broadcast language after English. Although there is a fairly close correlation between number of hours broadcast by a particular station and size of the Italian community in the reception area (thus most of the hours broadcast are in cities like Brisbane, Sydney, Melbourne and Adelaide) some broadcasting is carried out in areas where there are relatively few Italians resident.

While Italian print media in Australia are not necessarily tied to print media in other languages (indeed they have at times had considerable independence of action), Italian-language programs in the electronic media are invariably tied to more general forms of multilingual broadcasting on the various radio and television stations. However, in 1989, an Italian/English commercial station, Radio Italia, was established in Melbourne as a subscriber-based

Mamma Lena who started a weekly radio program in the 1950s called 'Arriverdeci Roma', is shown here at the microphone of 2CH in 1976. Her years of broadcasting on 'Foreign' Language Radio brought enormous benefits to the Italian community. (*Australian Official Photograph*)

station and was claiming in excess of 20 000 listeners after the first few months of operation.

By contrast with the 'mddle-of-the-road' SBS, some public community access stations broadcast to specific sectoral groups within the community. The 3CR FILEF program is almost entirely in Italian, uses some 'alternative' news sources, presents a left-wing, worker-oriented viewpoint and concentrates on the dissemination of information about Australian conditions to Italian immigrant workers. Compared to the somewhat bland programming provided on the EA stations, Italian language programs on some public stations (particularly 2SER in Sydney, 3CR in Melbourne and 5EBI in Adelaide) are tailored to meet the special needs of the particular segments of the communities they serve, admit the airing of varying and contrasting viewpoints, encourage participation and attempt to avoid any kind of censorship other than that stipulated by legal requirements and station policy.

These differences are in part due to the differing objectives of the government-funded SBS and independent public sectors. The prime aim of the SBS service is assisting the integration of NESB people into a now consciously multicultural society, especially through the provision of appropriate information. The public sector, on the other hand, presents a somewhat more pluralistic, fluid and less monolithic concept of programming for the ethnic communities, with the opportunity to express cultural identity both within and among the group as a basic tenet of programming policy.

Television programs in Italian are broadcast by the government-run SBS television which now networks to most of the major population centres. Broadcasting time allocated to Italian language television programs averages some six to eight hours per week. However, unlike radio programs which are almost exclusively produced in Australia (apart from *Tutto il calcio minuto per minuto* [All the soccer minute by minute] received from Italy via satellite link and transmitted live on the EA and some public radio stations), television programs are imported from Italy (a major supplier being RAI), are subtitled in English and are hence accessible to audiences which do not understand Italian.[4] Selection of Italian material for television is based generally on cost considerations. However, a further principle seems to be the avoidance of those issues relating to Italian culture and society which may be considered extremist or avant-garde.

Media and community

The language-specific media (particularly the print media) services for the Italian community in Australia have, overall, reflected a sense of community which is partisan and fragmented, a multiplicity of a somewhat contradictory nature rather than a monolith. They have provided at times a forum for the debate of some of these differences, but often a vehicle for submerging them. Potential instruments of ethno-cultural control, the print media have at times acted as a mouthpiece for Italian political and religious interests, while the electronic media have represented the Australian power elite. The definition of community provided by the Italo-Australian media has tended to be vague, multiple and shifting (except perhaps the SBS monolithic view) although there are cases where the media have united in presenting or defending a commonly perceived community cause. Media services have generally reflected the politically conservative nature of the Italo-Australian community.

Conclusion

As the nature of Italian migration and settlement has changed over the last 150 years, different types of institutions have been generated and those that have survived for long periods have usually undergone substantial transformations.

In the case of the Church, the early missionary role played by Italian priests and brothers has disappeared, and the need for Italian-speaking clergy is also fading as the first-generation component of the Italian population declines. New, pressing needs have emerged: in particular, ministry to older Italians, who are a growing section of the Italian population and who generally have fewer people upon whom they can rely for help and support than their Australian-born counterparts. A recent inquiry into the needs of aged Italians in Melbourne found that the parish clubs and associations of the Catholic Church were the institutions that were best-known to otherwise isolated older people, and indeed recommended that less widely known welfare bodies should use the parish club network to establish contact with aged Italians (Guthrie, 1983).

Likewise, in the case of welfare organisations, the need to respond to the immediate difficulties of settlement has diminished over the last twenty years as Italian immigration has been substantially reduced and the majority of Italians have acquired English and use it (often in conjunction with Italian) at home and at work (Bertelli, 1988: 632). Many of the early mutual assistance associations were formed around groups of migrants who had emigrated from the same region or village and who lived in close proximity, and these too tended to outlive their usefulness as immigrants' residences became more dispersed and their social and support networks focused more on the extended family and neighbours. New welfare needs have emerged and both FILEF and COASIT have, in the 1980s, placed considerable emphasis on dealing with the issues relevant to second-generation Italians. COASIT in Sydney was the first (and to date the only) ethnic welfare body to employ a specialist drug and alcohol counsellor. It also places considerable emphasis on general youth work, including responding to intergenerational conflict and establishing 'safe' and 'therapeutic' social groups for young people (COASIT, 1989).

The clubs also, in endeavouring to remain relevant to the Italian-background population and compete with the mainstream commercial entertainment industries of the capital cities, have dramatically altered their foci and activities. The large, non-regional clubs have been able to survive by modelling themselves on the Leagues and Returned Servicemen's League clubs, opening up to members of

Italian senior citizens from Werribee play cards in the park at Lake Mulwala near Yarrawonga, Victoria, during a club excursion. (*F. di Blasi, Italian Historical Society, Melbourne*)

non-Italian descent and broadening their focus from the early days of soccer. In 1980, the APIA in Sydney reported 60 per cent non-Italian members, though the governing bodies of both Marconi and APIA remained largely composed of Italian–Australians (Burnley, 1988: 629).

Of course, none of these changes have taken place independently from the broader context of Australian society, and in particular the role of the State as it adopted multicultural policies and enhanced ethnic welfare services in the 1970s and 1980s. The new forms of Italian-language media evident today perhaps best demonstrate these impacts. Government funding and support for ethnic radio and television in the 1970s brought a dramatic expansion in the Italian-language media available to Italian immigrants in Australia. Italian-speakers can now hear a radio broadcast in Italian every day and watch an Italian program on television for up to eight hours of the week. The funds and infrastructure needed to establish such services are qualitatively different from those available to voluntary organisations or most Italian small businesses. However, the increased role of the State in service provision for ethnic communities in Australia has had contradictory effects. While creating more and more varied services, it has also led to an increase in regulation and control of the 'private' lives of Italian migrants, over the information and entertainment available to them, and in the case of the welfare organisations, over what services are provided and how they are delivered.

9 Italo-Australians and politics

Stephen Castles, Gaetano Rando and Ellie Vasta

At first sight, the impact of Italian settlement on Australian political institutions and culture appears small—indeed most observers argue that postwar immigration in general has had little effect. Jupp et al. write that, 'Australians of non-English-speaking background are marginal to the exercise of political power and influence in Australia' (1989: 51). McAllister states that postwar immigration 'has not resulted in any discernible change in the overall pattern of voting behaviour. Despite large-scale immigration, social class, not birthplace, has remained the basis for divisions between political parties' (1988: 919). Examining Italians in the 'Little Italy' of Leichhardt in Sydney from 1961 to 1973, Di Nicola found that their 'political impact has been slight' (1984: 177). Can the lack of specific migrant or minority politics be seen as a measure for the success of assimilationism or multicultural policies? Or do the reasons lie in specific characteristics of the migrants, such as peasant or working-class origin, their desire to escape from conflictual politics as experienced in the homeland, or their primary concern with economic security in the new country? Whatever the reasons, there is no doubt that migrant or ethnic politics are not a major issue of debate in Australia.[1]

The very lack of political mobilisation on ethnic lines, which differs from the experience in the USA or Canada, is something which needs investigation, as it helps us to understand the migratory process and the way the political system has responded to it. Moreover, the apparent absence of ethnic groupings in mainstream politics makes it necessary to look for alternative ways in which the interests of Italian migrants have been articulated. These include the role of migrant and ethnic organisations as lobby groups, and the incorporation of migrants into state consultative bodies of various kinds.

Political emigration from Italy

Among the Italians who migrated to Australia in the second half of the 19th century were some who sought refuge from political upheavals at home. A few of these political refugees participated in the social and political debates. While Raffaello Carboni's contribution may be seen principally as that of the chronicler of the Eureka Stockade, others such as Francesco Sceusa and Pietro Munari, who arrived later in the century, participated in more active ways.

Sceusa arrived in Sydney in 1877, having been 'encouraged' to leave his native Trapani because of his political activities, and was an active participant in the Australian socialist movement over the 30 years he resided in Australia. Sometimes accused by the more conservative elements in the Italian community of being a socialist, an atheist, an anarchist and a bandit, he was nevertheless active in promoting its welfare, being among the founders of the first Italo-Australian welfare organisation and the first Italo-Australian newspaper (see Chapter 8). Among his major concerns were the promotion of the rights of Italo-Australian workers and the links between them and Australian labour organisations.

Munari, a textile worker from Schio, emigrated to Australia in the 1890s after being sacked because of his political activities. He took an active interest in Australian politics, participating in the debates which gave birth to the Labor Party and contributing to the founding of an International Socialist Club in Sydney. Like Sceusa he also acted as correspondent for the socialist press in Italy, reporting especially on the Australian labour movement and the Federation debate (Munari, 1897). Another Italian, Pietro Baracchi, was a member of the committee appointed to choose a design for the Australian flag in 1908, while his son Guido Baracchi was a founding member of the Communist Party of Australia (CPA). In the 1920s and 1930s left-wing activists such as Omero Schiassi and Francesco Carmagnola emigrated to Australia as a result of fascist oppression but their involvement was mainly restricted to politics within the Italian community (see Cresciani, 1981: *passim*).

There are also sporadic examples of second-generation Italians elected as members of parliament. Camillo Lazzarini was elected in New South Wales as member for Marrickville in 1917, a seat which he held until 1952 (with a brief interruption from 1931 to 1934), while his brother Pietro was elected to the federal seat of Werriwa in 1919, becoming Minister for Home Security in 1942. Giuseppe Lamaro, elected to the New South Wales state seat of Enmore in 1927, was Justice Minister from 1930 to 1932.

At the end of World War II, the major impetus to emigrate was provided by the harsh economic circumstances and the poverty existing in many localities. However, according to Cinanni important additional factors in forcing the emigration of southern *contadini* were the failed agrarian reforms: '. . . De Gasperi . . . chased the peasants not only from the land, but also from their homes to marginalise them in the ghettoes of emigration' (Cinanni, 1979: 115). Those who had taken a prominent part in the various agitations and uprisings, especially if associated with left-wing political movements, were 'encouraged' to emigrate by threats, by being denied employment and by other forms of harassment (Cinanni, 1979: 68). There is no specific evidence that the local authorities altered the records of some of the political activists in order to make them acceptable to countries requiring immigrants, but according to hearsay both in Italy and Australia, this definitely appears to have been the case.

Migrant social and political rights

In the early postwar years, according to the *Aliens Act* 1947, all non-British migrants were classed as 'aliens' by law. British migrants were privileged over other migrants with regard to allocation of housing, choice of occupation and availability of social services. Non-British migrants had to be naturalised (which meant a five-year waiting period) for the same concessions (Vasta, 1990b). In fact, under common law, 'aliens' were subject to severe restrictions, one being that they could not buy or own land. The object of this restriction was to 'prevent the nation being subject to foreign influence' (Pryles and Bravender-Coyle, 1988: 904). Also, as late as 1959 all non-British migrants had to register their names since they were not on the electoral roles. This was meant to make them 'feel welcome' and to help organise and assimilate them. Thus, an 'alien' still had to notify the Department of Immigration of changes of address, employment and marriage (see Vasta, 1990b: 160).

Civil and political rights of non-citizens have been improved over the years through legislation. For instance, non-citizens resident in Australia are protected by Australian law and 'have the same criminal and civil liability as citizens'. All immigrants are protected by the provisions of the 1975 *Racial Discrimination Act* (Pryles and

Bravender-Coyle, 1988: 904). Although migrants have now achieved equal rights through legislation, it would be misleading to assume that racist ideologies and practices can be legislated out of existence (see for example Mitchell, 1988; de Lepervanche, 1990). Furthermore, the Minister for Immigration, Local Government and Ethnic Affairs has the power to order the deportation of any non-citizens.

One example was the deportation of a FILEF organiser, Ignazio Salemi, which attracted much attention in the late 1970s. Salemi's deportation was linked with the differing welfare styles and ideologies of the two main Italian welfare agencies in Melbourne, COASIT and FILEF (see Jakubowicz et al., 1984: 47–63). The ideology and the organisational style of the two organisations differed dramatically, producing many conflicts. In the 1970s COASIT was a conservative organisation, and its founders, the Vaccari family, had established links with extreme anti-communist groups like the National Civic Council and the Democratic Labor Party (see below). The FILEF strategies were concerned with the social and welfare rights of working-class Italians in Australia. The Salemi affair 'was essentially the denouement of the FILEF/COASIT conflict' for when in 1975 Salemi sought to extend his visa, Jakubowicz et al. claim that '[a]t the insistence of conservative Italians and other people associated with the Liberal Party, Mackellar (Minister for Immigration) rejected the request' (1984: 81). In 1975, the Melbourne premises of FILEF were broken into and an attempt was made to burn down the building (Cresciani, 1988b: 281). Salemi's connections with the Italian Communist Party provided a scapegoat in a country which has hysterically feared communism throughout the 20th century. In 1976, Salemi was refused permission to remain under the Immigration Amnesty. He fought his case through the courts and lost, and was finally deported in October 1977.

Political representation

In this section we examine the extent to which Italian migrants and their descendants have become members of the Commonwealth or state parliaments, or of local councils. Only Australian citizens can stand for elected office, so the precondition for becoming a member of a parliament or council for first-generation migrants is naturalisation. As pointed out in Chapter 3, the 1986 census showed that 76 per cent of the Italian-born had become Australian citizens, but many of these have done so fairly recently, so that they were ineligible to stand for public office for many years. Nevertheless, many of those who are not naturalised do have permanent residency status which provides them with all other civil rights.

Commonwealth and state parliaments

No figures are kept on the ethnic origins of members of parliaments, so the only way of estimating them is by the somewhat unreliable practice of guessing from their names. It is thus impossible to distinguish between first and subsequent generations. According to one estimate, only 23 people of Italian origin have ever been members of the Commonwealth or state parliaments.[2] In 1982, out of the 189 members of the Commonwealth House of Representatives and Senate, there was not a single Italian. Looking at the 399 members of state lower houses, five members were of Italian origin. If Italians had been represented in proportion to their share of the population, there should have been eight in the Commonwealth parliament and seventeen in the state lower houses. Italians shared this underrepresentation with members of other NESB groups and with Aborigines (Jupp, 1984b: 190). In 1990 there appeared to be two federal politicians of Italian origin—Con Sciacca in the House of Representatives and J. Pannizza in the Senate. As Jupp points out, Australian political elites are still overwhelmingly of Anglo-Saxon Protestant background (1984b: 182).

Even where Italians have been elected to parliament, to achieve nomination has meant joining an Australian party, undergoing complicated preselection procedures, and being willing to accept party policies and to represent constituents of all ethnic backgrounds. Unlike the USA, Australia has no areas dominated by any single ethnic minority population (Jupp et al., 1989: 32). There have been no ethnically based political parties in Australia, partly because the electoral system would make it very hard for them to get representation, but also because the mainstream parties have, in the long run, found ways of incorporating minority interests, as will be seen below. At present, the majority of Italian parliamentarians are members of the ALP. They generally represent central city constituencies, with electorates of both migrant and working-class background. Some Italian politicians have maintained close links with the Italo-Australian community, and have attempted to secure recognition of their needs (and indeed of those of migrants in general) in politics and government. State members like Giovanni Sgro in Victoria and Franca Arena in New South Wales typify this approach.

One of the few instances in which a person of Italian origin has played a decisive role in Australian politics should be mentioned here. Bartholomew Santamaria, born in 1915 as son of an Italian immigrant, became leader of Catholic Action, a militantly anti-communist movement among Australian Catholics. After World War II, Santamaria and his supporters—known as 'the Movement' or the 'Groupers'—set out to combat communist influence in the trade unions and the ALP. In 1954, ALP leader Evatt denounced the outside influence in the party, and many 'Groupers' were expelled. Santamaria was instrumental in establishing the breakaway right-wing Democratic Labor Party (DLP) in 1955 (Ward, 1977: 311–14). Although Santamaria's power base was the Catholic Church, his politics had little to do with Italian immigration, and were not based on the Italian community.

Local councils

Italians have secured more representation at the third level of government, the local councils, than at the other levels. There were Italians on the councils of Northcote, Coburg and Richmond (all municipalities of Melbourne) by the mid-1960s, and the first Italian mayor was elected in Coburg in 1968 (Jupp et al., 1989: 37). In Sydney, things moved more slowly. Di Nicola (1984: 171–4) reports that the New South Wales ALP was suspicious of migrant participation and few Italians joined. In the 1968 municipal elections, three Italians were candidates in Leichhardt (a municipality of Sydney), but all were defeated, leading to disillusionment with electoral politics. Di Nicola attributes the defeat to the relatively small proportion of naturalised Italians at that time, as well as difficulty in understanding the complex preferential voting system.

Nonetheless, by 1981–82 there were NESB members on seventeen councils in Melbourne, ten in Sydney and six in Adelaide (Jupp et al., 1989: 37). Representation continued to grow through the 1980s, with considerable NESB representation in the four major metropolitan areas of Melbourne, Sydney, Adelaide and Perth. An Italian, John Catalini, was elected as mayor of Fremantle in the 1980s. Brisbane was the only exception, with just one councillor of Italian origin and one of Scandinavian origin in 1988 (Jupp et al., 1989: 36). However, there are many councillors of Italian origin in other Queensland municipalities. A comparison of NESB representation by state indicates that the situation is most favourable in Western Australia and least in NSW. Jupp argues that the old style tightly controlled ALP machines in the inner suburbs of Sydney have been a barrier to migrant political participation. In any case, despite the growing number of councillors of NESB origin, migrants still remain underrepresented in relation to their share in the population (Jupp et al., 1989: 37).

Italians do, however, play a major role in the council of the large outer-western Sydney area of Fairfield, where in 1990 three out of fifteen elected alderpersons were of Italian background, while the deputy mayor was Vietnamese (Fairfield City Council, 1990). By contrast, in the area with the second-largest Italian community in

New South Wales, Wollongong, Italians seem to have played only a minor role in local politics. In 1990, they were not represented on the city council. One hypothesis to explain this is the greater concentration of Italians in manufacturing work (mainly in the steel industry) in Wollongong, compared with Fairfield and other areas. It seems likely that it is employment in the tertiary sector, and particularly owning a small business, which leads most readily to involvement in local politics. In rural Griffith, which has a substantial Italian population (see Chapters 4 and 7), there were three Italians on the twelve-member council in 1980. However, according to Kelly '[i]t was emphasised by several [Italo-Australians] that it was considered unwise to raise issues relating specifically to Italo-Australians because this could lead to accenting divisions and causing resentment from Anglo-Australians' (1984: 132).

Clearly, local politics provide the best opportunity for the development of ethnic representation, partly because it is possible to achieve some unity on local issues, and partly because ethnic concentrations are most felt in local voting wards. However, it must be remembered that there are no areas even at the local government level with an Italian population that makes up more than 22 per cent of the total population (see Chapter 3). State and parliamentary constituencies are much larger, generally including areas with diverse class and ethnic composition, making ethnic politics fairly problematic at these levels.

Voting behaviour

A crucial question for Australian political parties is whether there is an 'ethnic vote' which can be mobilised around issues of interest to immigrants by ethnic community leaders. In the early postwar years, little attention was paid to this question: assimilationist ideology made special attention to migrant interests anathema, and few migrants had become naturalised. Those who had been naturalised tended to vote for conservative parties (the Liberal Party and, in rural areas, the Country Party and its successor, the National Party). This applied particularly to eastern Europeans, who were refugees from communist regimes and distrusted even the mildly socialist ALP. In the 1970s, there appears to have been a swing of southern European voters to the ALP, which was maintained in the 1980s. McAllister (1988: 921) estimates that 82 per cent of southern Europeans voted for the ALP in the 1983 federal election (no specific information on Italian-born voters is available).

From the late 1960s, ALP leaders realised that migrants represented a significant section of working-class voters, and that their votes could be decisive in inner-city areas. The ALP set out to woo the 'ethnic vote', setting up Italian and Greek sections in some areas, paying attention to migrants' educational and welfare needs, advertising in the ethnic press and selecting migrants as candidates (Collins, 1988: 135–7). Party leaders attended ethnic community meetings and functions. Gough Whitlam's ALP victory in the 1972 election seems partly attributable to this policy. The Whitlam government's concern with migrant welfare, and the first steps towards multiculturalism (see Chapter 3) were logical consequences. In response, the Liberal Party, from 1975–1982, also became concerned with ethnic issues: it established the Australian Institute of Multicultural Affairs and the Special Broadcasting Service; set up an Ethnic Affairs Branch within the Department of Immigration, and funded welfare services provided by ethnic communities through the Grant-in-Aid scheme. Similarly, most of the states set up Ethnic Affairs Commissions, and announced their intention to make their services more appropriate to the needs of ethnic communities.

Most political scientists in Australia argue that there is no 'ethnic vote' in the sense of blocs of votes which can be controlled and manipulated by ethnic power-brokers. On the other hand, politicians behave as if they believe that there is an 'ethnic vote', in the sense that any policy measure which is seen as an attack on the interests of ethnic communities may produce an electoral backlash, which could be decisive in marginal constituencies with large immigrant populations. The clearest example of this was the attempt by the Hawke government to cut services to migrants in the 1986 budget (see Chapter 3). The ensuing protests by ethnic communities led to a very rapid policy reversal and a strong reaffirmation of multiculturalism by the government. Similarly, then-Opposition Leader Howard's attacks on multiculturalism in 1988 are generally seen as a major reason for his removal from the leadership soon after.

The political role of Italian associations

What has been said so far indicates a paradox: Italians (and other NESB migrants) have not managed to achieve much representation in state or Commonwealth parliaments nor in party leaderships, yet politicians cannot afford to ignore them as a political factor. Clearly the political influence of Italians is not reducible to their role in formal institutions. The attention given by politicians to the 'ethnic vote' implies other ways of participating in politics. The key to understanding this is to look at the way in which community networks and associations mediate between individuals and political institutions, acting as what political scientists call 'pressure groups'.

One early Italian pressure group was the *Consiglio Italiano del Lavoro* (Italian Labour Council), established by Captain Giuseppe Di Salvo in Melbourne in the mid-1960s. It did not achieve its aim of nominating Di Salvo for the Commonwealth seat of Batman in 1966, and this led to disillusionment with the ALP on the part of his supporters (Allan, 1984: 141). A more significant role has been played by Italian clubs such as the APIA in Leichhardt. The APIA was opened in 1954, soon becoming a focus for Italian social and political life in Sydney. It has been visited by leading politicians from both sides of the political spectrum, including Gough Whitlam, William McMahon and Bob Hawke. As Di Nicola (1984: 166–7) points out, the party leaders hope to gain Italo-Australian votes through their visits, but are also informed of community concerns, such as the transferability of Australian pensions to Italy. This is a very clear example of the two-way political function of such apparently non-political bodies. The Fraternity Club in Wollongong appears to play a similar role, being used as a meeting place by political parties and trade unions. It has also been visited by the Prime Minister and New South Wales premiers over the years.

However, more formal pressure groups linking all NESB ethnic groups have been established since 1975—the Ethnic Communities Councils (ECCs) in each state, and the Federation of Ethnic Community Councils of Australia (FECCA) at the national level (founded in 1980). These bodies are very much a product of the consultative strategies introduced through multiculturalism: they are a transmission belt between ethnic groups and the government, allowing the former to put forward their needs and interests, and the latter to gain assistance in the implementation of immigration and ethnic affairs policies. The ECCs and FECCA are frequently called upon by various state and Commonwealth departments to provide their views on specific government proposals, and they nominate participants to a variety of official consultative boards and committees. The quasi-state function of FECCA is shown by the fact that 72 per cent of its income was provided by public funds in 1989 (Jupp et al., 1989: 26).

Consultative bodies

There is currently a tendency in western democracies to formalise the role of pressure groups as representatives of sectional interests, through the proliferation of government consultative bodies. This trend became most evident in Australia from the time of the 1972–75 Whitlam government, and today there is a wide range of consultative or advisory bodies at the Commonwealth and state levels. Examples in the ethnic affairs area include the Australian Council on Multicultural Affairs (ACMA), which is chaired by Sir James Gobbo, a jurist of Italian origin; the National Population Council (NPC), which advises the Department of Immigration, Local Government and Ethnic Affairs; the Commonwealth/State Council on NESB Women's Issues, which advises the Commonwealth Ministers for Ethnic and Women's Affairs; the National Advisory Council on Skills Recognition (NACSR), which advises the Department of Employment, Education and Training; and the Ethnic Affairs Commissions, which advise state governments on issues concerning ethnic communities.

Consultative bodies assist in policy-making by allowing bureaucrats to test the acceptability of measures before making decisions on implementation. For ethnic groups, consultative committees have an ambivalent function: on the one hand they give an opportunity for organised ethnic interests to get direct access to government departments (Jupp et al., 1989: 43). They can thus partially substitute for the deficient parliamentary representation of ethnic groups. On the other hand, they can have a depoliticising effect: by making ethnic leaders dependent on government patronage, and allowing the government to choose which ethnic representatives are to be listened to, they can undermine other forms of political mobilisation (Castles et al., 1988: 77).

Recent research shows that NESB migrants are well represented on bodies in the immigration and ethnic affairs areas; less well represented on bodies concerned with educational, social and related topics; and not represented at all on bodies concerned with economic policy, industry, industrial relations, agriculture and banking. This indicates a continued marginalisation of ethnic groups: their representatives are not perceived to be competent to deal with central issues of government policy which concern society in general (Jupp et al., 1989: 43–5).

Trade unions

Australia has a powerful and militant trade union movement, which has been successful in incorporating workers of non-English-speaking background. In 1982 their rate of union membership was 60 per cent higher than the rate for Australian-born workers, which was 48 per cent (Collins, 1988: 138). Since most Italian migrants became blue-collar workers, their role in the unions is a key aspect of political involvement. In the early postwar years, the unions tended to see 'foreign' immigrants as a potential threat to wages and conditions, particularly during times of recession. This attitude often made migrants feel unwelcome in the labour movement. In fact, in the postwar years there developed an ideological pact between the State, employers, Anglo-Australian workers and trade unions against migrant workers (Vasta, 1990b).

One of the first instances of Italian migrant worker struggles against the State occurred in 1952 when Italian migrants in their early twenties staged a one-day hunger strike in Melbourne demanding 'work or repatriation', as some had been out of work for eight weeks. Many of these demonstrators had been brought out to Australia on a two-year work contract and had not found work weeks after arrival. The following year, Italian migrants sued the Australian government for breach of work contracts. The issue was finally settled out of court (Vasta, 1990b: 131–5).

Some of the major problems facing Italian migrant workers include lack of knowledge about their industrial rights; being played off against Anglo-Australians and other migrant workers for overtime and job allocations; and lack of proficiency in English. These problems have acted as major barriers to migrant worker militancy in Australia. Despite this, Italian migrant workers have been involved in numerous struggles over pay and work conditions. For example, in 1964 at General Motors Holden in Victoria there was a strike which lasted a month, in which the workers defied union requests to return to work. Union leaders blamed Italian and Greek migrants for the length of the stoppage and for their refusal to accept union recommendations (Quinlan, 1982: 364). At the Ford Broadmeadows plant in Victoria in 1973, migrant workers, including Italians, repudiated union leaders and refused to return to work. Overall the strike lasted more than nine weeks and 'demonstrated the depth of frustration, hostility and solidarity on the part of the migrant workforce which surprised both management and union leaders' (Quinlan, 1982: 365; see also Lever-Tracy, 1984). This strike did secure pay increases and improved work conditions.

These incidents led union leaders to realise that they were out of touch with workers (see Martin, 1978) and around 1975 they began to take notice of the migrant presence. However, a study carried out by Nicolaou in New South Wales between 1982 and 1986 indicated that most unions had still done very little to deal with the needs and difficulties of migrant workers. Nicolaou found that immigrant men and women were severely underrepresented in union bureaucracies, which were dominated by men of Anglo-Saxon background. This led to isolation and lack of participation in union activities. Nicolaou concluded that this situation was the result of closed and centralised power structures within the unions, as well as assimilationist and sometimes prejudiced attitudes on the part of some officials (Nicolaou, 1988: 961–3). Although migrants have often resisted class exploitation, in the Australian context there were no distinct political 'cultures of resistance' by Italian migrant workers (Vasta, 1990b: 140). However, as Lever-Tracy and Quinlan suggest (1988: 316), migrants' experiences of Australian class relations and institutional structures, during the first three postwar decades, played a more influential role in terms of ethnic class consciousness than did their ethnic cultures or ethno-historical past.

One interesting question which arises from this situation is to compare the low political profile of Italo-Australian migrants with the militancy of southern Italians in the industrial towns of northern Italy. Such a comparison raises three points which need to be placed within the historical and political contexts of assimilation and multiculturalism. First, the southern Italian workers in northern Italy were invited to be active members of their unions. In Australia, as noted earlier, migrants were mostly ignored by their unions even though migrant membership was high. Second, it is easier to be militant in one's own language and with institutions of which one has some knowledge. Third, the emotional strain and investment involved in moving to such a distant and alien language and culture also had the effect of producing low political involvement.

Italo-Australians also appear to have been less militant than Italian workers in west European countries. One possible reason is that there were effective communication channels between immigrant workers around Europe, whereas immigrant workers in Australia were rather isolated from their compatriots in other immigrant countries. Another reason is that Australia is one of the few immigrant countries which has adopted a policy of multiculturalism, and although this policy has provided migrants with certain benefits and rights, which reduces the need for militancy, they still have to guard against co-option.

Nando Lelli—an Italo-Australian trade union leader

There are numerous examples of Italian workers who have been elected as shop floor representatives or to other types of office such as the appointment of Joe Caputo as union organiser for the Clothing Trades in Melbourne in the mid-1970s (see Brunswick Oral History Project 1985: 88, 93), and Franco Mantino as Migrant Representative for the Building Workers Industrial Union in Brisbane in the late 1970s. One of the most outstanding examples is Nando Lelli. In the twenty years he led the Port Kembla Branch of the Federated Ironworkers' Association of Australia, representing the workforce of Australia's largest steelworks, he was instrumental in considerably improving the lot of its members, particularly of the

Nando Lelli receives his degree at the University of Wollongong. (*Turo Chiodo*)

large proportion who were migrants. In 1970 not one of the elected full-time officials was of non-English speaking background, and the number of multilingual clerical staff at the union office was very limited. Twenty years later, one-third of the elected full-time officials were of non-English speaking background, while all the office staff spoke at least one language other than English. In addition, there have been considerable improvements in the provision of language courses (including English courses at the workplace), and of information and other services for migrant workers (see Lever-Tracy and Quinlan, 1988: 167–236).

Ferdinando (Nando) Lelli was born in Ascoli Piceno and came to Australia in 1957 at the age of 25. After some three years spent in various occupations such as fruit picking and cane cutting, he obtained a job as a labourer with Australian Iron and Steel (AIS) at Port Kembla in January 1961. The local union leadership had worked closely with the employers, and imposed a rigid control on the membership. The branch did little to involve migrant workers, or to respond to their problems, which were particularly serious in view of the very difficult working conditions and the high accident rate. Thus began Lelli's involvement with the unions.

In 1970, after a hard-fought campaign against the old leadership, the rank-and-file group, of which Lelli was a leading member, gained control of the branch executive. In 1972, Lelli was elected Secretary of the Port Kembla Branch of the Federated Ironworkers' Association of Australia, one of the largest and most powerful union branches in Australia. There were barriers to be overcome, first and foremost the language barrier, then that of proving his commitment to the group's cause and his leadership qualities:

> During my commitment to the political movement to which I belong there were Italians who were not necessarily politically orientated the way I was. And I can assure you that they were very active in seeing if they could put the skids under me rather than assisting. So I never asked for a favour unless there was a political affinity between people. I don't want to be supported by the Italian community because I am Italian. I want to be supported by those who are politically orientated the way I think I am . . . Some of the Italians in this region were very, very active over the years in opposing my candidacy in the election and they were very, very, very solidly against my style of leadership.

He remained in this position until 1990. He led the workers of Port Kembla throughout the difficult period of industrial restructuring, during which the steelworks was threatened with closure, eventually reducing the labour force by more than half. By the time he retired as Secretary, Lelli had won widespread respect, not only from trade unionists, but also from AIS management and the community at large. On 12 October 1990 he was awarded an Honorary Fellowship by the University of Wollongong for his outstanding contribution to the trade union movement and the community.

Italo-Australians and political power

The findings of this chapter are ambiguous. Italo-Australians (and the same goes for other NESB ethnic groups) do not have a high political profile. They have not established their own political parties or trade unions, nor have they gained significant representation in parliaments. On the other hand, there are a large number of local councillors and some mayors of Italian origin, yet even at this level of government Italo-Australians are underrepresented in comparison to their share in the population. Despite this, the 'ethnic vote' appears to be an issue which influences the behaviour of Australian political leaders. Not only do they make efforts to approach Italian (and other ethnic) associations to mobilise electoral support, they also make concessions to ethnic needs and interests in their policies.

The explanation for this combination of a low political profile with fairly successful interest articulation seems to lie in the relative openness of the Australian political system for immigrant groups, at least at a superficial level. Postwar immigrants to Australia encountered a very different situation than the large pre-1914 influxes to North America. There, both employers and governments often followed exclusionary or divisive strategies, with new immigrant groups being used as cheap labour and strike-breakers. Where they resisted, the full force of the State was used against them. In Australia, governments and strong unions combined to guarantee orderly industrial relations, which would not threaten the conditions of local workers. Policies of assimilation may have been discriminatory because they set out to destroy migrants' cultures, but by providing civil rights and citizenship, they did lay the groundwork for political integration.

But the fact that ethnic groups were integrated and allowed to voice their interests does not necessarily mean that they obtained a share in real political power. As Jupp points out: '[p]ower in the corporate sector, in the parties, in the bureaucracies, in the professions, in the media and in the unions—is still in varying degrees, in the hands of people of British or Irish origin' (1984b: 182). Indeed, it might be added, it is still in the hands of white, middle-class, middle-aged men. One reason for the lack of first-generation Italo-Australian parliamentarians and party leaders is their predominant class background as former peasants who have become manual workers. There has been a strong tendency in the past twenty years for leading politicians in all political parties to be university graduates with middle-class occupational backgrounds (Jupp et al., 1989: 54). Small business may be a route into local politics, but not into state and national arenas.

Thus Italo-Australians and other NESB groups have obtained some political influence in ethnic affairs and welfare policies, and have been able to develop their own leaderships within the context of the Australian political system, but they are still far from having any measure of control in central political and economic areas. The question is whether this situation will change as the mainly poorly educated migrant generation leaves the centre stage, and is replaced by a new self-confident second generation, which has passed through the Australian educational system. It has yet to be seen whether this group will be able to create a new political identity within a changing society, or will become indistinguishable in its political orientations from other Australians.

10 Italian migrant women

Ellie Vasta

From the outset, women have been part of Italian migration to Australia. Their role has been crucial to the formation of the Italo-Australian community. Yet they, like many other migrant women, 'have been the Cinderellas of the immigration program: their sacrifices, their efforts, their difficulties have been overlooked; at times ignored' (Arena, 1985: 22). Italian migrant women, along with other non-English speaking migrant women, have had to deal with many of the contradictions of gender, class and ethnic relations both as these existed in their home communities and in the form in which they have emerged in new communities in Australia. They have experienced severe discrimination in the workplace, in the community and through the racist practices embedded in Australian government policies and institutions. Nevertheless, Italian migrant women have dealt creatively with an often hostile environment, making significant contributions in both the public and private arenas. Because there is very little systematic research on Italian women in Australia, this chapter relies heavily on individual accounts and case studies.

Prewar Italian migrant women

The first Australian census of 1881 recorded a figure of 1880 Italians based on declaration of nationality, of whom it is estimated that one in six were women (Cresciani in Arena, 1985: 22). The Italian community was still rather small in 1904, when two sisters,

Amelia aged fourteen and her older sister Matilde arrived, on their own, from the Italian Riviera to settle near Melbourne to look after an elderly uncle (Triaca, 1985). The life story of Amelia is valuable because it is one of the few biographies written about the lives of Italian migrant women in Australia in the early years of this century. Outside Melbourne, at Daylesford, they lived in an ethnically diverse environment having English, Cornish, German, Italian, Swiss–Italian, Chinese and Anglo-Australian neighbours (Triaca, 1985: 52). Amelia and Matilde kept house for their uncle while Amelia did all she could to learn English from one of her Italian neighbours. In the Daylesford district there were a number of Italians who owned small businesses—namely dairies, hotels, a spaghetti factory, and wine saloons. One woman, a Mrs Locantro, owned and ran her own fruit shop. Many of the women worked along with their husbands in their small businesses.

During her first year in Australia, Matilde discovered that her uncle, who was 50 years her senior, wanted to marry her. She had tried to put him off but in the end felt she had to succumb to this unwanted fate. On the day set for the wedding, the pair discovered, much to Matilde's and Amelia's delight, that an uncle and a niece could not marry. When Amelia had been in Australia for one year she wanted to go to school, but her uncle would not allow it, although he was not averse to her taking a job. She decided to become a nanny and found herself a job in Melbourne looking after the children of a wealthy Italian woman, Madame L'Hardy, and her French husband. In this job, Amelia became one of the family and received a legacy when Mr L'Hardy died. In 1918 she married an English returned soldier, lost her husband to the Spanish influenza and gave birth to their daughter five months later. Before her wedding she had bought a house in Melbourne with her L'Hardy inheritance, and after her husband's death she subdivided the house into flats. She was able to raise her daughter, provide her with a good education and take a trip to Italy. Earlier, she and her sister had brought their mother and younger siblings to live in Australia with them. When Matilde's husband died in the early 1950s, the two sisters lived together again for about twenty years until Matilde passed away in 1974. In 1985 Amelia was ninety-five and living with her daughter.

Italian migration to Australia increased significantly in the 1920s, though the number of women remained small. The average ratio between the sexes for Italians in the 1920s was 4.4 males to 1 female. In some areas the imbalance was even greater with 9 to 1 in South Australia, and 8 to 1 in Western Australia (Diana, 1988: 2). There were high concentrations of women in some areas such as the cane fields of northern Queensland, parts of New South Wales and Victoria. The general pattern for migration during the 1920s and 1930s was that the men came out first, worked and saved, and would then return to choose a wife. For others, women would migrate as wives, daughters, nieces, lovers. Such was the case for Dina Vasta and Angela Torristi (née Di Martino) aged 11 and 15 respectively, who arrived in 1937 along with their mother to join their father in the cane fields of northern Queensland. Dina went to school for a couple of years and eventually dropped out with very little English. One of her chores as a twelve-year-old was to rise at 3 a.m., summer and winter, to light the wood fire and prepare breakfast for her cane-cutting father. Often she fell asleep and would have nothing but cinders to offer her tired and hungry father. A hiding followed. At the age of nineteen she married and moved to Sydney, where she began to work in factories. She worked on the process line of a Sydney match factory for twenty years. Work conditions were often sweltering, damaging to the eyes and dangerous, since frequently matches would spontaneously combust. This job offered a bonus system, so for long periods Dina was up at 5 a.m. and returned home at 9 p.m., only to begin again the next day.

Frequently, women experienced the trauma of separation and isolation, all the while harbouring a strong desire to return to Italy. During the prewar years very few Italians returned since the majority were labourers, and lacked the money. For those who had bought farms or houses, mortgage repayments prohibited their retum. The strength of the family during these years became an important factor in dealing with an alien environment. Italian families tended to mix together, developed their own communities and, as far as possible, continued Italian child-rearing practices, cultural traditions and customs. The role of the Church at the community level during the 1920s and 1930s was minimal except for its involvement in baptisms, weddings and funerals. Within the family, the men were the source of authority while the women were relegated to the 'domestic' sphere. Double standards operated for sons and daughters: the sons were allowed the freedom to go out as well as the possibility of following their fathers' trade or work. Parents had a stronger hold over their daughters, who were expected to marry Italians, were not allowed out unchaperoned, and were expected to gain social mobility through their marriage. The men led a more 'public' life, socialising in pubs and billiard rooms (Diana, 1988: 70–1).

Nevertheless, in northern Queensland Italian women planted cane, worked as cooks, and contributed to the running of shops, boarding houses and pubs (see Menghetti, 1988: 602). In the fruit-growing areas of the Murrumbidgee Irrigation Area in New South Wales the women worked as fruit pickers and performed other horticultural jobs on the farms, as they had in Italy (Diana, 1988: 68, 74). In the cities women shared much of the work in family businesses, cooking, cleaning, running boarding houses and working in textile factories (Diana, 1988: 75). In contrast to the work they did, their involvement in political activities appears to have been minimal. In northern Queensland for example, where there was a fascist movement, there appears to have been no women's involvement. In the 1930s Italian women around Australia donated gold and wedding rings to the fascist funds. In Sydney and Melbourne the Women's *Fascio,* founded in Sydney in 1927, organised balls, charities and receptions (Diana, 1988: 76–7).

One reason for the strength of the Italian family and community and low rate of intermarriage with Anglo-Australians was the Italian migrants' experience of racism. A 1933 report commissioned by the Queensland government on racial problems in northern Queensland stated:

> [t]he vials of popular wrath and enmity are reserved for the Italians and other foreign elements from southern Europe . . . In the eyes of the wage earners the Italians contemptuously known as 'Dagos' are the very scum of the earth, who live on the smell of an oily rag, undercutting all competitors for work on the cane fields . . . dirty in their habits, exclusive and unsociable . . . They are a menace to the country! (Ferry in Diana, 1988: 69).

This racist attitude was fanned by the war and continued after the war as the numbers of Italian migrants reached unprecedented levels. During the war, many Italian women suffered further isolation and loneliness as their husbands, defined as enemy aliens, were interned.

The experience of Maria Paoloni reflects the experience of many Italian women during the war. She and her husband had bought a small mixed business in Balmain, an inner-Sydney suburb, and while her husband Gino was away working during the day, Maria ran the shop. Maria describes the experience in her own words:

> Houses were searched, men taken away to camps for enemy aliens and women and children left to fend for themselves . . . Gino was arrested and I was shunned by everybody. To be *internati*—interned in an enemy alien camp—meant not only loss of one's freedom and separation from the family, but also financial ruin. In my case many customers stopped coming into the shop . . . But the worst terrors and insults came from bands of young, sadistic vandals whom I had never seen before . . . One night they smashed the shop window (Paoloni, 1989: 69–70).

Maria had to close the shop to go and seek work to keep herself and her son alive. She ended up at an isolated poultry farm working for her keep, experiencing further cultural and emotional loneliness.

When her husband was released, they started all over again. Though it is difficult to ascertain the numbers, a few Italian women, some with young children, were also arrested and interned during the war.

Postwar proxy brides

Before the war, as after, the ratio of men to women was unbalanced and this affected Italian migrant marriage patterns. At certain times there were high proportions of unmarried men and this problem was dealt with by the community in several ways. If possible, Italian men would marry Italian women. There was very little intermarriage with other ethnic groups or with Anglo-Australians, one reason being their inadequate command of languages other than Italian. Many returned to their village, married and returned with their new family. Others arranged proxy marriages where the ceremony was conducted in the Italian village for the bride while the groom was in Australia. These marriages were registered in Italy (Price and Zubrzycki, 1962a) and the women became known as proxy brides. Or some women would join their fiancés and marry within weeks of arrival or on the day of arrival at a church nearest the landing wharf (Price and Zubrzycki, 1962a: 65)—wharf-side brides.

The imbalance of the sexes persisted into the 1960s (Price and Zubrzycki, 1962b). One report claimed that southern European single men were developing social problems because the traditional social customs of southern European national groups in Australia precluded a balanced social life for their unmarried young men and also because there was antipathy on the part of Australian girls towards southern European males (IAC, 1969a: 11). The imbalance of the sexes was officially viewed as a problem because there was concem that migrant men would become an unruly force without the tempering influence of women. It was felt that due to the chaperone system for Italian girls, many Italian men were pursuing an 'espresso-bar' life-style which often led to 'unhappy social consequences' (IAC, 1969b: 7). In the early 1960s, Immigration Minister Downer gave an assurance that absolute priority would be given to nominations on behalf of parents, wives, dependent children, sisters, fiancées and other single women (Downer, 1961: 17).

The selection of single migrant women raised a number of significant contradictions. The problems of southern European migrant women, defined as 'semi-illiterate and unskilled', were explained as emerging from 'the age-old custom throughout southern Europe which regards literacy among the women folk as unnecessary, even undesirable' (IAC, 1963). So while women were viewed as illiterate, dependent and unproductive, they were sought to pacify southern

European men who were considered to be more unruly and disruptive than Anglo-Australian men. Therefore, women were needed as sexual partners to contain their male nationals. Clearly, through cultural explanations, the women were being defined into racially constructed gender roles.

Further, as Anglo-Australians wanted them to train as domestics and acceptable housewives, migrant women were seen to be incapable of contributing to Australia's industrial development. Migrant women's participation and contribution in the labour market was seen at best as temporary. Yet, from the 1950s onwards, migrant women in fact made an enormous contribution. This has been discussed in Chapter 5 and will be examined more fully in a later section of this chapter.

Italian women in rural Australia

The work of rural women has also been ignored in the histories of Italian migration, reflecting the attitude that men manage and work the farms while women run the households and merely provide some help on the farms when there is a shortage of male labour. The experience of Italian migrant women in some rural areas defies such classification. For instance, in her study of Griffith, Huber discovered that '[t]he women worked side by side with the men in the fields, and the children joined them as soon as they were old enough. Australians were shocked to see Italian men allowing their wives to perform tasks regarded as strictly for males. Their success aroused much animosity, suspicion, and friction' (1977: 58).

The family became the main working unit because if they had employed outside labour they would not have been able to afford to buy their own farms. Typically, the farms were passed on to the sons while the daughters were expected to become upwardly mobile by marrying men with property. Generally, the second-generation women did not work out in the fields, some having gained secretarial skills and the like. After marriage, the young women tended to stop paid work, especially after the arrival of their first baby. Then the first-generation women would get down to work for their daughters, sewing, knitting and mending. Mothers and sisters were a ready source for baby-sitting and any other help required. These support networks remain informal and intergenerational, for example children often translate for parents (see Kelly, 1985: 298).

In Griffith Italians are involved in local business and farming associations, in charities and in Italian regional organisations which are mainly concerned with the maintenance of the ethnic culture (Kelly, 1985: 290). Kelly suggests that although 'some group organisations are open to all . . . many are organised along sex and ethnic lines' (1985: 288). Regional allegiances remain important to many Italian migrants and northerners continue to manifest superior attitudes towards southern Italians. Besides their regional biases, 'these clubs have a sex bias in the sense that they operate mainly as male social clubs. The membership is predominantly male and the activities of the clubs reflect this' (Kelly, 1985: 290). There are, however, Anglo-Australian women's clubs which have a very low Italo-Australian participation rate because many operate within an assimilationist framework where structures and organisations do not reflect the interests and needs of the Italian women. As a result of this sense of exclusion, the northern Italian women have formed their own social club which, although there are no membership restrictions, is not frequented by southerners, while Anglo-Australians make up only about 20–25 per cent of attendance (Kelly, 1985: 295–6). The southern Italian women spend much of their social time with their families and especially their children when their husbands are at their clubs. Kelly concludes:

> [i]n Griffith, older Italian–Australian women are socially marginal in a double sense. In the wider Griffith society, their marginality stems from their minority status as Italians; while in the Italian community, it stems from their status as women. Community for these women is largely based on the strong allegiances of family groups and regional ties (1985: 298).

The isolation of the older Griffith women, living in a fairly dense geographical area, presents a stark contrast to the isolated Sardinian women of rural Ashford, a declining tobacco-growing area in northern New South Wales. In an ethnographic study of the Ashford Italian community conducted by Andreoni (1983), it was found that the migration chain to Ashford mainly leads back to one small village in Sardinia called Santu Lussurgiu. Typically, the migration pattern began with the men coming out first to establish themselves and later calling for wives or fiancées, or going back to find a wife.

Despite coming from a culture where women's and men's roles were often segregated, in Ashford women work with their husbands in the fields, where both partners depend on each other for survival. Although there appears to be a separation between the public and private domain, and women's public shyness and hospitality may be misinterpreted as signs of subservience, women in this community share in the family decision-making process. As Andreoni suggests:

> [w]hen a woman wishes to have time to think about an issue or wishes to consult first with her family before making a decision, she will often express the need to ask her husband first. This may be a

> delaying tactic rather than an indication of absolute deference to the husband's wishes (1983: 9).

In this isolated community, the women, many of whom migrated to break out of the poverty cycle, run frugal and self-sufficient households where everything is self-grown if possible, including fruit trees and sheep, calves and pigs. Their main reason for migration was to secure an economic base which would improve the life chances of their children. Rural life or tobacco-growing for these people was only a means to an end. However, the tragedy which has unfolded for them is that, with the downturn in the tobacco industry, they now barely achieve a level of subsistence from their farms. The problem is felt more intensely by the women 'because they have lost their support network which the men to some degree have recreated through their contacts with other tobacco farmers, and English-speaking members of the community that service the tobacco industry' (Andreoni, 1983: 10–11).

The children have become one group of mediators between the two cultures. Through their schooling, they have become bilingual and bicultural, and while both girls and boys have been encouraged to complete senior high school, many of the boys have been encouraged to further their education through technical college or university after which they are expected to return to the farm. However, problems have arisen when some sons have married non-Italian-speaking women who have little knowledge of the Sardinian culture. This introduces a further sense of isolation for the Sardinian mother, who 'in such cases finds herself with a daughter-in-law with whom she can barely communicate and who shares few of her values and priorities. This is a high price to pay for migration and improving the life chances and education of one's children' (Andreoni, 1983: 16). Indeed, this is a frequent complaint of Italian migrant mothers whose children marry outside the Italian community (see Vasta, 1985).

Table 10.1 Employed women: status of worker by birthplace, per cent, August 1987

Birthplace	Employers	Self-employed	Wage & salary earners	Total per cent	Total absolute
Australia	4.1	7.5	87.0	100.0	2 153 700
UK & Ireland	2.3	8.9	88.2	100.0	237 800
Asia	3.6	8.0	87.8	100.0	110 200
Sth'n Europe	5.4	10.3	83.4	100.0	111 200
Greece	*	16.7	76.4	100.0	25 400
Italy	*	12.0	78.2	100.0	39 900

Note: * indicates figure not available.
Source: ABS, 1989:106.

Andreoni found little outside interaction for the women except on special occasions such as weddings and christenings, or during times of crisis such as sickness and childbirth. However, co-operation between the Italian- and English-speaking women was enhanced by the establishment in 1980 of the Ashford Sardinian Craft Co-operative. Through this venture the Sardinian women have been able to pass on their skills to English-speaking members of the community. It has also helped break down the isolation experienced by the Sardinian women in that the Centre has operated as a means of disseminating information about the health and welfare systems, and providing translations of the traffic codes so that the women could try for a driver's licence (Andreoni, 1983: 19).

Despite these positive changes, the tobacco industry's rapid decline in the late 1970s and early 1980s had left many farmers on the verge of bankruptcy and despair. Many families had difficult decisions to make, whether to continue to eke out a bare subsistence or to move on at an inhibiting financial loss. The feelings of this tobacco farmer were shared by many: 'Ashford has destroyed the flower of my youth without my knowing why. It's an illness. You have a couple of good seasons, the years pass and then it's too late. My life has been that of a lonely slave' (taped interview, Andreoni, 1983: 22).

Andreoni concludes that the sacrifices made by this Sardinian community seem 'to have fallen disproportionately on the shoulders of the non-English-speaking women. Any successes that may have been gained have been at the expense of the women's self-fulfilment. Only time will tell if they can find the energy to start yet again' (1983: 23).

Italian women workers in urban Australia

The majority of Italian migrants have congregated in the urban areas of Australia. During the early postwar years when there was a shortage of housing, many Italian migrants along with other migrant groups lived in the lower end of the housing market, paying the cheapest rents possible, sharing with family and friends in dilapidated and cramped housing.

Some lived in backyard garages until they were able to afford to buy their first home. Typically, the desire for their own homes and a better education for their children drove Italian women and men to work long, arduous hours in often exploitative work conditions.

For Italian migrant women this exploitation has often gone unnoticed. While the census shows an overrepresentation of migrants among small business owners, very little information exists on the participation and contribution of women in family and other small businesses (Alcorso, 1991: 19). There is evidence which indicates that women's work in the family business is mostly unequal in that men often control the enterprise and women have little control (Phizacklea, 1988: 21–2). In fact, women's work in small businesses is unaccounted for and frequently occurs as the primary labour because the business often is owned by the husband who holds a day job in a factory. Consequently, many businesses registered in the husband's name are actually run by their wives and children.

Italian women have not only experienced the loneliness and frustrations of immigration, they have also experienced problems of discrimination within the context of Australian society and the ideological structures generated from that society. These ideological structures include the gender, class and ethnic disadvantages and stereotyping to which they are subjected, thus highlighting the ways in which migrant women's gender identities and class position are racially and ethnically constructed by those in positions of power. Italian women's position in the labour market illustrates this problem clearly.

The 1986 census showed that around 42 per cent of women working in the manufacturing industry were migrant women, doing unskilled or semi-skilled manual and piecework in household equipment, food and clothing industries. The number of first-generation Italian women in the workforce has declined in the 1980s due to the decline in the overall rate of Italian migration and the ageing of the migrant population. For instance, the 1986 census showed that there were 41 470 Italian migrant women in the workforce. Of these, 26 per cent were in manufacturing, compared with 62 per cent in 1954 and 55 per cent in 1966. Although the percentage of Italian women in manufacturing had fallen, it was still double the figure of 13 per cent for the total female population.

On the other hand, as Table 10.1 demonstrates, 1987 figures show that there was a higher incidence of self-employed Italian migrant women compared with other southern European women. Moreover, there is an even higher incidence of self-employed Italian migrant women compared with women from Asia and women of English-speaking background, including the Australian-born. Although the figures for Italian female employers are unavailable in this table, Collins indicates in Chapter 5 that in 1981, 17 per cent of Italian-born women were either employers or self-employed. The contribution of Italian women has certainly been concentrated within the manufacturing industries, but as these figures below indicate, compared with other national groups, Italian migrant women have also contributed significantly in small business.

Labour force participation and occupational status provide only part of the picture of the work experience of Italian migrant women. Within the labour market, migrant women have had to deal with institutional racism and sexism. Research conducted among long-settled Italians in Brisbane (Vasta, 1985; 1990a) provides an illustration of the difficulties experienced by 56 Italian women (and 46 men)—mostly Sicilian—who arrived in Australia between 1949 and 1966. Their experiences are typical of the experiences of Italian women in the workforce throughout the 1950s, 1960s and 1970s (see also Alcorso, 1991).

Many Italian women worked long, arduous hours in poor conditions and found their jobs very difficult and different from any previous work they had done. On arrival, the majority of the women went straight into factories, including process work in food canneries, on the assembly line of various manufacturing industries or at sewing machines piecing together garments. Some were compelled to undertake outwork due to inadequate child-care. Apart from being aware that they were often the last hired and the first to be fired, once they had work they were often maltreated by employers and foremen. Until recently, unions have not taken seriously the needs of migrants in the workforce (see Zaccari, 1986). Many women in the Brisbane sample complained that Italians were given the hardest, dirtiest and heaviest jobs. These women often performed jobs which were repetitive, tedious and monotonous. Not only did they feel discriminated against by employers, often they experienced racism from their fellow workers. Some had often felt humiliated either because they had not understood what was being said, or they had been called derogatory names. Further, reports of sexual harassment at work are not uncommon (Alcorso, 1991). The positioning of migrant women in the workforce clearly illustrates racially constructed class exploitation.

Often migrant women report that they are played off against each other in terms of payment systems or by supervisors with regard to work performance. One Italian machinist in a clothing factory put it this way: '[w]orkers were jealous of each other—hostile if you were faster than them' (Alcorso, 1991). Another study found that employers believed that migrant women were suited to these types of jobs because they were seen as lacking intelligence and were defined as 'dumb peasant types' (see Storer, 1976). One of the most significant issues, however, to emerge from the Brisbane sample was that on arrival most of the women in the artisan/trade category (seamstresses, lace-makers etc.) became deskilled. Indeed, of fifteen of the women in this category, on arrival only four continued their skill in paid work and one woman lost clerical skills (Vasta, 1990a: 122). The skills of migrant women have persistently been ignored. Employers and the State have categorised migrant women as dependent wives and mothers, unproductive, illiterate and isolated from the outside world.

The public face of Italo-Australian migrant women

In public and political life, Italian women have also made their mark. In the 1950s Lena Gustin, affectionately known as 'Mamma Lena', became involved with the Italian community at a time when 'Italian language, food, dress and customs were resented, shunned and ridiculed not only in small-talk and back-chat, but in the streets and shops, even in publications' (Anon, 1977: 25). While still working in a coffee shop and writing a weekly column for *La Fiamma,* she began to realise the magnitude of desolation and isolation experienced by migrant women. Through her column and her weekly Italian radio program—*Arrivederci Roma*—in the 1950s, she reached out to the Italian migrant community. At a time when there was a strong bias against female radio announcers, Lena became very popular amongst the Italian community.

Through her program she began to seek assistance from parliamentarians and local government leaders and many others to help migrants sort out numerous and complex problems. The program opened up opportunities for Italian businesspeople, and the need for advertising support meant that small businesses such as delicatessens, chemists and butchers could reach more Italians in the Sydney region. Furthermore, apart from *La Fiamma,* Australian newspapers, radio and magazines 'rarely published any news about Italy . . . thus the large migrant population was left completely ignorant of what was happening in their homeland' (Anon, 1977: 76). Lena's husband, Dino, would link up with shortwave radio program from Italy to provide news and sport from Italy.

In 1968, Lena was awarded the Order of the British Empire and celebrated the academic successes of her two children who graduated from university. In the early 1970s, Mamma Lena's Sorella Radio was formed to assist with welfare and charity work. Mamma Lena was instrumental in the building of a welfare centre in Fairfield (Anon, 1977: 83–4). And as late as December 1990 she was out in the streets petitioning for signatures in protest at the government for whittling away the teaching of Italian in schools.

Another Italian migrant woman who has made a substantial contribution to Australian public and political affairs is Franca Arena, who arrived in the late 1950s as a single woman on an assisted passage. Arena worked for *La Fiamma* for seven years and later became involved in ethnic affairs and was one of the few women involved with the establishment of the Ethnic Communities Council of New South Wales. In 1973, she joined the ALP and in 1981 was elected to the New South Wales Legislative Assembly (Arena, 1987). In her maiden speech she made the point that given the multi-ethnic composition of the Australian population it was anachronistic that Australia should continue to owe allegiance to the British monarchy. Thus she called for an Australian republic. With Dorothy Buckland she set up a Migrant Women's Association as early as 1973 and, in 1985, Arena inaugurated the National Italo-Australian Women's Association. This group organises to develop solidarity, share information and set up networks to help Italian women of all generations.

Italo-Australian women's independence

Despite the racially or ethnically defined gender and class experiences of migrant women (cf. Bottomley, 1984a and 1984b; Martin, 1984), many Italian women have achieved a measure of independence in Australia which they believe they would not have gained had they remained in Italy. As Kasnitz suggests: '[w]omen's new opportunities and experiences in Australia allow them to develop new roles which emerge to fill power gaps in modern life which occur when traditional roles and knowledge have no precedents, or when traditional male attempts at control are inappropriate and fail' (1983: 243). Italian women have been the 'cultural custodians' of the Italian community. They have taken a major role in maintaining language and traditions within the home and have acted as intermediaries between the Italian family and institutions such as school and social services.

For the sample of Brisbane women, there was a strong indication that they had a relevant and, to them, satisfactory power base. While sharing many problems with their Anglo-Australian sisters, these Italian migrant women had other more pressing issues to deal with. These concerned the necessary adaptations brought about by migration: stresses on their marital relationship, their relationship with their children, adaptations to new work conditions, new social, political and institutional conditions. Italian women have taken more and more responsibility for major family issues, and indeed, the family unit has provided a source of power and strength for them. For example, as cultural custodians, many of these women on their daughters' behalf, fought to change patriarchal practices. Although many Italian migrant mothers still support the patriarchal value of honour and virginity, others recognise the contradiction of their own female and patriarchal upbringing and are aware of the inherent double standard (Vasta, 1990a: 129). They have, in fact, developed their own forms of resistance[1] as well as forms of accommodation and often, as many migrants do, develop their own cultural traditions as a means of support.

Many Italian migrant women, while complaining of the difficulties of maintaining dual working roles, feel that migration has provided them with the freedom to accomplish their aspirations. This was often expressed by the Italian women in the Brisbane sample in the following terms: 'I had the aspiration to have a house with all the comforts. I got it. I see my children with a better education and it fulfils my ambitions' (Vasta, 1990a: 125). Certainly in financial terms, through long and hard work, they have achieved security, and all the women in this sample in partnership with their husbands own their own homes. Despite the fact that some women felt they had not had the opportunity to train for more satisfying work, some claimed to have definitely achieved greater happiness and freedom in Australia, and many others felt they had gained more freedom in helping the family financially. Their paid work outside the home had provided them with a degree of independence.

Nevertheless, Italian migrant women continue to experience many forms of institutional racism: inadequate services, especially English-language classes and health facilities; racism from bureaucrats who misinform or do not adequately inform migrants of their rights and available services and make racist remarks about migrant clients (see Mitchell, 1988). As a result, these migrant women have many difficulties in challenging Australian institutions such as their children's schools, and legal and health institutions, although many Italian migrant women have become intermediaries between their families and institutions (Kasnitz, 1983: 259).

Conclusion

To conclude, Italian migrant women have often been portrayed as oppressive to themselves and to their families, as helpless, passive and illiterate 'peasant-types'. In fact, Italian migrant women have, in their own right, significantly contributed to the development of this country. They have worked in the cane fields, in the vegetable and tobacco farms, in shops and in factories, as well as running the household and taking chief responsibility for rearing of their children. Italian migrant women's multiple identities as working women, migrant women, wives, mothers etc., do not remain static. Rather, the women re-make their own cultural–political traditions and engage in their own 'cultures of resistance'.

As noted earlier, these women have gained more freedom here through paid work, and this freedom has flowed into their family relationships. Martin suggests that for many migrant women although 'the family is the site of female oppression, it is an extraordinarily ambiguous and contradictory site' (1986: 245) where historical, political and cultural perspectives must be taken into account. Therefore, as cultural custodians and cultural brokers, Italian migrant women have been protagonists in the maintenance of Italian language and culture, all the while negotiating new cultural and political practices.

11 The second generation

Ellie Vasta

Although Italian migration diminished to a trickle by the early 1970s, the children of Italian migrants, the second generation, provide the social and historical links between Italian and Australian culture and identity. Many of the second generation grow up with the experience of 'cultural ambivalence' which, during the uncertainties of adolescence, can provide the basis for severe conflicts between parents and children. The second generation are also involved in the process of developing identities which have to deal with racism. As adults, they become 'cultural brokers' who, in a variety of ways, represent their communities and negotiate Australian institutions as well as socio-political and cultural practices. This chapter provides an account, both from a sociological and personal perspective, of the lives and experiences of the second-generation Italo-Australian.

There is no agreed formula for an exact definition of 'second generation'; it is one of those terms which everyone understands but which is difficult to define precisely. Three definitions are commonly used. The first is a statistical definition, as used in Chapter 3, which refers to the Australian-born children of overseas-born parents. Census data provide figures for those who have either one or both parents born overseas. The second, which is a social definition, includes those people born in Australia with overseas-born parents, as well as those who arrived in Australia during infancy or early childhood.

A third definition has more to do with the subjective construction of identity in that there are many who consider themselves to be either Italian, Australian or Italo-Australian. This definition, which raises the issue of 'multiple identities' emerging from the cultural ambivalence experienced by the second generation, shall be explored more fully in this chapter. Because there is very little systematic research available about prewar, first-generation Italo-Australian youth, we shall begin by taking a look at the lives of some of the young Italian migrants of that time. This chapter, however, concentrates on the second generation and the terms 'second generation' and 'migrant children or youth' will be used interchangeably.

The school-aged children of Italians who arrived during the 1920s and 1930s experienced chequered careers in the Australian education system. Many went to school for only a year or two; others stayed longer and carried with them into adulthood the institutional and personal racism of teachers and fellow students. Oral histories from the prewar years provide a poignant picture of the experiences of the young. Gina, who grew up in an inner-city suburb of Melbourne in the 1930s, found that her experiences in secondary school left her with a strong attachment to her Italian identity. For Gina, her school days were 'horrendous' because she was 'fighting the whole time' with teachers and classmates, and later with employers:

> How we managed to learn, it's unbelievable. Any questions to be asked, anything we didn't understand, it was just left for the next day. Would you like to be in a classroom and you put up your hand and you've got the answer and you're just overlooked, not worried about? Where do you go? What happens to a child? You're ignored. Your work . . . not recognised, that's the part. Believe me, it was hard, it was plain discrimination. To try to be accepted I called myself Jean, that wasn't foreign, but I got no medals for that. I still had an Italian surname . . . From the Italian community I got warmth, the importance of family life, acceptance as a person, and sharing our troubles . . . we had a lot of fighting to do, even as far as jobs were concerned. You applied for a job, they'd ask if you were Australian, you'd say yes, but your name would be Italian and the fact that you were Catholic made it not on (Loh, 1980: 21–3).

Assimilationism and the second generation at school

During the 1950s and 1960s, with the influx of Italian migrants, there was a dramatic increase in the number of school-aged Italian children. According to official rhetoric, assimilation policy was proceeding satisfactorily: Anglo-Australians desired and insisted that migrants should assimilate, and their desire was sufficient grounds for them to believe that migrants were assimilating without too much difficulty. For migrant school children, the ideology of assimilation brought about frequent confusion and conflicts at home and at school (Vasta, 1980). Although specific pedagogical and language issues were ignored, research was commissioned in the late 1950s to investigate the progress and assimilation of migrant children.

The Dovey report, produced by the Commonwealth Immigration Advisory Committee (IAC, 1960), concluded that 97 per cent of young migrants settled down well to life in Australia and that they were above-average in scholarship, though in social activities they lagged behind Australians. The report's claim that migrant children had 'so adapted themselves as to lose their identity as migrants', was clearly an example of assimilationism taken to the extreme. By ignoring the specific disadvantages experienced by migrant children in the Australian education system, the ideology of assimilation in fact reproduced a particular form of structural racism. The Director-General of Education in New South Wales, Dr H. S. Wyndham, claimed that the Australian school was caught between two cultures (Wyndham, 1963: 22) rather than attending to the position of migrant children who were (really) the ones caught between two cultures.

While the language and traditions of the children were mostly ignored, the importance of teaching migrant children English drew some effort from authorities. As Martin states, '[t]he school returns consistently revealed the assumptions that migrant education meant teaching English, that assimilation was the ultimate goal, and that "national groups" in community or school hindered assimilation and were therefore to be discouraged' (1978: 92). Italian children received the wisdom of assimilation through a variety of discourses. One came via the school which encouraged children to speak only English. Parents were frequently discouraged by teachers from speaking Italian at home to their children. The authorities assumed that because the children of migrants were becoming proficient in English that they were assimilating.

On the other hand, Italian parents were doing all within their power to ensure that their children, while learning English at school, would continue to speak Italian or the dialect at home. For Italian migrants in Australia, maintenance of the Italian language was seen not only as the one lasting link between the first and second-generation but also as a link between Italian and Australian culture, especially as their children were assimilating into Anglo-Australian society. In the late 1960s, Saturday morning Italian language classes, the ethnic schools, were established by interested associations in the Italian community (and subsidised by the Italian government from the early 1970s) (Di Biase, 1989: 186). Despite the availability of these classes, many second-generation children resisted their parents' demands to speak Italian at home, and especially in public, because it was frowned upon by teachers and because of the racism they experienced on account of being Italian or speaking Italian.

The result of this three-way tug-of-war between the ideologues of assimilation, Italian parents and their children is that the children, as adults, have mostly become proficient in written and spoken English and, at least, in spoken Italian dialect. Contrary to the assimilationist argument that maintenance of the Italian language would hinder assimilation into Australian society, the second generation provide the links between themselves and the first generation, and between the Italian and Anglo-Australian and other ethnic communities. There is some evidence, however, that language maintenance is being lost with the third-generation Italo-Australians, though the extent of this loss requires systematic enquiry.

Multiculturalism and the second generation at school

In the late 1960s, reports began to emerge that migrant children were having problems at school. Thus, the Child Migrant Education Program (CMEP) was established in 1970. This program was based on the premise that the problems experienced by migrant children were fundamentally 'problem[s] of communication located in the individual child', that they could be addressed through English language classes, and that no other changes were necessary (Martin, 1978: 113). However, the problems that were emerging were broader. These included a lack of awareness that many migrant children were learning English as a second language and that teachers were not trained for this; some schools were withdrawing children from the mainstream classroom and placing them in remedial classes which undermined the child's confidence; schools and teachers were ill-prepared for classes with a high migrant density; and the curriculum was geared towards the needs of middle-class Anglo-Australian students. Some studies indicated that migrant children performed less well than other students (Connell et al., 1975); while others indicated that students from non-English-speaking backgrounds lagged behind the Australian-born in their endeavour to gain Commonwealth scholarships to university (Taft, 1975), even though the second-generation immigrants tended to stay at school longer than their peers from the same lower socio-economic backgrounds (Connell et al., 1975).

With the weight of these results, which pointed to a serious level of disadvantage experienced by migrant children, and with the rising voice of the 'ethnic professionals', these and many other issues began to be addressed through the policy and programs of

Table 11.1 Occupational status according to birthplace of parents, 1981

Birthplace of parents	Occupational status (percentage distribution) Professional technical executive		Clerical		Sales		Farmers, fishermen, hunters		Tradesmen, process & production		Service, sport, recreation		Unemployed	
	Generation 1st	2nd	1st	2nd	1st	2nd	1st	2nd	1st	2nd	1st	2nd	1st	2nd
Australia	18.4	18.4	17.8	17.8	8.3	8.3	7.9	7.9	23.6	23.6	7.7	7.7	5.6	5.6
UK & Ireland (Rep.)	20.2	20.8	16.9	18.5	7.7	8.6	1.7	6.3	28.5	22.1	9.5	7.9	6.8	4.7
Germany	18.1	14.5	15.2	11.8	6.5	8.8	2.3	4.6	31.8	28.2	10.7	6.9	5.9	13.7
Netherlands	20.3	16.1	14.5	17.1	7.1	9.5	4.7	3.4	33.8	27.4	8.0	8.2	4.8	10.4
Poland	15.5	22.9	9.1	22.8	6.8	8.2	1.4	0.9	35.5	19.0	11.5	6.9	7.4	8.6
Greece	5.7	17.4	4.8	21.3	13.8	11.6	2.4	1.2	47.1	20.9	11.5	6.9	7.4	8.6
Italy	7.6	12.6	7.1	20.1	6.0	11.6	5.4	6.1	51.3	25.5	9.0	6.2	3.8	7.7
Malta	5.7	6.6	7.9	13.8	3.8	7.2	4.3	3.6	51.6	40.7	11.4	6.0	4.9	10.2
Yugoslavia	4.9	14.8	5.0	19.9	3.6	7.4	1.6	2.3	58.6	25.0	8.9	7.4	8.2	14.2
Middle East	6.4	17.5	6.8	19.8	8.5	15.9	1.0	5.6	47.8	15.1	6.8	6.3	12.7	9.5
Asia	25.5	22.6	17.0	17.1	4.5	10.1	2.1	2.0	22.2	23.1	10.4	12.1	10.3	6.5
New Zealand	19.7	21.6	15.9	18.0	8.4	9.6	2.8	4.9	26.4	18.6	10.7	8.7	7.1	6.1

Source: ABS (1981 census, one per cent sample tape of individuals), in Hugo, 1986: 255.

multiculturalism. In schools this meant an introduction of 'specialist teaching of English as a Second Language (ESL), the valuing and accreditation of "community" languages, bilingual teaching, the employment of teachers with overseas qualifications, and socio-cultural programs trying to foster positive self-images in children of non-English-speaking background' (Kalantzis and Cope, 1984: 84). Often, multiculturalism has been conveniently interpreted and delivered in such a way as to concentrate on migrants' ethnicity and culture, while class and gender issues are ignored (see Kalantzis and Cope, 1984).

Some studies, which rely on empiricist and statistical analyses of the 1981 census, attempt to demonstrate that migrant children have few problems in the education system and in the labour market (Mistilis, 1985; Bullivant, 1986). Researchers such as Birrell and Seitz (1986) state that second-generation students 'are, if anything, doing better than Australian students' and so they question the need for multicultural policy in education. They argue that the 'ethnic movement' has succeeded in turning multicultural education policy into 'ethnic studies' (stressing ethnic language fluency and cultural maintenance) rather than 'intercultural studies' which would ensure 'that all students are exposed to Australian and other ethnic studies . . .' (Birrell and Seitz, 1986: 3). Ultimately, they suggest that all multicultural education, save English-language classes for migrant children, should be abandoned. Basically, their conclusions are that migrant children stay at school longer; that there is considerable intergenerational mobility into white-collar work; and that the children of Anglo-Australian blue-collar workers are remaining within the manual working class. Furthermore, these authors explain this in terms of an 'ethnic work ethic', which makes the most of an education system based on 'egalitarian, non-ascriptive values' (Birrell and Seitz, 1986: 28).

This debate demonstrates the need for a closer look at the labour force and occupational status of second-generation Italo-Australians as compared with other ethnic groups and with first-generation Italians.

Italo-Australian youth at work

The majority of Italian migrants of the 1950s and 1960s entered the Australian labour market as unskilled workers in construction and manufacturing. The labour market status of their children has improved by comparison, though simple statistical presentations do not explain the complexity of the issue, requiring a more thorough sociological analysis. To begin with, figures for the occupational structure and labour force status of the second generation are unavailable from the 1986 census. Therefore, we have to rely on the 1981 census figures, which provide a comparison between the first generation and second generation of several ethnic groups (see Table 11. 1 below).

One of the main factors motivating Italians to migrate to Australia was to provide their children with educational and occupational opportunities which were not available to them in Italy (see Vasta, 1985). Although the Italo-Australian second generation, as well as other non-English speaking migrant children, experienced difficulties at school, recent evidence suggests that these problems have begun to be redressed. For example, Table 11.1 indicates upward educational mobility for second-generation Italians, Greeks and Yugoslavs, the majority of whose parents arrived in Australia more than twenty years ago. However, when compared with Anglo-Australian children, and children of British-born parents, the incidence of second-generation Italo-Australians going into the professions is still significantly lower. This result calls into question the argument presented above that it is migrant students who have been privileged by the Australian education system.

Secondly, as can be seen from Table 11.1, the Italian and Greek second generation have moved in large numbers into clerical positions. However, they tend to be employed in the bottom levels of the clerical occupations which suggests that the mobility from the blue-collar status of their parents to the lower end of the white-collar status is minimal (Collins, 1988: 190). Further, the fact that there is a higher proportion of Greeks and Italians in clerical occupations does not necessarily mean better paid work (Bertelli, 1984: 13). Thirdly, Table 11.1 indicates that unemployment is higher amongst the second-generation southern Europeans than it is for Anglo-Australians and those of British-born parents. Therefore, this downward mobility needs to be weighed up against the upward mobility into the professions as well as against the 'sideways' mobility into the clerical occupations. Although the figures indicate that the second generation had higher rates of unemployment than the first generation, the figures are not comparable since unemployment is age-specific in that younger age groups are likely to experience a higher incidence of unemployment than older, more experienced workers. On the other hand, the Italian, Greek and Yugoslav second generation are likely to have higher school retention rates, which are often a form of concealed unemployment, especially for girls (see Castles et al., 1988: 33–5). In addition, many students who experienced language difficulties in the early years will stay on at school longer to gain minimum school leaving credentials.

As mentioned earlier, the statistical data needed to make accurate

Figure 11.1 Intergenerational mobility

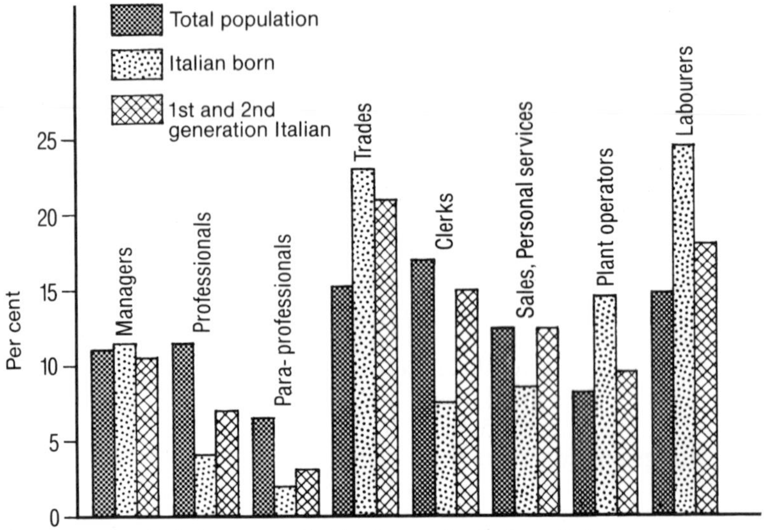

Source: Census 1986, figures provided by Census Applications, Sydney.

comparisons of the second generation with Italian-born parents and with the overall population are not available from the 1986 census. However, there are some figures (see Figure 11. 1) which show the difference in occupational position between the first and second generation combined, the first generation and the rest of the population. Note that the groups have been redefined compared with those used in 1981, and are therefore not comparable with these.

These figures need careful interpretation. The first column in each case shows the percentage in a given occupational group for the total workforce of Australia, the second column shows the percentage for the Italian-born, and the third shows the percentage for Italian-born combined with Australian-born persons with at least one Italian-born parent. In nearly every case, the third column shows a situation intermediate between that of the total workforce and the Italian-born. This indicates that the second generation are moving out of the concentration in manual occupations shown by the first generation, towards occupational distributions fairly similar to those of the total workforce. However, the data is not precise enough to show how far the trend has gone.

To conclude, the above analysis indicates that there is considerable intergenerational mobility, but that there are still substantial differences to the profile for the total workforce. Second-generation Italians are still somewhat disadvantaged in occupational terms, compared with the total population.

Identity, culture and community

Concern with the second generation is a relatively recent phenomenon, which has emerged as more and more Italo-Australian children have been through the Australian school system. As was noted earlier, the school experiences of migrant children during the first three postwar decades were mostly ignored, both from a pedagogical and cultural perspective. And many of those who arrived in their early teens dropped out within a few years (Cahill, 1986). During the 1950s and 1960s, for many Italo-Australian children, their first experiences of 'being Italian' probably occurred at school, creating many conflicts relating to their sense of identity and culture. Having Italian surnames, speaking very little English and even dressing differently set them apart in the eyes of their schoolteachers and peers. The following excerpt illustrates how the issue of identity and culture was dealt with by young migrant children within the ethnocentric climate of assimilationism:

> The way I looked to others was another surprise. I had never realised that I was classified as different because I didn't know that blonde hair and blue eyes was seen as normal . . . As I noticed these differences, and I was hurt, I tried to change myself in order to be accepted. The first thing I learnt was no salami sandwiches for lunch, and instead I wanted to order a meat pie or a vegemite sandwich. I also realised that mum didn't use Kraft cheese in my sandwiches but the smelly one. In the classroom situation, when it came to tell the class 'news', I'd find myself changing the stories so that mine wouldn't sound so different from the others. The day we spent making salami at Zio Rocco's turned into a family barbecue and watching a soccer game became an afternoon at the footy (Lombardo, 1985: 49).

Even in the 1980s migrant school children are dealing with similar problems relating to their culture and identity as they saw the attitudes of teachers placing ethnic parents in a subordinate status in the school: '[i]t's not really that my father can't speak English, he can speak English well, but because he's got a heavy accent, they don't bother with him' (Malpantidis, 1986: 262).

There were a number of reactions to the racism experienced by the second generation. It was not unusual for scuffles to break out when young Italians were called names such as 'wog' or 'dago'. A group of Italo-Australian boys interviewed, in the late 1970s by this author in a Brisbane boys' high school made the point that the worst kind of name-calling which they could offer back to their Anglo-Australian racist peers—words such as 'convict' and 'skippy'—did not have the same derogatory value as 'wog' and 'dago'. Clearly, the power to define cultural symbols lay in the hands of the

Anglo-Australians even when the majority of boys in that school happened to be Italo-Australians, and the dux of the college was Italo-Australian. Nevertheless, many of these boys were able to assert themselves by working towards good grades and being part of the soccer team.

Whereas many of the adult first-generation migrants resisted direct racism and the ethnocentrism of assimilation by closing themselves off against Anglo-Australians and by sticking mostly with the Italian community, many of the second generation began to reject their parents' culture and often found themselves caught between the two (see Vasta, 1979; 1980). Rejection often meant that children would refuse to speak Italian at home and in public, and their family and Italian culture often became an embarrassment to them:

> My Italianness stood out in me as if I were wearing a constant sign . . . I even started believing the images they [Australians] had of my culture, and if they made fun of it, I'd find myself laughing with them rather than defending myself. To be accepted, I was agreeing with their comments and ideas about my culture and family: my grandmother wore black; my parents had an accent; I had garlic breath; I only washed once a week; I had spaghetti for breakfast; my father was a mafia godfather, my uncle owned a fruitshop . . . Walking down the street, I tried to avoid relatives and family friends so as not to be stopped and kissed and hugged. I'd hate running into school friends while out with my parents (Lombardo, 1985: 50).

The rejection of language and other cultural symbols and practices has created much conflict between parents and children. These conflicts are more than the usual intergenerational conflicts of adolescents. They tend to emerge from racism experienced within Australian ethnic relations and the power operating within Australian State, class and gender relations.

The evidence presented above indicates that the State has managed the problem of migrant children's identity in two contradictory ways. First, their identity was managed through assimilation by devaluing the children's cultural and socio-economic backgrounds. Secondly, in contrast to the assimilation period, through multiculturalism migrant children can take pride in their cultural backgrounds. However, as was mentioned above, by concentrating mostly on cultural issues and ignoring the socio-economic position of migrants, migrant children have not achieved the same occupational status as their Anglo-Australian peers. Therefore, many migrant students also suffered class disadvantages along with other working-class children because they were congregated in working-class areas where schools tended to be under-resourced.

While the State has played a major role in managing migrant

youth identities, it has been unwilling to confront gender inequalities through multiculturalism. Italian and Australian gender relations are also a source of conflict for Italo-Australian second-generation women. Italo-Australian girls, like the majority of girls, have not had the same kind of encouragement to work towards careers in the professions. In one study conducted among second-year high school migrant children in Victoria in the mid-1970s, it was found that the aspirations of Italian boys were high compared with the 'very low' aspirations of the girls. Taft reports that '[o]nly 10 per cent of the Italian working class girls intended to reach Form IV, 38 per cent below the figure for the boys, thus confirming the generally held opinion that working-class Italian girls are discouraged from pursuing a higher education' (1975: 58).

Furthermore, Italian girls have had to deal with the sexist restrictions of family honour and female chastity (see Huber, 1985). This has often meant that girls are not allowed out unchaperoned and their experience of family life is quite different from males. For females, conflicts often centre around questions of freedom and independence and as one woman has put it, it means that 'the only way she could get out of this place [her parents' house] was in a wedding dress or a coffin' (Hampel, 1984: 173). Nevertheless, as noted in Chapter 10, many migrant women as cultural custodians have resisted certain forms of sexism which pass as cultural practices, and the results have benefited their daughters (Vasta, 1990a). Many Italian mothers have quietly fought for their daughters' freedom, not only through long, tedious work in the factories in order to provide them with a better education, but also through slowly chipping away within the family, at their daughters' lack of independence (Vasta, 1985; 1991).

These experiences of racism and conflict, often reinforced by the media, have frequently led to the second generation being ashamed of their background. As a result, Di Pietro remembers:

> . . . spending endless nights with friends discussing our identity in the hope of finding a label that would fit neatly and nicely . . . so I began to realise that the point wasn't so much who I was but how I was going to be an active and informed member of my society (1987: 38).

Some fear that the second generation have become so well assimilated that their sense of Italian identity and culture will disappear with that generation, as occurred in the USA. One American observer has claimed that the second generation lost familiarity with the Italian language and culture but that there was a resurgence of interest among the third generation (Hansen, 1938). Another suggested a typology of three categories, namely the 'rebel', the

The future is assured for the Lia family, whose four generations were photographed at the 80th birthday of great-grandfather Domenico. (*F. di Blasi, Italian Historical Society, Melbourne*)

'in-group' and the 'apathetic' reactions of second generation Italo-American males to the contradictions of adjustment to American society (Child, 1943). According to Child, the rebel seeks affiliation with the American group and tries to circumvent barriers of prejudice by making out that he is not really a member of the Italian community. The in-grouper is the opposite of the rebel in that he obtains his rewards from the Italian community even though these rewards are seen to belong to a group with lower status (Child, 1943: 188). The apathetic reaction is considered by Child to be more complex than the other two. The apathetic individual was, in his analysis, one who accepted being both Italian and American in identity and who also avoided conflicts about the contradictions between the two. For example, the apathetic individual often did not feel too strongly about Italians being called 'wops', using the explanation that all nationalities had their prejudices (Child, 1943: 155).

In Australia neither of these theories seem to apply. Although it is true that many of the second generation, during adolescence, rejected their parents' language and culture, this rejection, though often seen in personal terms, has several more complex causes. These include the vulnerability of adolescence, the embarrassment caused by racism, and recognition that the adoption of middle-class Anglo norms was the price that had to be paid for educational and occupational success. However, it would appear that as adults, many of the second generation are highly involved with their Italian heritage to the point of operating comfortably with a bicultural ethnic identity. Therefore, there is a return to their Italian culture and identity within the one generation and, as adults, they are neither 'rebels' nor 'in-groupers' and certainly not 'apathetic' individuals, for in providing links between the Italian and Anglo-Australian communities, second-generation Italians are directly and indirectly breaking down the many barriers which exist in communities.

Conclusion

The adult second generation—those who range in age between 25 and 45 years of age—have become the 'cultural brokers' within the Italian community. Many of the business and professional people such as builders, tilers, doctors, chemists, lawyers and welfare workers have set up their businesses and services in the communities in which they grew up. They not only maintain and foster the Italian language and culture but they also provide the link into Anglo-Australian institutions for working-class migrants, for the older generation, and for the third and subsequent generations. They maintain the connections between Italian culture and the community, which cut across class relations in that they incorporate family-orientated culture with the individualism of Australian capitalist society (see Hampel, 1984). For many of the upwardly mobile second generation the Italian family and community remain a central focus. And certain cultural symbols, such as weddings, holy days and saints' days remain the cultural cement which binds first, second and third generations and working-class, petit-bourgeois and middle-class urban Italians. These and many other cultural practices act as a source of strength for the Italian community, especially in combating racism.

Despite the ambivalence the second generation experiences in operating within the Italian and Anglo-Australian cultures, they have developed 'double cultural competences', and can represent their communities in a variety of ways. Ethnicity is thus continually negotiated, and remains a source of transformation for second-generation Italo-Australians. However, it can also be a source of contradiction especially for the upwardly mobile who absorb the ideological structures of the middle class but who, at the same time, are linked to the Italian migrant working-class identity of their parents and community. Since Italian migration has come to a virtual standstill, the strength of Italian identity, culture and community to sustain itself into the 21st century rests with the second and third generations of Italo-Australians.

12 The Italian language in Australia: sociolinguistic aspects

Gaetano Rando and Franko Leoni

At the beginning of European settlement it is estimated that there were some 600 Aboriginal dialects in Australia.[1] Less than 20 per cent have survived to the present day. However, despite the existence of these dialects, the presence of speakers of Gaelic languages and, later in the 19th century, of German, Chinese and Italian, English was the language of power and the undeclared official language of the fledgling colonies. Other languages, apart from French, German and Italian, were neglected if not actively discouraged. Australia was on the way to becoming one of the most monolingual countries in the world. Indeed, the attitude that immigrants should conform to the cultural and linguistic models of the host society discouraged the teaching of community languages in schools even after the post 1947 immigration boom (Taylor, 1984: 13). Over the last twenty years, however, there has been a growing realisation that the language skills of over two-and-a-half million Australians constitute an invaluable asset to a nation which has espoused the tenets of multiculturalism and one which should not be lost.

Central to the debate on multiculturalism (no matter how vague or undefined the concept) is the public recognition that a significant minority of Australian residents desire to maintain their cultural and linguistic identity, and that this can be fundamental to cultural interchange and thus lead to an enrichment of Australian culture (see, for example, McLean, 1982: 17; Wilton and Bosworth, 1984: 32). Some proponents of multiculturalism argue that a truly multicultural society is one in which the various languages of the component groups (called 'community languages') are maintained and transmitted to successive generations. Insofar as language forms the very basis of culture (see Smolicz, 1980; 1981; 1985), it is thus seen as desirable that a substantial number of people should be able to use the spoken and written forms of their language in all domains as well as of English.

In 1987 the federal government adopted a National Policy on Languages with the aim of encouraging bilingualism and the maintenance of the languages of the population (Lo Bianco, 1987). Among Australian residents aged 15 and over in 1983, 1.7 million people had a language other than English as their first language. Of these, 85 per cent were born overseas. The ten main languages were Italian (440 776 speakers), Greek (227 167), German (165 633), Dutch (110 540), Polish (86 016), Chinese (85 000), Arabic (77 565), Croatian (65 882), Maltese (60 000), Spanish (56 500), Serbian (27 000) and Vietnamese (27 252) (Lo Bianco, 1987: 24–5).

In the last 40 years the proportion of monolingual English speakers has been somewhat reduced (from approximately 97 per cent to 82 per cent (Lo Bianco, 1987: 13) due to immigration from non-English speaking countries. Despite this reduction there remain deeply rooted in Australian society considerable economic, political, social and cultural factors which guarantee the hegemony of the English language and which ensure a more or less gradual transition to monolingualism in English in successive generations if not in the first generation.[2]

The National Policy on Languages recommended that: an active competence in standard English be accessible to all; languages other than English be maintained and developed in Australia; and opportunities for learning a second language be offered to all Australian students (Lo Bianco, 1987). Nine languages (Arabic, Mandarin Chinese, French, German, Modern Greek, Indonesian/Malay, Italian, Japanese and Spanish) were identified as being of particular cultural, geographic, strategic, economic or political importance to Australia. The provision of courses in these languages was discussed as well as the urgent need to upgrade language teaching. The formal acceptance of the National Policy on Languages may be seen as indicative of a change in official attitudes with respect to the traditional position of monolingualism.

Two main forces drive Australia's language policy choices in the early 1990s. The first, which might be called 'multiculturalist', derives from an openness in public policy towards linguistic minorities. This is expressed through official encouragement for the maintenance of minority languages; support for the teaching of minority languages at school; 'ethnic' broadcasting; and the provision of interpreting and translating services. The second main force is the 'pragmatic Asianist' approach, which argues that Australia's geographic proximity to largely non-English speaking nations in Asia makes it necessary to prepare the population for economic, diplomatic and other interaction with 'the region'.

Both these forces have engendered slogans: 'Italian/Greek/Maltese is an Australian language'; 'Australia's future is in Asia'. Such slogans would have been unthinkable or seditious in 1950; hard to believe or understand in 1960; mildly amusing in 1970 and probably still so in 1980. But in 1990 a dramatic reappraisal of the national ethos and self-image of Australia has brought about these changes. Although divergent in their short-term goals, the two driving forces have much in common. Both express a linguistic correlate of changed international and internal reality and both converge on the issue of immigration. As Australia's immigrants increasingly come from Asia, the society becomes Eurasian in composition and orientation, and the linguistic index of social and political dominance by the anglophone world is subjected to challenge within Australia as well as externally.

Language is a resource to be cultivated to help Australia's commodity-dependent exports penetrate largely non-English speaking markets. What do such national needs mean for the self-perception of Australia? The 'multiculturalist' answer is for societal multilingualism and individual bilingualism. The 'Asianist' answer is for the widespread acquisition of 'key' Asian languages in the belief that 'the future' of the world will be driven by the powerful econonomic nations of the Pacific rim, especially the north-east Asians (OMA, 1989; Garnaut, 1989). What we are seeing is a new political discourse, a new way of conceptualising the diversity of Australia's population, no longer just about enrichment or about equality but now about economics. For instance the Prime Minister's Advisory Council on Multicultural Australia has emphasised the importance of multilingualism in achieving economic efficiency: '[cultural and language] concerns go to the heart of contemporary economic priorities. They recognise that the cultural diversity of Australia is not a problem. Rather it gives us resources, and provides us with assets, that can help secure our future in an increasingly competitive world' (ACMA, 1988).

In recent years state and federal governments have adopted strongly positive language policies, with substantial financial and human resources. But despite this, the erosion of minority languages persists. In immigrant situations, where one language controls the domains of power and the reward systems, transgenerational language shift is the norm. Language policy has primarily dealt with formal language study in school settings. This is a very different matter from the maintenance of minority languages in a society where their attributed status is inferior and their domains of use are subordinated. When the social status of two languages is unequal, schools sometimes merely serve to showcase the inequality and may hasten the abandonment by children of their minority language if the material rewards of the society are exclusively associated with the dominant language. Thus bilingualism in Australia is mostly among the 25 per cent of the population born overseas in non-English speaking countries and their children, and is often a transient phenomenon on its way to extinction.

The current shift of language policies away from monolingualism has much to do with a changed national self-perception. No longer will Britain's geography determine Australian educational content. The key factors in planning language policies are the competing claims of geography and demography—but the changing pattern of migration will assist to reconcile these. The European outpost in the South Pacific will look more like its neighbours and will inevitably see its bridges and links to Europe as a strength. The national image is already cultivating a self-description in which monolingualism occupies the past, and linguistic diversity, cultural pluralism and multilingualism occupy the future.

Italian as an 'Australian' language

Within these contexts the Italian language in Australia currently enjoys a relatively favourable albeit contradictory position. It is recognised as the most widely spoken community language after English, with currently 420 000 regular speakers. For census and other statistical purposes it is assumed that all speakers of 'Italian' in Australia use the same language, and a distinction is not made between speakers of dialects and of the different varieties (regional, popular, etc.) of Italian. The real life situation is, however, much more complex: most Italian immigrants speak varieties other than the standard one and perhaps as many as 45 per cent use a dialect habitually or exclusively. This complex linguistic situation has important ramifications for the second generation: a significant minority find that standard Italian is for them virtually a foreign language. Further, as a community language Italian does not hold any particular position of prestige. It is only standard Italian, particularly the literary register, which is considered a language of considerable cultural prestige, ranking with French and German. And, despite the fact that Italy is not currently among Australia's most important trading partners, there is growing recognition of the value of Italian as a language of economic importance given Italy's position as a major economic power in the Western world.

However, it cannot be taken for granted that the position of the Italian language in Australia is a stable and favoured one in the long term. In September 1990, rumours that the federal Minister for Education was examining a proposal which favoured Chinese, Japanese, French and German as languages to be taught in secondary schools and universities, generated considerable protest from the Italian community which saw the teaching of Italian in the Australian school system as being under threat (see *La Fiamma,* 3 September, 10 September, 10 October and 19 November 1990). Some community groups attempted to seek clarification and reassurance by calling meetings, contacting the Minister for Education and other politicians and organising petitions to parliament. That the controversy was created months before the publication of the discussion paper on the federal government's proposed Australian Literacy and Language Policy may perhaps be seen as indicative that the position of languages other than English is subject to the dictates of political expediency.

It can be claimed that the Italian language was present in Australia almost from the beginnings of white settlement as the acquired cultural language of a minority of the educated elite. Italian music and opera were very much in vogue, so much so that Italian singing teachers and musicians were found in Australia as early as the 1840s. Italian was also an important language for the hierarchy of the Australian Catholic Church since bishops were selected from among those prelates who had travelled to or studied in Rome.

However, it was only with the establishment of Italian immigrant communities that Italian in Australia became a language used for other than cultural purposes. Throughout most of the 19th century the small numbers and relatively high education levels and occupational status of many Italian immigrants meant a rapid acquisition of proficiency in English, although not a complete abandonment of the source language. With the establishment of Italian rural communities at 'New Italy' (northern New South Wales) in the 1880s and later, after the turn of the century, in north Queensland and the Riverina, some Italian dialects became the everyday language of a substantial number of the residents. However, these dialects were not maintained by subsequent generations. In time Italian also became the everyday language of the 'Little Italies' which were established in Sydney and Melbourne.

Research into the history of the teaching of Italian in New South Wales (Totaro, 1988) has revealed that Italian studies in the Australian education systems have been officially present for over 50 years (French and German were present in the school curriculum from the 1880s). It was a recognised subject for the matriculation examination (although it was generally unavailable as a teaching subject) and it has been taught at university level since 1929. However, until the last fifteen years or so it had experienced relatively little growth, lagging a distant third behind French and German. Since 1982 there have been spectacular advances in the study of Italian at secondary level, with a 200 per cent increase over the 1982–87 period. This has been in part inspired by a complete review of the secondary syllabus bringing in a functional–notional approach at the junior school level and a communicative approach (as opposed to the old grammar–translation method) at the senior school level. On an Australia-wide basis French (7.4 per cent) remains the most popular language taught in secondary schools, German (4.5 per cent) is second and Italian (4.1 per cent) now rates a close third (Totaro, 1988: 193–201; Lo Bianco, 1988: 193–4).

The expansion of the teaching of Italian in the tertiary sector in the 1980s has also been rapid although not as spectacular. Currently 26 Australian tertiary institutions teach the subject with a total student load of 885 EFTSUs,[3] making it the most widespread language after Japanese (taught in 28 institutions) and after French and Japanese in terms of student numbers (1998 and 1295 EFTSUs respectively) (*Widening our Horizons, 1991:* 64, 66). In some institutions specialised degree courses for community interpreters and translators have been developed.

There is no doubt that the expansion of Italian studies has helped to positively alter the perception and attitudes which Australians have of Italy and the Italians, and has influenced the way in which the descendants of Italian immigrants in this country see themselves and the land of their parents or grandparents. Indeed the commitment with which community organisations such as COASIT and FILEF have actively promoted language teaching may be taken as an indication of the perceived role of language in the definition of the community and its culture (not necessarily the same to each organisation) as well as in partially blocking the assimilation process in the second generation.

The rapid expansion of the teaching of Italian has been accompanied by considerable debate not only on policies but also on directions, practicalities and language teaching methodology. This has led to the adoption of new types of courses and approaches at the school level. However, the tertiary sector has come under criticism for failing to provide for the specialised development of teachers of Italian as well as for its continued focus on Italian literary studies (Totaro, 1990: 123). Further, it is necessary to be aware of its importance as a useful tool of communication in the fields of commerce, science and technology (Totaro, 1990: 124). These considerations have led to the positing of the need for considerable diversification in areas such as Italian for special purposes (Lo

Bianco, 1988: 195) and purpose-designed undergraduate degrees (Lo Bianco, 1987: 134) so that those entering the teaching or other professions can use the language in the context of the trade and other relations between Australia and Italy and as an Australian community language.

These proposed changes not only respond to perceived current needs of the country but are also more in line with student motivation for the study of Italian. Surveys on this, undertaken in the early 1980s, suggest that Italian is studied in Australia both for cultural (access to literature and art, study of music) and practical motives (communication with friends or family, for work). Most students at all levels study the language for the latter rather than the former set of reasons (Ministero Affari Esteri, 1981: 112). At university level too, motivation tends to be more for practical purposes than for strictly cultural ones (Hawley, 1982).

As a community language, Italian in Australia is used predominantly in the domestic and private domains for communication between first-generation extended family members and *paesani* as well as in religious services. Australian English is the predominant language outside these domains.

In the workplace Italian is used in Italian-run businesses whose employees are mainly first generation. It is also extensively used in Italian-owned shops in areas with a concentration of Italian-speaking residents. Indeed in these areas an Italian speaker can shop without having to use any English at all!

Italian as an Australian community language has other uses as well: in the Italo-Australian press, where it has registered a presence for just over a century; and in recent years in the electronic media (see Chapter 8). Italian-language newspapers have had a significant role in regulating the use of Italian in Australia as they have presented a model for the standard written language, although exceptions, including the use of Australian Italian (see below), may also be noted. Since its inception some ten years ago, SBS television has consistently provided contact with the contemporary linguistic situation in Italy through the transmission of films and documentaries and, in particular, of the neo-standard variety of Italian provided through the coverage of major sporting events. Public libraries are also a minor, though not unimportant, area where the Italian language is present. In places which have a concentration of first-generation Italians, libraries have been adding books and, more recently, non-book materials produced in Italy, to their collections.

Table 12.1 illustrates the use made in various domains and registers of the language by first- and second-generation speakers and provides some quantitative confirmation of the remarks made above relating to the use of Italian as a means of interdomestic commu-

Table 12.1 Percentage of people of Italian background In Australia who use 'Italian' language, by country of birth

		Country of birth	
		Italy (per cent)	Australia (per cent)
Speaks the language:	at home	88	69
	at work	52	29
	socially	98	91
	elsewhere	71	44
Reads the language		75	37
Writes the language		74	29
Speaks but does not read or write		18	8
Does not use the language but understands		—	6

Source: Victorian Ethnic Affairs Commission, 1984: 11.

nication. It may also be noted that the second generation scores relatively low in reading and writing skills while 6 per cent do not possess an active use of the language.

As Genovesi (1990: 71) points out, language is perceived by Italians in Australia as an important factor in the definition of community and as a central issue in the retention of cultural identity. First-generation Italian speakers show considerable language loyalty, being surpassed on an Australia-wide basis only by the Greek and Yugoslav communities (see Table 12.2). Among the elderly there is a tendency towards the abandonment of the acquired language (English) in favour of the mother tongue. The measurement of language loyalty is based on the rate of language shift. Language shift refers to the numbers of first-generation speakers who abandon the use of their mother tongue and 'switch' completely to English. The following data are extrapolated from the 1986 census (Clyne, 1988: 23).

Variations in the percentage shift among the Italian (as well as other) groups are influenced by factors such as cultural core values,

Table 12.2 Language shift among selected groups of non-English speakers

Language group	Percentage of group displaying language shift
Greek	3.5
Yugoslav	9.5
Italian	10.5
Polish	16.0
Maltese	26.0
German	40.5
Dutch	48.0

degree of cultural/linguistic similarity to the dominant group, the extent of intermarriages. Other factors that may play some part in governing language shift are: multicultural history and language policy of state; urbanisation; numbers of non-English speakers; size, concentration and immigration history of the speech community; individual characteristics (period of residence, age, sex, attitudes) (Clyne, 1982: 34–55). On these criteria Italian displays an overall high rate of maintenance among the first generation, even among those who have been in Australia for over twenty years (Victorian Ethnic Affairs Commission, 1984: 20–1). While some 10 per cent of the Italian-born make the shift to English, at the other end of the scale some 17 per cent speak little or no English (in this group 54 per cent are women aged over 64) (Ware, 1981: 29). The remainder use both English and Italian (Ware, 1981: 23).

Another linguistic characteristic of the Italian-born is language change (the abandonment of one variety of Italian in favour of another). The most noticeable type of language change occurs through the adaptation of elements from Australian English, which has led to the formation of a distinctive variety of the Italian language called, variously, Australian Italian, Italo-Australian or Australitalian. Fieldwork data obtained in October 1990 by Mario Bonaccorso from immigrants from the province of Catania (Sicily) residing in the western Sydney area indicates that Italo-Australian elements in the speech of first-generation speakers ranged from 10 to 30 per cent, while for second-generation speakers the range was 20 to 40 per cent. In general terms it can be said that Australian Italian is a particularly marked characteristic of the speech of the second generation, although there is a tendency in a small number of speakers to change, wholly or partially, to standard Italian as a result of having learned this at school and/or at tertiary level.

There is considerable language attrition among the second generation which is largely correlated with age. According to Ware (1981), some 15 per cent of school-age children of Italian immigrants use only English. This figure increases to 20 per cent in the 20–29 years age group, 36 per cent for the 30–50 age group and 59 per cent for those aged 50 and over. Further, unless the second-generation speaker has had formal schooling in the language, comprehension is not likely to be good, the standard of speaking lower, and reading and writing very limited. Interviews conducted with eight second-generation Italian youths in their early twenties found that all the interviewees stated they thought exclusively in English; Italian was used only in the domestic domain but never to the complete exclusion of English; and that they had extreme difficulty in using Italian to speak to their parents about their work or on abstract topics such as politics. However they were unanimous in stating they were conscious of an 'Italian' identity: all maintained close ties with parents and relatives, all declared a marked preference for forming friendships with persons within their own sociocultural group (but only English was employed in communication with this group), and all had a preference for Italian food (see Rando and Teh, 1981).

There is, in fact, a general tendency among the second generation to answer their parents principally in English. According to Smolicz and Harris (1976: 137), Italian can be perceived by some, if not by all, second-generation speakers as the language of age and local ethnic parochialism. Important factors in the use and maintenance of Italian among the second generation are the presence, either permanent or on a visit, of grandparents; trips to the parents' homeland; availability of the language as a school or examination subject; its regular (or uncompromising) use by parents; and the presence of older (Italian-born) siblings living at home (Clyne, 1982: 28).

The main element which distinguishes the Australian variety of Italian from that of mainland Italian among Italian-born speakers is the use of vocabulary items adapted from or influenced by the superstratum of Australian English which also influences syntax, although to a lesser extent. There are perhaps some 300 lexical items which are relatively common to all speakers in all areas but there are considerable oscillations in use, both in terms of geographical distribution and from one individual speaker to another. Some individuals may minimise interference (using far less than this number of Australian Italian items), some may maximise it (using much more). Further, Australian Italian terms are most often used by a minority of speakers and not to the complete exclusion of their Italian equivalents.

Observations on relative word usage (Rando, 1971b; Basili, 1983: 368–459) have been based on small samplings and have provided data which probably present a bias towards the use of the 'standard' Italian term. Because of this it is difficult to argue, as some have (Andreoni in Leoni, 1981: xii), that Australian Italian constitutes an autonomous and self-sufficient code, for its basis remains the variety of Italian or the dialect which the speaker brought from Italy with the addition of a more or less conspicuous superstratum from Australian English. Indeed the speech of many speakers can be constituted by a mixture of all three varieties:

> Per passatempo mi piace fare un **picnic** ['pikiniki] a fare un **barbeque** ['babakiu] sotto *l'alberi*. Andiamo a trovare una mia *commare* a **Shepparton** ['*f*Σpto], Vittoria. Lì abitano nelle **farme**,

cianno delle **farme di frutta**. C'è più, più spazio, più aria fina. A me mi piace solo per **holiday** ['olidai].

A me mi piace ordinare la casa . . . questi figli disordinati . . . che mi *dunanu tantu travagghiu* da fare. *Puru* che mi fanno arrabbiare non ci faccio caso. Se vengono a casa mi *mettunu tuttu* sott'e sopra.[4]

The Australian variety of Italian

A local variety of Italian was already in use in Australia towards the end of the 19th century. In Sydney in 1885 Francesco Sceusa commented in various articles in *L'Italo-Australiano* about the existence of a local variety of Italian. His writings were followed by Nibbi (1937) and Sacchi (1973). However the study of the phenomenon on a systematic basis did not commence until the publication of Andreoni (1967a) and Rando (1967). An excellent, penetrating and comprehensive analysis of studies on Australian Italian is provided in Kinder (1990).

The base language for Australian Italian is Popular Italian, a variety of Italian in common usage amongst Italian immigrants during the 1950s. Popular Italian can be briefly defined as a social variety of Italian used by the lesser educated, mainly dialectophones, who, guided by the model of Standard Italian, try to achieve a common linguistic denominator which might enable communication beyond the limits imposed upon them by their dialects.

When Italian immigrants came into contact with Australian society in the 1950s and 1960s, a significant number possessed considerable competence in Popular Italian, as well as in their dialects. The assimilationist policies of the time strongly discouraged the use of migrant languages in favour of English. However, it could be argued that, faced with a threat to their cultural identity, many immigrants reacted defensively and tended to maintain their community language.

Of course not every influence on language can or should be entirely repelled. In fact a certain degree of interference is virtually essential if the language is to remain an effective means of communication, particularly when the speakers find themselves in a completely new situation. In almost every respect Australia proved vastly different from anything that the migrant had previously experienced in Italy. It was frequently necessary, therefore, to find new words and new expressions to describe unfamiliar situations and experiences. So, just as Popular Italian arose from the efforts of dialectophones to speak Standard Italian, the contact between Popular Italian and English in Australia gave birth to 'Australitalian'.

By far the most common influence found in Australitalian occurs when words from English are transferred to Popular Italian—these are called lexical transfers, and they are not unusual occurrences, since the lexicon of any given language presents a high degree of accessibility to elements from other languages, particularly when this latter language is a prestigious and dominant one.

So, for example, 'Ho lavorato per sei *monti* a taglià la *cana'*, where the terms *monti* 'months' and *cana* '[sugar] cane' are nouns transferred from English, and adapted phonetically and structurally. Amongst the verb borrowings one can find *scracciare* 'to scratch', *pusciare* 'to push', *bettare* 'to bet' and many others. *Cleva* 'clever' and *cranchi* 'cranky' are two examples of borrowed adjectives, whilst *fulli* 'fully' and *notaim* 'in no time' are examples of adverbs. According to Bettoni (1981b: 115–16) interjections such as ié 'yeah', *iuno* 'you know', *detsrài* 'that's right' are also widely used.

Semantic transference occurs when the meaning only of a given word is transferred into the recipient language. For instance synonymic transfer in words such as *droga* (from 'drug, medicine'), *accidente* (from 'accident') and *quota/quotazione* (from 'quote'—*preventivo* in standard Italian), or compound terms (also called loan translations) such as *fratello in legge* 'brother-in-law', *giusto un momenta* 'just a moment', *australiani nuovi* 'new Australians'. In these the Anglo-Australian meaning has been transposed into Italian lexemes, which are then used in an Italo-Australian context.

Another category of semantic transfer is constituted by homologous diamorphs when the English and Italian words have part of their semantic content in common. In this case the Italian word takes on an additional meaning: for example, *moneta* (from 'money'—standard Italian *soldi, denaro), crema* ('cream'—standard Italian *panna)* and *guardare* ('to look like'—standard Italian *sembrare*). Semantic transference occurs also in homophonous diamorphs where an Italian word is used because of close phonic similarity with the English one but has no semantic content in common with it: *introdurre* ('to introduce'), *bucare* ('to book'). There is also the odd case of para-etymological word creation, such as *dolori* (from 'dollars').

Syntactic transference, though very limited, is also found in Australitalian. This occurs when English syntactic rules regarding word order are applied to an Australitalian context, often with disconcerting results (*giovanile delinquenza* 'juvenile delinquency', *sta bene abbastanza*). Such transference can often occur in the case of prepositions (*le ho portate swimming, se in caso, per la radio*).

Other transferences, although less common, include phonic transference (the transference of an English phoneme)—the Italian term *musica* is pronounced *miusica*; prosodic transference, when words transferred into Popular Italian maintain the tonic accent they had in English—*macchìna* rather than *màcchina*; and finally, pragmatic transference, when norms regulating English speech, and related to spelling, word order and numbers, are applied to the language of the Italian immigrants—'*un film nero e bianco*' instead of the Italian *bianco e nero*.

According to Bettoni (1981b: 73–9, 118–20) code switching, the change by a speaker from one language to the other within the one unit of discourse, accounts for some 10 per cent of transference phenomena and occurs predominantly among the second generation (over 77 per cent of cases). Such switching is triggered primarily by interjections, conjunctions or the introduction in the discourse of lexical transfers.

The influence of Italian on Australian English

In the Australian context, Italian and English are languages in close contact. Because of its position of power and prestige, English has had a considerable role in changing the spoken, and in some cases the written, Italian of immigrants. The Italian language has in turn had some influence on Australian English, although it has been much less radical and profound than the influence of English on Australian Italian. The influence of Italian on Australian English can be noted almost exclusively at a lexical level, Italian being the fifth-most important language of influence after Latin, French, Greek and the Scandinavian group of languages. About 0.55 per cent of the Australian English lexicon is of Italian origin; however, some 85 per cent of this is common to the lexicons of the other varieties of English, particularly the British and American, and is due to cultural influences (such as in the case of music terminology), not to the close language contact due to the migrant presence (see Ransom, 1973). The migrant presence, however, seems to have had some influence in gastronomic-related terminology and it is in this area that Australian English seems less tied to the other varieties.

Thus in the *Macquarie Dictionary* a number of Italian gastronomic terms are to be found, such as: *antipasto, Asti spumante, bianco, bolognaise, cacciatore, gelateria, macelleria* (often written *macellaria), pepato, savoiardi, spag* (abbreviation of *spaghetti*). As well as these terms there are a considerable number of other gastronomic terms which Australian English shares with other varieties of English: *cappuccino, cassata, espresso, fettuccine, zucchini* (used in Australian and American English in preference to *courgette* used in British English). In particular *vino*, according to Taylor (1989: 124), is used as 'a middle class non standard term for "wine" in place of the working class *plonk* with its pejorative connotation "cheap wine'', itself a World War I transfer of Fr. *(vin) blanc,* "white (wine)" '.

Other commonly used terms are individual lexical items like *mafia, biennale, veneto, confetti* (It. *coriandoli*). There seems to be little else at an overall level although an investigation of local usage would certainly reveal many other lexical features such as *Alfieri toscani* (a group of local Italian children who perform a flag-waving ceremony in the manner of the *Palio* of Siena) in Wollongong and *Calos* (from *calabresi*) in Griffith.

Italian influences on Australian English would thus seem to be strictly limited to the lexicon. The particular characteristics found in the pronunciation, morphology and syntax of adult first-generation Italian speakers of English seem to be completely contained within the group defined by Horvath (1985: 49) as a 'group of frozen interlanguage speakers'. Some of these characteristics may be passed on to some of the second generation although it has been observed (Mitchell and Delbridge, 1965; Horvath, 1985) that, in general, second-generation Italians use Australian English in a way identical with their Australian peers.

Conclusion

The Italian language in Australia has thus progressed from a 'cultural' language to its present binary status as both a language of culture and a 'community' language within the current context of the attempt to redefine Australia as a multicultural and possibly multilingual nation.

Along the way it has given rise to a local variety of overseas Popular Italian (*italiano popolare*) similar in many ways to the type of language which has developed among Italian immigrants in the USA, Canada and the United Kingdom. The establishment of this variety is to be seen primarily as a result of changes brought about by the close contacts Italian immigrants have had with Australian English, although there may also be some element of truth in the claim that Australian Italian is an aspect of Italo-Australian cultural identity: '. . . Australian-Italian is the linguistic result of a significant reaction to the often brutal pressure of Australian society on the Italian migrant community, (Leoni, 1988a: 212).

On the future of Italian in Australia little can be taken for granted. It depends both on Australian attitudes towards the language (including 'competition' from other languages) as well as on the propensity or otherwise on the part of the Italian community to find exclusive areas of use for the language such as to guarantee its survival. According to Kinder (1990: 81), 'studies of intergenerational language attrition and language attitudes suggest that there is much to be done to prevent the complete abandonment of Italian within three generations'; and 'research into the attitudes of the Italian community towards the linguistic varieties spoken in the community suggests that one of the main obstacles to language maintenance and even language recovery is precisely the set of linguistic attitudes of Italian Australians themselves' (Bettoni and Gibbons, 1988). Lo Bianco neatly sums up the current state of thought on language futures by saying:

> The two faces of Italian, as a cultural language and as a community language constitute both its weakness and its strength . . . If the community will not promote and use Italian, one of its strong points will collapse, i.e. the fact that there is an Italian speech community in Australia . . . If its cultural prestige is not recognised and maintained then Italian will not be a language considered worth studying (1988: 196–7).

The nature of Australian society is such that because of a strong monolingual tradition and the lack of any basis which might lead to cultural negotiation between ethnic minorities and the mainstream, English will no doubt remain the official and predominant language. Nevertheless there may be some grounds for arguing that the conceptualisation of Italian and other non-English languages as Australian languages could well imply that the traditional Australian conformity towards monolingualism is not necessarily a foregone conclusion. If its implementation is not carried out in the spirit of mere tokenism, language policy in Australia is a promising development in that, tied to a concept of politicised multiculturalism, it may well prove a point of departure for some transformation of traditional language values and hence become a determining factor in the problematic process of redefinition of national and cultural identity.

13 Narrating the migration experience

Gaetano Rando

The presence of large numbers of Italian immigrants in Australia has led to the formation of a complex community structure covering not only social and sporting activities but also religion, welfare, culture, education and language. The various community associations constitute perhaps the more formal and visible element of the non-economic activities of the Italo-Australian community. Their existence may be seen as an articulation of Italian migrants' desire not to lose their social, cultural and linguistic identity, and perhaps a confirmation that the aspirations of the immigrant group do not turn to bread alone. Among these aspirations is the literary and artistic articulation of the migration experience. It is an activity which is undertaken by a very small minority, but nevertheless one which has its place and importance in the totality of endeavour by the community.

Memoirs and personal accounts

The production of memoirs and personal accounts is almost as old as the beginnings of an identifiable Italian migrant presence in Australia. Some of the political refugees (Carboni, 1855) and activists (Sceusa, 1881 and 1888; Munari, 1897), missionaries (Salvado, 1851) and professional people (Amati, 1886; Gagliardi, 1881; Riccioli, 1883, 1886) who went to Australia in the 19th century produced their impressions and reflections on their experiences.

The first such book to be published in Italy is probably *Memorie storiche dell'Australia* (Salvado, 1851). It provides an exhaustive and encyclopaedic account of Australia in the late 1840s, but perhaps the most fascinating aspect of the *Memorie* is Salvado's story of the founding and early years of the New Norcia mission, and of his experiences in the bush where he initially shared the nomadic life of the natives, thus gaining appreciation and an understanding of their customs and outlook.

The Eureka Stockade (Carboni, 1855), a moving and passionate eyewitness account of Australia's best known attempt at rebellion against British rule, is widely hailed as a document of fundamental importance for Australian social history. More than a chronicle, it contains Carboni's views and attitudes towards this new land seen as a culturally deprived, rough and tough frontier governed by the mores of crass materialism and pragmatic expediency.

The various later accounts of Australia produced by Italian writers of the 1920s and 1930s, such as De Scalzo (1938) or the lively but schematic Cipolla (1928), were written by visitors and not immigrants. After World War II the first book-length works in prose produced by Italian immigrants are non-fiction works which narrate the writer's experiences as an immigrant or, in one case (Strano, 1973), life before coming to Australia. Curiously enough it represents the revival of a genre which, as outlined above, was particularly in vogue among Italian writers in Australia in the mid-1800s but had subsequently died out.

Accounts such as *Italians as They Are* (Luciano, 1959) and A *Migrant's Story* (Bonutto, 1963), relate the experiences of Italian immigrants who came out to Australia in the 1920s and who have felt the need to tell their story after having lived 30 or so years in the country. A particularly interesting and sensitively told story is Maria Thriaca's account of her grandmother, Amelia Musso Tilbury, who emigrated to Melbourne from Liguria at the turn of the century (Triaca, 1985), and became a matriarchal figure surrounded by her extended family, being 96 years old at the time the book was published (see Chapter 10 for more detail). Alfredo Strano (1986) has recreated the story of Ezio Luisini who emigrated from Umbria to Western Australia in 1908 at the age of seventeen and by sheer hard work was eventually able to set himself up in a draper's business, becoming wealthy and very well known. The *Shoe in My Cheese* (Baggio, 1989) is a vivid tongue-in-cheek account about growing up in an Australia in transition written by a second-generation Italo-Australian born in 1937 at Little River in Victoria who, despite his attempts to 'fit in' finds that ethnicity is an eternal marker of differences:

> Over the weeks with my expanding knowledge of English came also

> a vague, uncomfortable feeling that maybe I was not the same as the other children. When they talked to me in the school yard, my colleagues would insistently call out the words, 'dago', 'wop', 'greaser', and chant the strophe, 'Dago Dick with the cast iron prick'. I didn't understand any of this talk. All I knew was that it was used only in talking to me, that the words were always accompanied by scornful merriment, that it was unfriendly talk, and that it marked me out as different. Children never want to be different . . .
>
> When my own children came home from school and asked me, 'Papà, what is a Wog, and what does it mean?', it startled me to reflect that my contemporaries were still at it, and were teaching their children the same, old, sad, hurtful things. New, multicultural Australia was about to be born, but it would be a painful process, after a gestation of thirty years, and under the threat of a still birth (Baggio, 1989: 25–6).

A collection of memoirs by eight women immigrants is presented in *Give me Strength—Forza e coraggio* (Kahan-Guidi and Weiss, 1989). The book is the successful outcome of a national competition held in 1987 by the National Italo-Australian Women's Association[1] which attracted 30 essays from around Australia on the general themes of life as a woman, as an immigrant and as an Italian. The essays evoke the feelings of isolation and exclusion, the difficulties faced by immigrant women, but they also highlight their achievements, tenacity and courage. Highly innovative aspects of *Forza e coraggio* are the ways in which it raises the question of a possible correlation between migration and the creation of the dysfunctional family and the emotionally charged descriptions of rites of passage which somehow never seem to be total. A. Marino, among others, graphically describes the important but unassuming role Italian migrant women have played in the migration and settlement process:

> Even though I was born in a village, I've never felt like a village girl. I always worked hard to rise above the situation into which I was born. Sometimes, when our accountant or our lawyer comes over for dinner, they compliment me not only on my cooking, but also on my high standard of English. This annoys Mario. He feels threatened. He thinks if I know too much, I will try to be boss. That's why he won't let me do further studies and wouldn't even let me go to English classes . . . Since Mario bought the grocery shop in Melbourne, I have always played a part in running his business affairs. Slowly, as my English became better than his, he would ask me to make his telephone calls and enquiries. Yet he's never openly admitted or appreciated the important role I've played. One thing I must say, though, is that Mario always asked my advice on his business deals, even though he didn't always take it. So far, my advice has always been right . . . I think the family takes me for

> granted sometimes—they don't realize what would happen if I were to go . . . I feel like a vital link in some construction: pull me out, and everything will fall apart (Kahan-Guidi and Weiss, 1989: 27–8).

Oral histories

An interest in the collection of oral histories developed in the late 1970s. While the written accounts (such as Luciano, 1959; Bonutto, 1963; Baggio, 1989) present a predominantly middle-class experience (with the exception of the interclass conceptualisation in Kahan-Guidi and Weiss, 1989), the oral histories contain a predominantly working-class viewpoint (with some exceptions in the Brunswick Oral History Project 1985—see below). With the publication by FILEF of *With Courage in Their Cases* (Loh, 1980) it was possible to obtain a direct account of immigrant workers' experience seen in the multiple aspects of their everyday lives.

Perhaps the most interesting and vital aspect of Loh's collection is the way in which it presents flashes of perceptive insight which are as varied and different as are the people who relate them. Reminiscences of the very hard times of the prewar years, the feeling of helplessness in being caught up in the tide of war-time events ('It was not our fault. We did not like to be in these things' [Loh, 1980: 25]) led to the hard work and massive readjustments of the postwar years. The accounts not only present the practical difficulties (language, establishing a home, work: 'Everyone who works for a living got problems I suppose . . . but us migrants have a few extra!' [Loh, 1980: 78]) but also the metaphysical travail this has entailed. A few have found success or happiness, some have never shaken off the feeling of being strangers in a foreign land, still others have never resolved the vexing question of identity ('What am I? Italian or Australian?' [Loh, 1980: 134]; 'We went back [to Italy] feeling Italian, but we found that we're Australian Italians somehow . . . We've developed here independently, we speak differently, we've become more self-contained, more disciplined, more reserved' [Loh, 1980: 131]).

For most the resulting long-term situation has been an uneasy compromise between preserving some base values and adjusting to new ones, usually at the expense of sacrificing ideal desirable states. In a few cases results have been extreme. If Giacomo (Loh, 1980: 68–72) can relate a story of material and personal success, Concetta (Loh, 1980: 84–8) has had to cope with severe mental stress and Joe (Loh, 1980: 122–3) ends a life of unhappiness and frustration through suicide. For the second generation too there have been these problems and compromises, a strong indication that the cost of migration is a long-term one (see Chapter 11) and involves all family members—those who came from Italy and those born in Australia, as Valeria so succinctly points out:

> It's funny what emigration does to identity. We all feel Italian but I feel I belong here. I'm quite settled. Mum feels she *doesn't* quite belong anywhere. Dad had no doubts. He wanted to go back permanently. It wasn't spoken about directly but we felt it and we were uneasy. My father never resigned himself to living here. Because he couldn't speak the language he couldn't settle down heart and soul. There weren't many skilled workers coming out and skill qualifications weren't recognised here. He couldn't do night classes for Australian qualifications because he couldn't speak the language and he couldn't go to night school to learn English first, because after you've worked all day you're so tired and the process seems to take so long. When we came home we were often too tired to listen to Dad talk about religion or politics, or have a discussion. 'Dad, please. We don't want to listen.' He always felt that, always . . . And then there's my brother. He's Italian alright, he loves the food, thinks no-one cooks better than his mum and whether he's wearing casual clothes or is more formally dressed he always has style somehow. But he's very much Australian, the most Australian of all of us. He has a real 'ocker' accent, likes a beer and goes to the pub from time to time. He loves soccer but likes Australian Rules too. If you gave him a choice tomorrow to go back to Italy, he'd go. Straight away. It's inexplicable. One family, four different positions. A mass of contradictions (Loh, 1980: 134–5).

For a Better Life We Came (Brunswick Oral History Project, 1985) records the experience of sixteen Greek and Italian postwar immigrants who have settled in the Melbourne suburb of Brunswick. This collection features accounts of both workers and those who began as workers but have managed to achieve some upwards socio-economic mobility. Hence Franco Schiavoni and Joe Caputo begin as workers but become a teacher and a trade union official respectively, while Nancy Torresi and her husband begin life in Australia as pieceworkers to become proprietors of their own factory, and Ruggiero Sernia finds fulfilment as a musician and music teacher. In a sense these accounts present the more positive aspects of the migration experience. Despite the difficulties encountered, results are obtained through sheer hard work and a determination to succeed, in some cases through commitment to participation in political and/or social activities with the objective of bettering the migrant condition.

An exclusively women's viewpoint of the migration experience is presented in *Le signore di Albion Street* (Pettini, 1989). It evokes memories of the place of origin—sights, colours, smells—which can never be forgotten, tells how most of the group reluctantly accepted their menfolk's decision to migrate, only partially consoled by the thought of a better life to be had in Australia. It also tells of the trauma of the transition from the *paesetto* to a strange new country half a world away. As with the women's accounts in Loh (1980), most women emigrated to Australia subsequent to a decision taken by their husband, father or brother and there was particular anguish at parting from family and friends. After so many years in Australia many still cannot come to terms with the people ('One thing I still don't like about the Australians is their reserve' [Pettini, 1989: 107]) or the fact that they are still not fully accepted by the host society ('I would like to scream out that it is fifty years since I tried to become Australian' [Pettini, 1989: 107]) or their children marrying Australians. In fact, the generation gap and changing times are much more exacerbated by ethno-cultural differences ('Also our way of thinking is completely different from the way of the young people today' [Pettini, 1989: 120]), more accentuated by the realisation that as Italians in Australia they have become different from Italians in Italy although it is admitted that Australia 'is a lot better for the future of a woman' (Pettini, 1989: 133). In the final analysis there is no definitive conclusion to these experiences: 'Has it been worthwhile? I don't know. Here there is everything but nothing at the same time' (Pettini, 1989: 137).

What emerges from the oral histories is the narration of a collective experience, perhaps much more fragmented, less articulate and certainly less 'polished' than the memoirs written by individual writers but more spontaneous, more visceral, and much more varied. These accounts, presented in a matter-of-fact fashion and relating highly personal stories also contain a vast mine of information of historical and social value, such as the 1952 Bonegilla incident, the experiences of the prisoners of war and of the civilian internees (see Chapter 2), the attempts to relate to the Australian political system or the trade union movement, the dangers of flood and bushfire.

Different from the male-dominated formal memoirs, women's accounts feature prominently. They tell of difficulties such as the wife left behind for many years in Italy having to cope with young children and insufficient money or in a similar situation in Australia during the war when the husband was interned. They relate the poignant moments of families separated for so long that they had become strangers, and, in the postwar period, when, more isolated and alone than the men, they often had to face the double burden of housework and work in the factory. But as well as the difficulties they also tell of the strength which comes out of having to deal with all these problems (as in *Forza e coraggio*). Fear of loss of cultural identity is rarely stated but often implied, one particularly significant instance being found in Loh (1980: 129): 'Migrants want to defend it [their culture] because they're scared not only of losing their children but even themselves. It's a protection more for themselves than their children . . . Underlying all these stories are the everyday complexities of coping with a new environment: difficulties with language, the search for security, selling labour in return for wages, exploitation in the workplace because of lack of knowledge of their rights, finding a house, isolation, discrimination, sometimes alienation.

While there are many accounts of the experiences of Italian immigrants in Australia, virtually nothing has been done about the experiences of returnees or of those who have remained in Italy, but whose lives have been touched by migration to Australia. Yet untapped resources exist, as revealed by preliminary research carried out at Filicudi (province of Messina)[2]. Among the stories are those of Pino, who emigrated to Sydney at the age of seventeen, built up a successful transport business, but after several years there, had a nervous breakdown and was told by his doctor that he would end up in a mental hospital unless he returned to Filicudi. The return was instrumental in dissipating much of the stress and he has established himself in a small business on the island, but his wife has decided to remain in Australia. Egidio, who left his parents and a sister to emigrate to Australia, eventually decided to return and rejoin his family even though his economic future in Australia was more prosperous and secure compared with the employment he has found locally. Stefano emigrated briefly to Australia but found that work in the building trade there was not to his liking and is now established as a successful building contractor on the island.

As a generator of separation and loneliness, migration seems to have been a much more difficult and unacceptable experience for those like Bartolo and Francesco who are very much tied to the island's maritime traditions and have the sea in their blood. The two best fishermen on the island, they have both been unable to stay away. Bartolo went to Melbourne in the early 1950s to join his only son but the heat and the confusion of a big city where he felt absolutely land-locked, proved too much. He soon refurned to his beloved island where he has now become old and alone but contented. Francesco had a life-long history of migration to America with periodic returns to the island. He finally emigrated to Australia at a relatively late age to join his children. However, after eight years he returned to live out the rest of his life on the island while all his immediate and extended family remained in Australia.

Some of the women who remained on the island have particularly poignant stories of family break-up to relate. Caterina's husband abandoned her and their two baby daughters shortly after he emigrated to Australia. When the money he sent to support them stopped coming and he did not arrange for their passage out, Caterina had to fend for herself and bring up her daughters on her own. Angeluzza, too, found herself on her own after her husband and sons emigrated to Australia. She was reluctant to leave her house and land and so remained, although in the last few years she has made a number of visits to Australia to see her sons and their families. At age 89 she still tills the land, harvests grain and makes her own bread.

The oral histories thus provide a hitherto untapped facet of the narration of the working-class migration experience. Some of the protagonists of these stories find fulfilment in the 'lucky country' but most have to cope with difficulties related to their role in the workplace which can manifest themselves through injury, illness, mental disorders, and failure to achieve initial aspirations.

Creative literature: narrative

Despite a somewhat sporadic beginning in the 1930s (Ercole, 1932; Nibbi, 1937; Sacchi, 1932), a coherent body of Italo-Australian narrative did not begin to appear until the 1950s. Two prose writers, Nibbi (1965) and Cappiello (1981), have been distinguished by a modicum of success in Italy and also, in the case of Cappiello (1984), by some recognition from the Anglo-Australian literary establishment. Both writers are critical, ironic and incisive, but vastly different in style and technique. Nibbi is a detached observer, traditional if not slightly old-fashioned in style. Cappiello's approach, on the other hand, is highly subjective and her language charged, impetuous, aggressive.

With few exceptions, Italo-Australian fiction concerns characters and situations connected with migration and its consequences. It comments directly or implicitly on Australian society and the migrant's relation to it. Attitudes to migration range from qualified optimism to bleak pessimism. Some writers such as Bosi (1971a) have de-emphasised the problems it causes; others, like Cappiello (1984), have given full recognition to its painful implications, the disappointments, losses, loneliness, despair. Autobiographical elements are strongly present, though Cappiello manages to go beyond her immediate personal experience to universal aspects of the human condition. There is a widespread tendency to overwrite, a flaw shared by Nibbi but not Cappiello, and structure and technique are sometimes shaky, almost always conservative. Many comment favourably on the natural features of the new country (the harbour, beaches), but few venture in writing beyond the city limits. Even fewer attempt to theorise about a multicultural Australia.

Substantially Italo-Australian narrative treats seven broad themes—the Italo-Australian community (Bosi, 1971a); Italy (Tedeschi, 1986); bush and outback (Andreoni, 1967b; Abiuso, 1984); personal reactions to migration (Borghese, 1984; Di Stefano, 1975); the question of identity (Abiuso, 1984; Andreoni, 1982; D'Aprano, n.d.); racism (Andreoni, 1978; Cappiello, 1984) and multiculturalism (Andreoni, 1982).

Whilst with most of these writers there is a rejection, or at best a wary and uneasy acceptance, of the human environment, there is an almost universal acceptance of the Australian natural setting. It is this aspect of Australia which perhaps best serves to define both the uniqueness of the country and, in some cases, the justification for the decision to remain there. The protagonist of *Oltre il mare* (Bertozzi, 1984), newly arrived from Italy, finds the urban setting of the Italo-Australian community stifling and restrictive but revels in the beauty and splendour of the Victorian coastline. Cappiello, too, revels in the superb natural setting of the Sydney cityscape ('I discovered the marvellous beaches' [Cappiello, 1984: 3]) but is much less enthusiastic over the social landscape ('What sort of people were these Australians? . . . In the[ir] little square asymmetric red brick houses as arid and depersonalised as their souls' [Cappiello, 1984: 11), and is scathingly critical about the Italo-Australlian community which is seen as a ghetto and a 'prefabricated hell' rather than 'a cohesive basis for race or tradition' (Cappiello, 1984: 4).

Nibbi (1965) appreciates the primitiveness and tranquillity of the Tasmanian bush, although he is somewhat less enamoured of the Australian tropics, perhaps because the tropical landscape is too alien to his European perspective. The bush and outback as mystique is an important feature of the writing of Abiuso and, particularly, Andreoni. In an episode in the novel *Martin Pescatore* (Andreoni, 1967b: 161–3), the protagonist, after listening to the narration of an Aboriginal legend, reaches an understanding of the unique quality of the Aborigine's mystical feeling for the land which is the result of living for millennia in close and direct contact with nature without any of the mitigating effects of so-called civilisation. Through this newly acquired understanding, he is finally able to find a familiarity and acceptance in the Australian bush and thus to dispel the feeling of alienation which it had previously contained for him.

Surprisingly uniform is the presentation of the migrant work ethic theme which is found in Cappiello (1981), Di Stefano (1975) and, to a certain extent, Bosi (1971a) and Andreoni (1982) as well as in Nino Sanciolo's short story, 'Vito Quattara' (Rando, 1983: 260–7). Nearly all writers tend to regard this salient characteristic of Italian immigrants in negative terms, although according to Hempel (1959)[3] it is one of the more positive aspects of Italian emigration to Australia. In Bosi, the work ethic is closely identified with pride in *italianità* and the achievements of Italian immigrants. Yet despite this, the successful *fruttivendolo,* Gerolamo Scabbia, is presented in a rather pompous and vainglorious vein when he extols the virtues of hard work and the rewards it can bring (Bosi, 1971a: 15). At the other extreme, Rosa Cappiello presents a vehemently grim and bitter picture of the abject existential state of the immigrant woman factory worker who is driven by the dictates of a crassly materialistic and exploitative host society:

> This is the female factory worker, wife of the modern coolie and coolie herself, who has got down to a fine art the act of tying her baby to the bed or to the downpipe of the kitchen sink so as not to forgo the happy hour on Friday which is pay day. Slave of the dollar, she sends her newly-born babe to relatives in Egypt, Yugoslavia, Spain, Greece, and after a few years back it comes like a postal package by sea or by air . . . Structure of modern society. You have to adapt. Go along with it. Those who have no possessions aren't worth anything (Cappiello, 1984: 14).

It is interesting to note that Cappiello's position parallels, in fact, the way in which piecework is viewed in the oral histories (see, for example Loh, 1980: 60–1).

Perhaps these are the themes which are of more immediate interest to the writer, closer to his/her 'reality' and that of the intended reader (*Paese Fortunato* and Nibbi excepted). Nevertheless they do have a limiting effect and very rarely does a work transcend these limits to attain more universal values. Further, although 'migration' literature in Italy deals with the experience of the emigrant both in the host and in the home country, Italo-Australian narrative has, to date, not dealt with the migrant experience in the home country (Italy) to any great extent.

Largely lacking in the memoirs and oral histories, perhaps because in the final analysis there is a balancing out between 'racist' and 'friendly' Australians, racism is not a particularly well-developed theme in narrative although more emphasis is given to it in poetry. Nevertheless the discourse on racism is present and incipient in a number of the prose writers, albeit not always presented explicitly. It takes on particular emphasis in Abiuso, D'Aprano, Andreoni and Cappiello.

The question of Italo-Australian individual and cultural identity is an overriding theme with which many writers grapple but with which few manage to come to terms. Outcomes and resolutions to the debate on identity are varied, and at times contradictory. It is an important and interesting aspect of Charles D'Aprano's as yet unpublished novel *The Swallow* whose protagonist, after decades of indecision and oscillation between identification as an Italian or as an Australian, finally arrives at the articulation of an Italo-Australian identity which is a viscerally felt reconciliation of both worlds.

For Andreoni too, the resolution of Italo-Australian identity lies somewhere between the two cultures. Attempts at assimilation such as the anglicisation of names (sometimes imposed by the host society) and the imposition of Anglo-Celtic behaviour patterns are doomed to failure. The Italian-born protagonist of 'La Giornataccia di Montefiore' (Andreoni, 1978: 50–7), the bank manager Phillip Montefiore, has taken great pains to assimilate but despite his status in the New England rural community, he is still considered a 'dago' and outsider by the conservative and racist locals. On the other hand, Bosi advocates the resolution of identity through a sense of belonging to the new country while at the same time not losing sight of one's roots (see, for example, Bosi, 1971a: 100 and 125–8). Overall, Bosi's basis for an 'Italo-Australian' identity is constituted by a strong sense of pride which Italian immigrants have in their achievements and a close-knit solidarity within the Italo-Australian community, a survival strategy in that it constitutes an implicit defence mechanism against the 'outside'.

Diary of an Italo-Australian Schoolboy (Abiuso, 1984: 100–160) investigates what it means to be Australian for an adolescent immigrant, Mario Carlesani, thrust into the bewildering atmosphere of a state high school in a working-class inner Melbourne suburb. The issue is seen not only in ethno-cultural terms, but also as a class issue. Mario's understanding of the Australian spirit is brought about through his contacts with the history teacher's discussions on Australian culture, the encouragement by another teacher and his peer group towards commitment to political issues of immediate concern, and solidarity with his peers. Through these contacts the immigrant (Mario) is led to become an active participant in Australian society even though he may not fully accept it.

Creative literature: poetry

With the exception of a few poems by Raffaello Carboni and Pietro Baracchi the production of poetry by Italian immigrants to Australia can be relegated in a chronological sense to two periods—1922 to 1940 and after 1947.

Much of the poetry produced by Italian writers in Australia (especially post-1947 production) is preoccupied with 'universal' issues—such as love, death and other thoughts or experiences which are not necessarily tied to migration. Some however does deal with the social realities experienced and observed by the writer.

Most pre-World War II poetry deals with the migration experience at an external level and as a collective phenomenon, an important aspect being the relationship between the immigrant and the host society in a climate characterised by racism and hostility. Examples can be found in 'Il Monito' (Rando, 1983: 31–2) and 'Dici lu ngrisi' by Gaetano De Luca (Rando., 1983: 32).

In post-1947 production the migration experience is internalised, rendered partial and subjective and subject to alteration over time. A common starting-point is that of nostalgia for one's place of origin (Sardinia in the case of Concas, 1977) or the feelings of isolation and exile which such thoughts provoke (Coreno, 1980; Di Stefano, 1978). Forced to live away from his/her native land, the poet can only find happiness in memories of a time that came before the isolation as an exile in Australia, some thing which does not represent a new life, but which is destructive, fatal, and heraldic of melancholy. As time progresses there is a critical re-evaluation of this position. The native land is seen not only through the nostalgic eyes of the exile but in terms of the conditions which had instigated the poet to leave it. Australia is seen as less alien, particularly because of its acceptance of the various manifestations of the Italo-Australian community (Concas, 1988). In her latest volume Di Stefano (1988) reaches the conclusion that while time has tended to weaken the ties with the native land, the reality of the adopted country does not completely fulfil all the immigrant's spiritual needs, despite its positive and satisfying aspects.

The most prolific and best known poet is Luigi Strano, who between 1959 and 1989 published twelve volumes of poems written over a 50-year period. Initially emanating from a classical, humanistic context closely linked to his pre-emigration cultural experience, Strano's poetry experienced a significant structural and stylistic transformation in 1934 with 'Giardini Bui' (Rando ed., 1983: 124–5), a metaphysical image of Sydney in the grip of the Great Depression. His poetry is acclaimed for its ring of sincerity, its anti-sentimentalism and its ability to transpose the many facets of the migrant experience in poetic terms. It tells the personal 'inner' story of the migrant experience, from the initial nostalgia to the physical presence in the host country; the slow and suffered acceptance of life in the new land and the re-evaluation of attitudes and sentiments related both to the country of origin and the adopted country. It also succeeds in externalising the migrant experience by presenting portraits and comments related to specific cases, such as the poignant lament of the grandfather from Calabria who cannot adapt to his new environment and bitterly regrets ever having left his native village ('Un pappu a l'Australia' [Strano, 1964: 39]—the poem is, significantly enough, written in dialect). Another recurrent theme in Strano's poetry is the variable and sometimes problematic relationship between Italian migrants and the host society as in the poem 'Australian alien':

> It all depends
> on what happened yesterday;
> it all depends on
> what the papers say;
> whether today
> you are a wog,
> a New Australian
> or an alien (L. Strano, 1986: 6)

Among the more recent Italo-Australian poets may be mentioned Rosa Cappiello, whose poetry reflects the savage irony and the linguistic disruption evident in her prose works; Cristiana Maria Sebastiani who, while appreciating the social and physical aspects of the Australian scene, nevertheless accuses the host society of rejecting the cultural contribution of the non-Anglo-Celtic immigrant; Emilio Gabbrielli, who has so far concerned himself with his reaction to the cultural and the physical contrasts between the old country and the new; Walter Cerquetti's prose poems of subjective introspection captured not so much as a fleeting fragment but at a more discursive level; Valerio Borghese, whose poetry presents hermetic fragments of existential introspection; and Paolo Totaro's finely written poems—many of the most recent in a multilingual mode—with their deep sense of anguish and irony, of linguistic and cultural disruption.

Theatre

The staging of Italian opera and plays has been a feature of local cultural activities since the mid-1840s. A performance of Verdi's *Attila* was given in Sydney in 1846 and performances of other operas followed in the succeeding years. In 1875 the famous Italian actress, Adelaide Ristori, completed a highly successful three-month tour of New South Wales. During the 1930s, performances were put on by amateur Italian community groups. In the early 1950s the Sydney University Italian Club performed plays for the Italian immigrants at Bonegilla, as well as at the university. It is during this period that Church-sponsored amateur theatrical groups were also formed. Only in the last ten years or so have Italian community, amateur and semi-professional groups included in their repertoires texts by Italo-Australian authors, and most of such activity seems so far to have taken place in Melbourne. To date the only instance of a performance of a play by an Italo-Australian author by an Australian group has been that of Nino Randazzo's *Victoria Market.*

Randazzo is a prolific writer, and his plays have been well received by Melbourne Italo-Australian audiences. Somewhat verbose in their formal aspect, Randazzo's plays present themes which are closely related to Italo-Australian social and historical reality: the 1934 anti-Italian riots in Western Australia *(Le Fiamme di Kalgoorlie,* 1987); the problems faced by the Italo-Australian aged *(Villaggio Paradiso,* 1983); the tendency on the part of the Anglo-Australian community to construct the Mafia myth within the socio-political context of the Italian community (*Mercato Victoria, Victoria Market* [*genesi di un mito*], 1982); the impossibility of communicating across languages and cultures and the dilemma which this causes for the Italian emigrant who returns to visit his native land (*Il Sindaco d'Australia,* 1981); and the themes of arrival, alienation and adaptation (*Il Pane e le rose,* 1980).

L'Ultima Flotta (1989) constitutes a break with Randazzo's tradition of social realism and takes an extremely pessimistic view of the future of Australian multiculturalism. Set in the year 2020, its protagonists are an embattled group of ageing first-generation Italians who came out to Australia in the early 1970s and now, some 50 years late, have to battle for collective cultural survival in a society which has done away with multiculturalism and has become fiercely racist and xenophobic.

Osvaldo Maione (also of Melbourne), on the other hand, has tended to concentrate on the more personal aspects of the migration experience. The Italo-Australian mother cult is the theme of *Il Bello di Mammà* (1984), Italo-Australian social traditions that of *Il Grande Ballo* (1983). How the immigrants manage to solve their economic woes by taking advantage of the Australian welfare and workers' compensation systems is explored in *L'Arte di Arrangiarsi* (1982). The legal complications caused by an insufficient command of English and an imperfect understanding of the local laws are a feature of *Bitch* (1979). The delusion of Italian intellectuals who emigrate to Australia and find that they cannot exercise their profession but have to take on manual work in order to survive is presented in *L'Attesa* (1979). The irrelevance of certain Italian folk traditions in the Australian context is the theme of *Il Nuovo Seme* (1979).

The generation gap exacerbated by the impossibility of cross-cultural understanding is the main theme of a play by Tony Giurissevich, *Mogli e buoi dai paesi tuoi* (published in Rando ed., 1983: 223–31). In it the hilarity of the situation does not mask the underlying 'serious' message that time does not stand still and that social change occurs in Italy as well as in Australia. On the same theme, and with a number of similarities, is Christine Maddafferi's *A Hard Bargain,* produced in Melbourne and televised by SBS TV in 1985, probably one of the best one-act plays produced to date. Its liveliness and zest blend well with the underlying serious impact of the situation. With great reluctance the parents finally agree to allow the daughter to continue her studies and not to force her into an arranged marriage with the son of *paesani.*

There are also examples of more popular forms of theatrical expressions such as *Il Cabaret dell'Emigrante,* performed in various Italian clubs in Adelaide during 1984–85 by Chris Bell and Teresa Crea. A similar sort of variety show is provided in *Ogni casa 'na croce,* performed during 1988–89 by the Melbourne group Broccoli Productions. This performance consists of a series of short skits, some farcical, some ironic, and a few songs on common aspects of the Italo-Australian experience.

Much more committed is the Sydney FILEF theatre collective which has produced some very effective and widely attended street theatre productions. Its first, *Nuovo Paese* (1984), which was performed outdoors at Leichhardt High School, explored the different experience, attitudes and life-styles of a group of Italian grandparents and their Australian-born grandchildren. Their second production, *Lasciateci in Pace* (1986) was a bilingual presentation on the theme of world peace and nuclear disarmament, a somewhat unsuccessful attempt at imitating Dario Fo, in that it lacks much of the zany humour and bitingly ironic elements present in the works of this master of modern Italian farce. *L'Albero delle Rose* by Sonia Sedmark, FILEF's third production, performed in Sydney in May 1987, is a bilingual presentation of the experience of Italian immigrant women and their daughters.

An interesting experiment in multilingual theatre is found in The *Journey TO ΤΑΞΙΔΙ Il Viaggio* by Tes Lyssiotis, performed by the Filiki Players of Melbourne in 1987. The dialogue is in English, Greek and Italian and the three languages are cleverly combined to create a dynamic dialogue accessible to everyone. The play portrays the lives, experiences and outlook of immigrants who came to Australia in the early 1930s and 1950s. It depicts the conflicts of these families and their children within an often hostile environment, and the interaction between the various new and old Australian cultures is depicted with bitter-sweet humour.

Doppio Teatro, a theatre group formed in Adelaide in 1989, is dedicated to the development and performance of original works that extend the understanding of Italo-Australian culture. It has performed a bilingual play *Ricordi,* about people who live in Australia but speak two or more languages and have memories and emotions rooted in another land. It is a kaleidoscope of characters and stories, some comic, some tragic, which together quintessentially present the multiple facets of the experience of Italian migrant women not only in their external aspects but through their desires, fantasies, expectations and regrets, their quest for identity and self-determination.

Italian immigrants and the Australian film industry

Somewhat different and less high-profile has been the contribution of Italian immigrants to the Australian film industry. Whereas creative writing in print has been produced in both Italian and English, film and television material, because of the need to appeal to a more general audience (despite SBS), has almost exclusively been produced in English.

The most notable contribution to date has been made by Giorgio Mangiamele, who emigrated to Australia in 1952 with the express purpose of founding an Australian film industry. Although his role in the emerging Australian film industry has been a relatively minor one, his is the only Italian name included in John Baxter's fundamental work on Australian cinema (Baxter, 1970: 102). Of his many productions only three—*Il contratto* (1962), *The Spag* (1962) and *99 Per cent* (1963)—are on a 'migrant' theme.

Among other Italo-Australians active in film is Rosa Colosimo (Melbourne), who made her debut in feature films as a production consultant for *Moving Out* (1982), a film which draws on material from Abiuso's *Diario di uno scolaro italo-australiano* (1975). Rick Cavaggion, who works for the South Australian Film Commission, has directed a number of educationally-oriented documentaries on Italian and more general migrant issues. He directed the videotape production of Osvaldo Maione's *Bitch* (1979) and among his latest offerings is A *Question of Identity* (1988) (co-directed with Bruce Ready), which deals with the relationship between the teaching of community languages and multiculturalism.

Monica Pellizzari (Sydney) has attracted considerable interest with her short feature films. *Rabbit on the moon* (1988) is the story of a young Italian girl growing up in the 1960s, confused by the conflicting values of her classmates and those of her Italian family; *Velo nero* (1988) relates the desperate loneliness and confused dislocation of an Italian woman who is widowed shortly after arriving in Australia to join her husband; while *No no nonno* (1990) is about an elderly Neapolitan's attempt to avoid being sent to the Sunnyside Rest Home by his family.

In the area of television, a significant contribution is being made by Australian-born Tony Luciano, who for many years has been producing the popularised *Variety Italian Style* for commercial television and, subsequently, SBS. Luciano has also produced a documentary on Italian immigrants in Australia for the Italian government (*Australia, terra promessa,* 1986) as well as a series of documentaries on Italian wines (1988–89). Luciano's work may thus be seen as an important link between the two cultures, presenting Italy not only to Anglo-Australians but also to Italo-Australians.

Conclusion

The production of personal accounts, creative writing and theatrical works seems, in part, to respond to an urge to articulate the hardships, the struggles, the material and metaphysical price paid for migration. Highly personal reflections on how some Italian immigrants see Australia and Australian society, how they react to it, their appreciation of the natural beauties of the new country, what they think of the land they left behind, are all salient elements. They are 'inside' stories told from a subjective and personal point of view. It is this particular constitution of the migration experience which makes these documents worthy of perusal by the second and third generation, as well as by Anglo-Australians.

Despite the importance of the Italo-Australian community in the settlement experience and the continuing support network it offers, the concept of community is not given a central role in the written memoirs and oral histories. Some of the written memoirs refer to some aspects of community organisations and the personalities which are involved in them. Mention may also be made of their settlement role, which is generally seen in a positive light. Critical views are, however, provided in some creative writing where the Italo-Australian community is seen as a fragmented and disrupted entity which has stagnated both in cultural and linguistic terms. For different writers it represents different things: a comfortable self-justifying close-knit survival mechanism for Bosi, a self-created stagnant prison for Bertozzi and Cappiello, a stepping-stone to the wider Australian community for Abiuso, a means of contrasting and comparing Italian and Australian cultural values for Nibbi.

In the final analysis accounts such as these, written by Italians and immigrants of other origins, may be seen as providing a new and different perspective on Australia and Australian society, a perspective which is impossible to obtain from a mainstream standpoint. They constitute, perhaps, the beginning of an answer to the question posited nearly fifteen years ago by Jean Martin:

> The crucial question in relation to public knowledge and public policy is whether the ordered production of knowledge and the complementary participation in social structure enable these diverse experiences to become publicly relevant, or whether—on the contrary—the experiences of only the favoured few are acknowledged as legitimate sources of social knowledge (Martin, 1978: 213).

These accounts have the potential for making a cultural and political statement to the extent of rupturing, perhaps permanently, the traditional homogeneous view of certain aspects of Australian society. The accounts by NESB immigrants tend to debunk such concepts of 'egalitarianism' and 'non-discrimination'. Despite all the good intentions of 'official' policy, these texts tell us that, in the main, the immigrant does not feel on an equal footing with Australian-born citizens. In particular, reference may be made to the powerful statements provided by writers such as Cappiello and Andreoni to realise that racism is still alive and well in multicultural Australia. These feelings, in turn, then reflect on the way the immigrant views the new country, substantially seen in a positive light in terms of what it can offer materially and in its natural setting, but as somewhat more problematical in terms of its human environment and cultural milieu. Certainly Italo-Australian writing represents a significant though hidden cultural contribution, since it is now impossible to discuss Australian letters without taking into account the production of non-English speaking immigrant groups. As such they provide a new dimension to the perception of national cultural identity.

14 Italian migration to Australia and Argentina

Michael Morrissey

In recent years a number of historical comparisons have been made between Australia and Argentina mainly at a macro-economic level, often with an historical focus (see Platt and di Tella, 1985). On the face of it, such comparisons are quite natural since there are a number of similarities between the two countries. Both were built on a foundation of genocide and in both the population is dominantly of European origin. Both have large areas and relatively small populations; in both the original engine of growth was livestock agriculture; both have attempted (with different degrees of lack of success) to industrialise; and, finally, both have declined from being amongst the very richest countries in the world to middle ranking, in the case of Australia, considerably less in the case of Argentina. Such comparisons tend to have a mirror-image function in Australia and Argentina (see Dingh and Menett, 1985). In this country there is an admonitory ring: we raise our game or we become another Argentina. In Argentina there is an exhortatory function: raise our game and be prosperous like Australia.

Assimilation, adaptation and cultural survival

The historical similarities between Australia and Argentina can be illustrated by comparison between the experience of Italian immigrants at periods crucial in the development of the two countries—from the 1870s to the 1930s in the case of Argentina and from World War II to the 1980s in the case of Australia. In both countries

Italian immigration formed an important fraction of population growth (although far more important in the case of Argentina). The role of these immigrants in the economic growth of the two countries, their processes of absorption, their influence on the mainstream culture, their socio-economic distribution, all differed enormously, however, and for this the following elements of explanation can be listed.

First, the sheer scale of Italian immigration into Argentina was much greater than to Australia, relative to the existing population of European origin. The changes which took place as a result of the process of cultural negotiation between host and immigrant populations had a strongly reciprocal character in the case of Argentina. In Australia, however, there has been far less reciprocity.

Second, Italian immigrants in Argentina arrived at a time and into a cultural context extremely favourable to a process of mutual host–immigrant cultural accommodation. By contrast Italian immigrants to Australia arrived into a situation where, for a number of reasons, the majority ethnic grouping(s) were relatively impervious to a process of two-way cultural negotiation.

Third, Italians in Argentina began to assume a position of dominance in the urban middle and professional classes within a relatively short time. No such phenomenon can be observed in Australia nearly 40 years after the beginning of large-scale Italian immigration to this country.

In the Argentine context, the result of these processes, it is widely argued, has been the development of what has been described as essentially a 'creole' society (that is a society which developed in Argentina but had its roots in Europe). More specifically, the historian Scobie states that the result of the immigration process '. . . was a culture, that by the early 20th century appeared to be Italianised Hispanic but that increasingly declared its "Argentinism" ' (Scobie, 1964: 192). It must be emphasised that the three major partners in this negotiation—the native Argentines, Iberian Spanish and Italians—were virtually the sole players. Many other national groups emigrated to Argentina and although, in many cases, they were extremely successful in a material sense, they virtually vanished without trace at the cultural level (Kroll and Sábato, 1981). Other groups remained and, to a degree, still remain marginalised from the mainstream of Argentine culture (Senkman, 1986; Avni, 1983; Graham-Yooll, 1981).

The important point for many Argentine historians and sociologists (Germani, 1974; Cortés Conde, 1964, 1979; Beyhaut, 1961) has been that the central dynamic of mass migration to Argentina led to the development of a unique Argentine culture which is different from that prevailing in the mid-19th century but still essentially unitary, or, at least, in the process of becoming so. Nothing could be more different from the conventional categorical progression of assimilationism–integrationism–multiculturalism which characterises the historiography of postwar Australian immigration (Castles et al., 1988).

A central problem of the Argentina–Australian comparison in this context is that in Australia Italian immigrants have relatively little effect on the mainstream culture. However, as Pascoe (in Chapter 6 above) points out, Australian-born children of these immigrants in large part identify very strongly with their parents' (or even grandparents') culture. In Argentina, however, the reverse was true: '. . . the children of these migrants . . . needed to assess their "Argentinism". They consequently sought to shed all traits which could link them to a foreign land' (Scobie, 1964: 134–5). This was by no means a product of lack of national identification on the part of the first generation. In fact, the Italian-born group in Argentina was characterised by a many-layered proliferation of fraternal, mutual aid, benefit and political societies which would make the structures of contemporary Italo-Australian society look fragile by comparison. For example, in 1914 there were 463 Italian mutual benefit societies with membership numbering over 166 000 (Bagú, n.d.: 59). Solberg (1970) records that on Italy's entry to World War I many thousands of young men elected to return to Italy in spite of the availability of citizenship (and neutrality) in Argentina. Yet only a decade later '[f]irst generation immigrant children were fervently identifying with creole culture' (Solberg, 1970: 171).

We are faced, then, with an apparent paradox. Whereas in Australia there is apparently a strong survival of Italianness into the second generation, in Argentina, where one might have thought conditions more favourable to such a survival, it did not happen. I shall attempt to explain this in two main ways. First, it will be proposed that the extent of cultural and socio-economic penetration of Argentine society by first-generation Italian immigrants in itself provides an explanation for the second generation's rejection of their parents' culture, just as the relatively shallow penetration by the first generation in Australia provides a framework of explanation for a high level of cultural survival. Secondly, it will be argued that the Argentine ruling class played a decisive role in fostering a unitary Argentine national consciousness whereas the failure of the policy of assimilationism in Australia, as well as the structural position of the Australian State has led to a fostering of cultural pluralism in which Italianness (and many other 'nesses') is encouraged to flourish.

Now, however, it is necessary to review and compare the characteristics of Italian immigration and settlement in Argentina and Australia.

Quantitative aspects of immigration

In Argentina, as in Australia, the nucleus of an Italian population existed before the advent of mass immigration.[1] At the time of the fall of the dictator Rosas, in 1852, the Italian-born numbered about 15 000—about 18 per cent of the total foreign-born population and 3.75 per cent of the population as a whole. This group, however, differed from the pre-World War II community in Australia in that it was in general prosperous and enjoyed high social status. From the 1870s, broken only by the depression of the early 1890s and by World War I, the Argentine economy grew strongly as the potential of the *pampa* was realised. In this immigration, the Italian component was always dominant (Baily, 1985).

The main contrasts to Australia, at the quantitative level, lie in two things. First, the existing population base of European origin prior to this era of mass migration was much smaller than in Australia and, second, the concentration of migration sources on two countries, Spain and Italy, was extremely pronounced compared to the much more diverse range of sources from which Australia drew its immigrants. From the 1890s to 1914 the Italian-born population of Argentina as a percentage of the total population of the country—12.5 per cent in 1895 and 11.4 per cent in 1914—was not far short of the percentage for all non-English speaking migrants in Australia for most of the period following World War II.

Social integration

Throughout the great period of immigration the nature of the Italian population was such that assimilation into the general Argentine population was promoted. Unlike Italian migration to Australia, the migrants to Argentina were predominantly male and unaccompanied by family. Thus Cacopardo and Moreno (1985: 45–65) estimated that, on average, 264 Italian men arrived for every 100 women over the entire period 1880 to 1930.

This demographic factor in itself would have promoted a degree of intermarriage between Italians and Argentines but this pre-existing tendency was strengthened by the disproportionate number of women in the Argentine population. Bourdé (1974: 203) estimated that the number of Argentine men for every 100 women was less than 94 for the entire period from the late 1880s to the 1930s and

Table 14.1 Intra-group marriages In Buenos Aires, 1882–1923 (average annual per cent marrying spouses of same group)

	Argentines		Italians		Spaniards	
Years	Males	Females	Males	Females	Males	Females
1882–1886	86.3	53.5	72.6	90.2	51.9	75.9
1887–1892	80.1	49.1	69.3	90.3	66.8	79.5
1893–1897	76.8	48.6	66.6	—	63.2	—
1898–1902	75.2	54.3	64.2	82.0	65.5	76.3
1903–1907	74.1	52.1	56.5	79.5	69.1	75.8
1908–1912	76.9	54.7	52.9	79.2	78.4	82.1
1913–1917	77.6	60.5	48.8	74.4	80.3	80.9
1918–1923	80.3	65.6	40.5	65.0	70.4	73.9

Source: Bailey, 1985:40.

sometimes dropped as low as 86. The resulting tendency towards mixed marriages can be observed from Table 14.1.

According to Germani (1974: 197–210), intermarriage was the major vehicle of change in Argentine society, taking place most frequently in the large towns. He also notes that such intermarriage was most easy and widespread among Spanish and Italian immigrants. Certainly, Szuchman's study of some non-Italian groups in the provincial city of Córdoba suggests lower rates of intermarriage than those for Italians in the capital (Szuchman, 1980).

This social welding at the level of intermarriage was paralleled on the other social and economic levels. The bulk of Italian immigrants had been farmworkers of various sorts in the period prior to emigration. In the initial period of mass immigration it is probable that it was the desire to acquire land which prompted the mass of people to leave Italy. By the turn of the century the engrossment of land by large owners made it increasingly unlikely that former peasants could do much more than become tenant farmers. Nevertheless, Italian migrants played a key role in building Argentine agriculture, both as tenant farmers and, in the provinces of Entre Rios, Santa Fe and Mendoza—where Italians formed up to 20 per cent of the population—as small proprietors.

The dominantly rural background of Italian immigrants did not mean that they became a rural group in their entirety, however. Throughout the period before 1914, Italians never formed less than 20 per cent of the population of Buenos Aires, and in the late 1880s constituted almost one-third of the total. The 'critical mass' that this presence provided in the process of cultural negotiation is of itself important and of a completely different order of magnitude from any non-anglophone group in Australia, Italians included.

However, there is another important dimension. Although in the main arriving to do manual work, a very high proportion of European immigrants in Argentina quickly became upwardly socially mobile.

Table 14.2 demonstrates the dominance of immigrants in the middle-class professional areas and this was strongly reflected in property ownership. One study (Germani, 1963), for example, demonstrated that of the Argentine middle class in 1914, two-thirds had at one time been in working-class occupations. Moreover, the rate of social mobility among migrants was appreciably higher than among the native-born, with over a quarter of the immigrant working class moving into middle-class occupations between 1895 and 1914, as opposed to only 19 per cent of the native-born. In all of this, figures for property ownership reveal a striking picture. By 1887, according to Korn and de la Torre (1987: 41–69), in Buenos Aires migrants formed 80 per cent of those engaged in industrial production, 77 per cent of those in commerce and 72 per cent of those in the service sector. In that same year migrants—of whom Italians constituted 60 per cent—owned 92 per cent of industrial and commercial enterprises.

This first-generation social mobility was continued into the second in no uncertain fashion. In his study of Argentine elites, de Imaz (1970: 182–3) found that no less than 77 per cent of Argentine bishops were sons of migrants and that 77 per cent of high-ranking army officers also came from immigrant backgrounds (26 per cent

Table 14.2 Urban middle-class occupations, Argentina (1914)

	Nationals	Foreigners	Total	Foreigners (per cent)
Commercial proprietors	56 021	117 382	173 403	67.7
Journalists	1 174	667	1 841	36.2
Employees:				
of commerce	40 781	39 484	80 265	49.2
of government	85 649	18 502	104 151	17.8
Lawyers	7 912	1 166	9 078	12.8
Pharmacists	1 427	1 211	2 638	45.9
Physicians	2 611	931	3 542	26.3
Teachers	22 939	5 527	28 466	19.4
Architects	335	619	954	64.9
Engineers & Surveyors	2 047	2 432	4 479	51.8
Theatre Artists	678	2 173	2 851	76.2
Others*	5 943	9 080	15 023	60.4
Total middle-class occupatons	227 517	199 174	426 691	46.7
Total workforce	1 670 545	1 356 438	3 027 033	

Note: *Others includes: contractors, distributors, bookkeepers, specialised teachers, and agronomists.

Source: Solberg, 1970.

of them Italian) (de Imaz, 1970: 60–2). Looking at the 50 per cent of the most prestigious firms actually owned by Argentines, de Imaz found almost half were owned by self-made men or their sons, typically of immigrant background (de Imaz, 1970: 145–6).

All this is not to say that all immigrants found in Argentina a land of milk and honey. It does indicate, however, that Italians in Argentina were much more socially mobile in the first generation than their compatriots in Australia and that the second generation penetrated elite groups in far higher numbers. Migrants had some advantages. The 1914 census (Bagú, n.d.: 61) showed that immigrants in the late 1890s had a literacy rate of 65.4 per cent compared with 47.7 per cent for the Argentina-born. The main advantage, however, and the main contrast with Australia, has already been alluded to. The period of mass migration coincided with (and was due to) massive socio-economic changes in Argentine society: an essentially two-class society was transformed by the creation of an urban middle class. The creation of this class was largely the work of migrants.

By contrast, the Australia of the 1950s and 1960s to which the majority of Italian migrants arrived was not in the process of such deep-reaching change. It was one where class relations were firmly established. In Argentina migrants effectively created a new middle class. In Australia they simply suffused the existing class structure.

Italian immigration and Argentine language and culture

Probably the most startling effect of Italian migrants in modifying late-19th century Argentine culture into the Italo-Iberian hybrid it later became, is the mutation of Argentine Castellano to the point where it stands as a unique language variety in the hispanophone world. By contrast Italian influence on the language usage of anglophone countries of immigration such as the United States and Australia went not much further than inserting individual words into the main language.

According to Aguirre (1979: 207–1) and Cara-Walker (1989), this process of mutual adaptation involved two intermediate linguistic forms, known respectively as *cocoliche* and *lunfardo.* Both had associated dramatic (particularly the former) and literary (particularly the latter) forms. The first stage of this adaptation, *cocoliche,* is described by Aguirre as 'an Italian, influenced by Spanish in its vocabulary, morphology, syntax and phraseology'—more succinctly, perhaps, an Italo-Hispanic pidgin.

The essential feature of *cocoliche* was that it was spoken only by Italian immigrants. The more sophisticated mutation, *lunfardo,* was evenually spoken by all the common people of Buenos Aires, and beyond—*criollo* and immigrant alike. It represents a true fusion of Italian and Castellano with trace elements of some other languages, notably English and Brazilian Portuguese. It became what the linguist Gobello called 'the alternative language' of the ordinary person (Gobello, 1974: 22).

Apart from linguistic influences, the national music of Argentina, the tango, is of directly Italian provenance, the most important sound being that of the accordion, fusing with Iberian rhythms. Certainly, it was widely seen as such at the time, the nationalist writer Manuel Gálvez describing this 'hybrid, unfortunate music' as the 'lamentable symbol of our denationalisation' (Gálvez, 1942). In a sense, of course, he was right.

Change in culinary habits is another significant area of cultural change. The modification of Argentine diet concomitant with Italian immigration would appear to have a distinct parallel in Australia. Virtually all restaurants in Argentina are, in part, Italian and so is virtually all home cooking. However, I would argue that Italian restaurants in Australia are simply one stop in the ethnic smorgasbord of food available in rich industrialised countries. Argentina does not have such a smorgasbord: it has a national cuisine revolving around the ubiquitous *bife* and a variety of Italian-influenced dishes. Once again the degree of Italo-Hispanic creolisation is extremely pronounced, although it must be remarked that, in the context of food, this does not always constitute an improvement. Argentine pizzas, for example, are a disgrace to the species.

The role of the State

In both Argentina and Australia the State was a crucial factor in shaping the process of absorption of the immigrant population but the precise roles of the two State apparatuses were very different as, indeed, were their composition and class base. There is, however, a perverse symmetry in the changing attitudes to immigrants of what one may loosely call the ruling class in Argentina and the State apparatus in Australia.

The Argentine ruling class consisted of a group of wealthy landowners which effectively dominated politics until the advent of Perón in the late 1940s. It was their changing perceptions of immigration and national priorities which were to dominate the activities of the Argentine State in the crucial period between the first great expansion of the Argentine economy in the 1870s and the depression of the 1930s. Schematically one may map out a change in the attitudes of this group over the 40 years preceding

World War I. Initially these rested on two main propositions: that a large supply of immigrant labour was necessary in order to open up the vast potential of the *pampa*; and that Argentina should be the site of a new and superior 'European' civilisation in which the supposed superiority of the European 'races' would come to flower in the southern hemisphere. Just as in Australia the slogan 'populate or perish' became a catch-cry, so in Argentina throughout the second half of the century echoed the political philosopher Alberdi's maxim: 'to govern is to populate' (Solberg, 1970: 7).

Given the fact that, on the eve of Argentina's great expansion something less that 1.5 million people inhabited a territory of over 1 000 000 square miles and given the enormous potential of the *pampa,* the emphasis on rapid population growth is scarcely surprising. Less susceptible to easy explanation is the anti-nativism, the emphasis on the civilisation which was to flow from immigration. This was due partly to the European education of many members of the Argentine elite and partly to the relatively high social status enjoyed by foreigners in the first half of the century. The ethos and presence of the *gaucho* were seen as an obstacle to economic development and as a permanent source of unrest, fuelling the endemic state of civil war or disorder which characterised the first 60 years of Argentine independence.

In the early period immigrants, of whom the largest group was always Italian, came into a country where a substantial section of the intellectual and political elite was busily repudiating its own cultural traditions and extolling those of the countries of emigration. It could be reasonably argued that such an atmosphere might have materially assisted in the very rapid process of mutual assimilation which took place between immigrant and native.

It is also a mirror image of the situation in which the first postwar Italian migrants found themselves in Australia. Here, the government was just as keen to import migrants as rapidly as possible but was faced with an organised working class which was traditionally suspicious of any kind of immigration, and particularly of immigration by people who did not originate in the British Isles. The result (see Chapter 3 and Castles et al., 1988) was the development of the ideology of assimilationism: essentially the proposition that immigrants—or 'New Australians'—could and should assimilate to what was proposed as, in essence, a British-derived culture.

In Argentina, Italian immigrants encountered a society which was culturally and, as we have shown, socially fluid. In Australia, the relative rigidity of ideology and social class, as well as the greater linguistic difference between Italian and English, had the effect of confining Italian migrants to a very constricted social space. (It is important to note that the vast bulk of Italian migration to Australia took place while assimilationism was official policy.)

Over the course of the first 40 years of mass immigration, the dominant ideology virtually reversed itself in both countries. In Argentina the europhilia, the expectation of cultural renewal by immigration, which characterised the mid-19th century was, by 1914, replaced by an aggressive nativism in which the most important features were the reinstatement of the *gaucho* as a positive and central cultural icon; and an increasing tendency to blame immigrants for creating a variety of social and political problems (Scobie, 1964: 195; Solberg, 1970; Rock, 1987). In Australia, by contrast, the initial insistence that immigrants should not be allowed to contest the homogeneity of a British-derived culture shifted, between 1967 and 1978, to a celebration of cultural pluralism based on ethnic groupings. The assimilationist phases of the two countries differed in one crucial respect, however. In Australia assimilationism was never much more than the blanket rejection of any possibility of cultural negotiation by the hegemonic group. In Argentina, by contrast, the State took active measures to create a unitary Argentine culture centred around nationalism and a series of traditional cultural icons.

Complex social and political processes underlay these changes which can be dealt with here in a summary manner only. It is, however, important to stress that in both countries the influence of the State was a key factor in determining the radically different forms of absorption of Italian immigrants. It is equally important to stress that the State did not and could not act autonomously from a wide range of socio-economic forces in both countries.

In Argentina the main reasons for the change in ideological emphasis are to be found in the ambitions and fears of the Argentine ruling class. Solberg (1970) stresses two factors: namely the very rapid expansion of an immigrant-dominated middle class; and a near-hysterical fear of anarcho-syndicalist doctrines which, it was believed, held considerable sway over Italian working-class immigrants. Both of these were seen as potential threats to the political hegemony of the *criollo* aristocracy and therefore, it is argued, the project was developed out of a social and political discipline based on nationalism and 'traditional' values. These 'traditional' values generally involved a rejection of cosmopolitanism and liberalism and an assertion of the supposed spirituality of the Argentine compared with the materialism of the North Americans and of European immigrants. Whilst frequently anti-immigrant in a generalised way (and invariably so in the case of Jews, 'Turks' and Asians), attitudes towards Italians in the literature of populist nationalism which began to dominate intellectual life in the 1900s were more ambivalent.

This was because a dominant theme in nationalist writing was the alleged moral superiority of the 'Latin'—a category which could easily include Italians.

Among the writers associated with the new nationalism, it was common to find a stress on education as a key vehicle in the development of national identity. Thus Ricardo Rojas in his book *La Restoración Nacionalista* states: '. . . it is now time to impose a nationalist character on our education through the study of history and the humanities' (cited Rock, 1987: 279). Rojas' book was one of the more significant and widely read texts of the new nationalism so it is significant that its research and publication were financed by the Argentine Ministry of Education, a body which, under the control of a violent xenophobe, José Maria Ramos Mejía, vigorously promoted the policy of nationalist education.

From the turn of the century onward, another highly assimilative force was the army. Under the influence of German officers the army was remodelled and universal male conscription introduced for Argentine citizens. In the period of military service a deliberate attempt was made to mix recruits of all backgrounds and classes (Scobie, 1964: 195; Atkins and Thompson, 1972: 257–74), and to inculcate patriotic attachment to Argentina. This formed almost a continuation of the nationalist school education.

Between the schools and compulsory military service we have a consciously assimilative system at work upon the children of immigrants and in particular on the Argentine-born children. In 1914 only 2.25 per cent of all foreign-born males in Argentina were citizens of that country (Solberg, 1970: 35), meaning that 97.75 per cent had never been subject to conscription, and also implying that a large majority had not been through the school system. By contrast, all Argentine-born children were citizens and, from 1900 on, were increasingly likely to be the objects of consciously assimilationist public socialisation throughout childhood and early adulthood.

Assimilationism in Australia was characterised neither by practices similar to the intellectual/mythological underpinning of the new Argentine nationalism nor similar to the systematic institutionalisation of assimilationist practice which grew up after 1900 in Argentina. Essentially Australian assimilation amounted in practice to little more than a demand that migrants as migrants should be neither seen nor heard. The main effect of assimilationism was, paradoxically, the cultural and social marginalisation of non-anglophone migrants. The gradual shift in the late 1960s and the 1970s to an ideology which is a celebration of cultural pluralism has its political and social origins in a series of processes too complex to explore in this context (Castles et al., 1988). Yet the results of this shift are beginning to become plain. Assimilationism, along with other factors, prevented mutual cultural negotiation between the host and immigrant populations in Australia. Australian multiculturalism celebrates diversity, but has nothing at all to say about intergroup negotiation. It does, however, provide some rudimentary structures for the continuing maintenance of ethnic group consciousness into the second and subsequent generations.

In Argentina, by contrast, the early policies of the State assisted (or, at least, did not hinder) early processes of mutual cultural adjustment. In the latter assimilationist phase, a genuine assimilation was possible partly because this earlier process of adjustment had taken place and partly because of a determined effort by the Argentine elite to institutionalise the process of assimilation in an active way. Not only were the Argentine-born children of Italian immigrants actively pressured to assimilate but the actual process of assimilation was facilitated by the fact that, by the turn of the century, Argentine society provided a number of intermediate structures, the products of cultural interchange between the host and migrant populations over the previous three decades.

Conclusions

I have proposed four main factors in the history of Argentina between 1870 and 1930 which ensured the development of a truly hybrid or creolised society. They are the sheer volume of Italian migration; the linguistic closeness of the Italian and Spanish languages; the social fluidity of a country which, in the space of 40 years, transformed itself from a state of semi-feudal pastoralism into one of the world's greatest trading nations; and the conscious and systematic way in which Argentine elite groups attempted to create a distinctive national identity in the first twenty years of this century.

By contrast Italian immigration to Australia was relatively small and inserted itself into a society which had already developed a strongly pronounced (albeit problematic) sense of cultural distinctiveness. It was also a society in which class relations were relatively ossified and in which a decentralised State apparatus was only occasionally capable of defining and imposing a sense of national purpose. In Argentina mass immigration meant radical mainstream cultural change at almost all levels. In Australia, by contrast, our options have always been posed at two extremes: total assimilation by migrants to the British-derived hegemonic cultural forms, or a *soi-disant* cultural pluralism which gives an uneasily turned shoulder to questions about the processes and limits of cultural modification between ethnic groups.

Two issues arise from the analysis presented in this chapter although considerations of space preclude anything but a mere mention of them. First a paradox: that in a perverse way, concentration on a single ethnic group (such as Italians) reinforces the thesis that mass immigration has had relatively little effect on mainstream Australian culture although it could be argued that mass non-British immigration as a whole has altered the political culture of this country profoundly. In 1945 most Australians knew exactly who they were: the antipodean modification of an essentially British culture. At the beginning of the 1990s we sail through the shoals of 'cultural pluralism' or 'becoming part of Asia'. Changes in the world trading economy account for this in part but so, too, does larger-scale non-British migration in which Italians have played such an important role. Perhaps this is a cultural transformation far more important than those I have attempted to portray in the case of Argentina.

Second, the basis of my comparison has been that of two countries, in two periods, when mass migration was one of the basic engines of change. Such comparisons are a little risky, however, since they abstract from a wider context. In the view of many people the nation state is increasingly anachronistic as a viable socio-political entity. A unitary culture of nationalism is fragmented into cultures of class, gender and diasporic ethnicity. Could it be that the survival of Italians as Italians in Australia, and the corresponding failure to survive as such in Argentina, can be explained better in terms of these geopolitical processes than in terms of the national peculiarities upon which I have chosen to dwell?

15 The Italo-Australian community on the Pacific rim

Ellie Vasta, Gaetano Rando, Stephen Castles and Caroline Alcorso

This book has described Italian migration to Australia and the emergence of an Italo-Australian community. It has shown how Australia has moved in the last half-century from being a monocultural society with a profound mistrust for anything foreign or new, to a more open and diverse society. One main cause has been mass non-British immigration, with Italian immigration as one of the largest components. This final chapter will start by examining the maintenance and transformation of Italian culture, and the development of the Italo-Australian community and identity. It goes on to discuss the consequences of the Italo-Australian presence on Australian culture and identity and, more generally, the emergence of a multicultural society. Another major cause for change has been the shifts in global economic and political structures which have made Australia's traditional dependence on Britain unsustainable. We will examine the effects of this upon Australia's geopolitical position and self-image. We argue that the changes in society and culture stimulated by increased ethnic diversity help Australia in developing the capabilities needed to cope with changes in its position in the world.

Six major aspects of Italian migration to Australia have been examined in this book. The first of these is the economic contribution: Italians have played a significant part in construction, manufacturing and farming, both as wage-earners and as entrepreneurs. A second aspect is the development of Italo-Australian social, cultural, religious and political networks. The third is the formation of Italian neighbourhoods and community spaces. Along with the socio-political networks, these have given rise to a sense of community based not only on geographical location in Australia, but also on premigration cultural, political and regional affinities. A fourth aspect is the linguistic, literary and artistic expressions of the Italian community and the effects these have had on Australian culture. Fifth, attention is given to the position of Italian women as 'cultural custodians' and to the second generation as 'cultural brokers' who have contributed to maintaining and building an Italian sense of community and identity. Sixth, this book has analysed the effects of Anglo-Australian racism on Italian migrants. Racism, such as the internment of Italians in World War II, and the policy of assimilationism, has been evident in many aspects of migrants' lives. The following section will draw these themes together, through an examination of the Italo-Australian experience with regard to culture, community and identity.

Culture, community and identity

Italian migrants have created cultural practices and strategies that have led to a specifically Italo-Australian culture. This, in turn, has influenced the wider Australian culture. However, the emergence of an Italo-Australian identity is in part a reaction to the exclusionary practices of the dominant Anglo-Australian culture and institutions, which created a feeling of difference, a sense of 'us' and 'them'. Thus, the cultural practices which may be grouped around the label of ethnicity work in a number of ways.

First, ethnicity works through a concept of community. Italians in Ausralia do not make up a single homogeneous and cohesive community, but rather a number of communities based on premigration traditions and regional ties, as well as on locality and social and economic interests in Australia. It cannot be claimed that these are 'culturally' cohesive communities. Even within working-class areas, there are differences based on economic interests, ethnocentrism between different Italian regions and gender inequality. Indeed people can belong simultaneously to different Italian communities, for instance to the Abruzzi community, which unites all people from a certain Italian region, and to the Fairfield Italian community. The socio-political strength of these varying groups depends on the goals around which they organise and on the success of their struggles.

Nevertheless, there exists a 'sense of community' which is tied up with a second way in which ethnicity works. This emerges from the discriminatory ethnic, class and gender relations experienced by migrants in Australia. Italian migrants resisted the racism of assimilation by guarding and using their own 'cultural baggage'. They did

The annual blessing of the fleet on the feast of Our Lady of Martyrs was established by the Molfetta communities in Port Pirie and Fremantle following World War II. At Farm Cove in Sydney, as elsewhere in Australia, the ceremony of the blessing of the fishing fleet now includes people from many different backgrounds. (*Our Lady of the Martyrs Association, Sydney*)

this in a number of ways including the insistence that the Italian language or dialect be spoken at home, and by establishing community language schools and language courses. They resisted intermarriage, retained their own child-rearing practices, formed their own social clubs, and set up their own community language newspapers. Often, migrants rationalise the situation in a manner which appears to express prejudice and a feeling of moral superiority: Italian parents are heard saying to their children, 'We have a better and more close-knit family life than they do' or 'We do things better than they do'. This kind of 'prejudice' should not be mistaken for 'reverse racism'. Rather it is a defensive mechanism in a situation of discrimination and marginalisation.

Third, many customs, rituals and traditions are expressions of ethnicity, though not an inert or static ethnicity, but one which is adapted to local conditions. The 'cultural baggage' which migrants bring with them is manifested through customs and rituals which often appear to be based simply on traditions. In fact, such rituals not only symbolise the need for attachment to common history and origin, but also to the need for reference groups when cultural confidence is diminished. For example, the celebration of holy days and saints' days is an expression of ethnicity in a new socio-political context. Many of these rituals operate as forms of social control in the ethnic communities. They also have an integrating function for both older and younger generations and provide forums for community solidarity and the development of new cultural competences. Given that culture is a social process defined through struggle, multiple meanings may emerge which centre on points of ethnic disadvantage. For example, action to gain culturally specific child-care services, or community solidarity to combat racism (Vasta, 1990a).

The poverty from which many Italian migrants escaped, aggravated by their new degraded status as immigrants ('We became like babies, insecure at the age when you must make decisions' [Vasta, 1985: 35]), leads many migrants to compensate with symbols of prestige and wealth (for example, 'spaghetti palaces'[1]). The ornate wedding, which has become the butt of much humour amongst Italo-Australians themselves, is another ritual which reflects a need for symbolic power. Sometimes this is taken to the extreme. For example, in Italy at the end of a wedding, the bride and groom formally thank the guests for their attendance by presenting each with a rosette of sugar-coated almonds (*le bomboniere*). In Australia, this tradition is maintained in most elaborate forms. As well, 'thank you' cards are posted to all the guests, an expression of an 'Australian custom'.

Another example of the expression of ethnicity in a new socio-political context may be found in certain work practices. Italian *contadini* were able to use their peasant skills and endurance to cultivate Australian land which hitherto had been considered unproductive (see Chapter 4). Similarly, the success of Italian small business may be in part explained by traditional family co-operation and solidarity.

Fourth, culturally based organisations constitute an important source of identity for first-generation Italian migrants, and are a means of articulating collective demands. Some Italo-Australian organisations, such as the ethnic welfare centres, are government-assisted. Others, especially sports and recreation clubs, are autonomous. Some of the large Italian clubs have taken on a political role. Local, state and federal politicians are invited to functions where community interests and demands can be put forward. In return, the politicans hope to mobilise the 'ethnic vote'. The existence of such organisations does not mean that these communities are homogeneous or politically united. They serve varying migrant interests, but in concert they do have some political clout in multicultural Australia. Their role can be ambiguous: by relying on the pre-migration past for symbols to maintain solidarity, they may strengthen nostalgic and conservative tendencies; on the other hand they may articulate working-class demands and contribute to cultural innovation in the context of the broader society.

For some people, the local community has become the main focus of political and social activity. If problems related to settlement and finding a job were vital in the 1950s and 1960s, currently the community is concerned with linguistic and cultural maintenance (see Chapters 11 and 12), and with the problems of caring for an ageing population. In the Illawarra, for example, this led to the formation of the Marco Polo Association which in 1988, after years of fundraising, built the Unanderra Nursing Home in conjunction with the Uniting Church. This nursing home provides the Italian aged with care from bilingual staff.

Italo-Australians and Italy

For Italo-Australians, the separation from Italy and the projection into a dominant Anglo-Australian culture has triggered a contradictory process: on the one hand some aspects of their ethnohistorical culture have become ossified; on the other hand, migration has been a powerful force for cultural change. Many Italo-Australians realise that over the years they have become somehow 'different' compared to the friends and relatives who remained behind. The variety of Italian spoken in Australia has changed compared with that spoken in the place of origin. Behaviour has also altered: 'we'd become more self-contained, more disciplined, more reserved' (Loh, 1980: 131). One perception is that the quality of life in Italy is better than that experienced by Italo-Australians.

Although most Italo-Australian migrants come from a working-class, rural, dialect-speaking background, the migration process seems to have triggered a closer orientation towards Italian national identity and 'official' Italian culture than is the case for those who remained behind. Furthermore, the regional dialects appear to have changed little, compared with the changes which have occurred in Italy (although the Italian spoken in Australia has changed in a different direction, incorporating English words). However, many Italo-Australians are aware that the society and economy are no longer the same as when they left ('. . . the people I left behind in Italy have become rich, and I am the poorest of all' [Pettini, 1989: 122]). Italy's new-found prosperity can be disturbing for Italo-Australians who were compelled to emigrate because of poverty. During the Bicentennial Conference on Italians in Australia (University of Wollongong, 27–29 August 1988) the local Italian community was invited to meet the participants from Italy. Discussion centred on the current presence of third-world immigrants in Italy. The most striking comment was an Italo-Australian migrant's poignantly perplexed question: 'But why hasn't the Italian government asked *us* to return to Italy?'

In fact, nearly one-third of Italian immigrants to Australia have decided to return to Italy over the years, and this rate may increase as Australia becomes less and less the 'lucky country'. In a study conducted among 100 long-standing Italian migrants in Brisbane, one outstanding result was that approximately two-thirds would return to Italy if they could. For many, the main barrier was that their children had settled in Australia (Vasta, 1985). The experience of re-migration, however, has often proved more difficult than the original migration.[2] One reason is that Italian bureaucracy is often cumbersome, so that resettlement procedures can be arduous and disruptive. Another difficulty is that Italian society has changed so much that it takes the returnees a long time to develop their old sense of belonging.

The presence of hundreds of thousands of persons of Italian origin in Australia has meant increased personal contact with Italy as many feel the need to keep up links with their past. Italian settlement in Australia has led to closer trade links, creating a demand for Italian goods. The Italian presence in Australia has also had a role in promoting closer ties at a formal and official level, such as visits by heads of state. Reciprocal social security agreements have been created for pension, medical and other benefits. There are also cultural agreements concerning collaboration between universities and research institutes, as well as a commitment to promote the teaching of Italian language and culture in Australia, and to establish an Australian Cultural Centre in Italy. Whether the Italian presence may serve to strengthen links with the post-1992 EEC remains to be seen.

Italian influence on Anglo-Australian culture and identity

The creation of 'Italian space' in areas like Fairfield, Leichhardt, Carlton, Griffith, and Fremantle is a highly visible aspect of the Italian presence. Such Italo-Australian neighbourhoods are based on the two basic distributive markets of labour and housing where Italian shops, cafés and clubs provide a distinctly Italo-Australian flavour. The construction and design of houses by Italian builders visibly influences the urban environment and this is evident in the widespread use of terrazzo, ceramic tiles, *lavori in muratura* (brickwork and stonemasonry), and the use of columns in a decorative/structural function.

There is another set of parameters which serves to define certain characteristics and contributions of the Italo-Australian community. The creation of informal networks may be seen as an Italo-Australian derivation of a southern European way of life, but the establishment of formal community structures (clubs, welfare associations) is an adaptation to Anglo-Australian patterns. Other visible changes have occurred with commodification of elements of culture by capital and their incorporation in everyday life through the consumption process. For example, the pizza has been industrialised by US multinationals (Pizza Hut). Similarly, Ferrari cars and Italian fashions, promoted as representing the good life under capitalism, are not dependent on an Italian migrant presence.

Perhaps the sectors in which Italian cultural practices have had the least influence are the professions and institutions. For example, the delivery of health and legal services has changed little to accommodate the specific needs of migrants. The development of interpreting and translation services over the past ten years can be seen as an institutional response to facilitate access to Anglo-oriented services and institutions. Although language services are necessary, they reduce the pressure for structural change in the long run. Within the education system, the teaching of community languages and the initiatives taken in multicultural education have had little impact on basic structures. Despite the implementation of multicultural policies for over fifteen years, institutions remain essentially Anglo-Australian in orientation and practice.

The majority of Italians who migrated to Australia have experienced dislocation, in many cases quite radically, at a personal, cultural, family and social level. Though significant, for Anglo-Australians the cultural dislocation brought about by the Italian presence has been less radical. Indeed, the Italian presence has broadened the Australian cultural landscape through agriculture, building and architecture, fashion, the arts and cuisine. Italians, however, occupy a 'contradictory cultural location'. In relation to Asian migrants, Italians are part of the European majority, long established and constituting the largest of the non-English speaking background immigrant groups. Paradoxically, however, they are part of a minority in relation to Anglo-Australians, still at the receiving end of institutional and informal racism.

One of the main ways in which Italian migrants have affected Australian culture has been indirectly made through their contribution to the move away from a monocultural definition of Australian identity. In the early postwar years, Australian identity was constituted through assimilationism, which set out to destroy migrant cultures while marginalising migrant workers in economic and social terms. When migrants resisted assimilation, by maintaining their cultures and building communities, the State was forced to find a new way of managing social policy and national identity. The result was multiculturalism. This does not exclude, but still divides and marginalises, and is thus fraught with contradictions.

To begin with, although multiculturalism has espoused cultural diversity and equal opportunity, it continues to stress the notion of social cohesion based on an overarching set of values, with stress on Anglo-Australian culture and institutions. Successive govenments have been more concerned with drawing people into the idea of 'nation' rather than with equal cultural, social and political rights. That appeal to national identity and interests obscures major social and economic inequalities and contains protest (Williams, 1962).

Another contradiction illustrates how multiculturalism is both liberating and marginalising in that it has provided necessary services for migrants, while it ignores the structural inequalities experienced by many migrants. As discussed in Chapter 3, however, multiculturalism has already been redefined several times. The 1989 *National Agenda for a Multicultural Australia* (OMA, 1989), did address the contradiction between cultural openness and socio-economic differentiation. This document is predominantly more concerned with increasing equality of educational and occupational opportunities, than concentrating on cultural pluralism, as multicultural policy has in the past. Yet a mere statement of principles cannot in itself remove the gap between the ideology of equal rights for all Australians and the reality of exclusion of non-Anglos from the centres of economic and political power (as described in Chapter 9).

Finally, there is the widespread uncertainty about cultural and national identity. Indeed, defining these remains a favourite Australian pastime. Many still believe that a *real* Australian is blond-haired, blue-eyed and that *he* prefers to spend much of *his* leisure time at the beach. Many migrant Australians also use these images to describe the *real* Australian, and the loss of identity is poignantly apparent when one often hears both first- and second-generation migrant Australians refer to Anglo-Australians as 'Australians' and to themselves as 'Italians' or 'Greeks'.

Despite all this, Australia has changed substantially since the days of the White Australia policy and assimilationism, and indeed has one of the most successful immigration and ethnic affairs policies in the world. Multiculturalism still has a long way to go to overcome racist practices and cultural domination, but it provides a permanent public arena for debate on the significance of diversity for national identity. This implies that Australian national identity remains fragile and unsure of an appropriate response to current global changes. The question is whether the Italian presence can play a positive role in the necessary process of redefinition.

The strength of Italo-Australian culture, identity and community in Australia will, in the foreseeable future, rely not only on Italian migrant women as cultural custodians but also on the second and third generations. As discussed in Chapter 11, the second generation, many of whom have become upwardly mobile and have developed dual cultural competences, often set up their businesses in the communities in which they grew up. Many are continuing the cultural traditions of their parents, such as hard work, Italian cuisine, and family gatherings centred around weddings and christenings. Although the second generation find themselves in contradictory cultural and class locations, they help provide links into Anglo-Australian institutions for working-class Italians and for older people. The position of the adult second generation is not altogether problem-free: there is some concern that those who have succeeded in mainstream business or entered the bureaucracy will lose contact with their communities of origin. On the other hand, the possession of double cultural competences raises another issue.

This underlines the fact that migration is not simply a once-and-for-all move from one country to another. Italian migration to Australia has helped develop permanent personal, economic and cultural links with Italy. The second-generation Italo-Australians who return to Italy (either temporarily or semi-permanently) have a foot in both countries, just like the first generation. As transport and communications improve, it becomes possible for them to form a permanent bridge. Their multiple identities are rooted in two societies, and they can help develop a process of interaction which embraces both cultures. In the light of the rapid and unexpected changes of the last half-century, who can tell what future interactions and links may develop.

Facing the Asian–Pacific challenge of the 21st century

This final section will discuss the effects of growing cultural diversity on Australia's international position. For the first 150 years of the existence of white Australia, the essential factors which structured the world for its inhabitants were dependence on Britain, and a strong eurocentrism—that is a belief in the moral, technological and cultural superiority of white civilisations based on European ideas. The Australian world-view thus had two central elements: the first was the 'cultural cringe', the taking-for-granted of being an adjunct of a more powerful and capable society. The second was the idea that other cultures—and particularly those of Asia—were inferior and threatening.

Britain's defeat in the Pacific in 1941–42, and the subsequent crumbling of the Empire, shook this world-view, but did not shatter it: Britain could for a while be replaced by our 'great and powerful friend', the USA. The real crunch for Australia has come since the 1970s. Today, the end of the Cold War, the economic decline of the USA, the move towards unification of western Europe, the rise of north-east Asia and the growing significance of transnational capital, are all leading to realignment of political, economic and military structures. The most significant factor is the economic ascendancy of Japan and other Asian capitalist countries. It is increasingly obvious that Australia needs to change its orientation away from Europe and the USA, towards the Asian–Pacific region. But not everybody in Australia agrees about the need for re-orientation and the feasibility of achieving it.

The best pet shop in the world

A widely held pessimistic scenario suggests that Australia with its small population and weak economy can do little to shape its destiny in view of overpowering external forces. As early as 1945, Arthur Calwell, the first Minister of Immigration, said: 'I wonder how many of us have ever thought how much we Australians are like the koalas. We both belong to dying races and both are well on the way to becoming museum pieces, along with the extinct moa and great auk' (quoted in Wilton and Bosworth, 1984: 1). Calwell was trying to convince the public of the need for mass immigration, which he believed would save Australians from extinction. The metaphor of the koala points to the dilemma of the Australian condition. Our relatively unspoiled nature is an asset because it offers unrivalled life-styles, but is also a trap because it leads us to rely on natural resources, and do little to develop technology or industry. More than 40 years later the same image appears in a report by the Japan Policy Section of the Commonwealth Department of Industry, Technology and Commerce which states: 'from the Japanese point of view a major barrier to such collaboration is their perception of Australia as a vast zoo and quarry with little to offer in the way of research and development' (quoted in David and Wheelwright, 1989: 51).

The novelist Peter Carey has taken Calwell's koala metaphor to its logical conclusion. His novel *Illywhacker* is about the post-colonial 'cultural cringe' and its role in perpetuating economic and cultural dependence. Australia has remained dependent on primary products and, increasingly, on tourism. In the biting satire which concludes the novel, the cuddly animals which draw tourists to 'the best pet shop in the world' are replaced as exhibits by typical Australians.

> There is a spirit in this place. It is this that excites the visitors. The shearers, for instance, exhibit that dry, laconic anti-authoritarian wit that is the very basis of the Australian sense of humour. They are proud people, these lifesavers, inventors, manufacturers, bushmen, aboriginals. They do not act like caged people. The very success of the exhibit is in their ability to move and act naturally within the confines of space. They go about their business, their sand paintings, their circumcision ceremonies, their strikes, settlements, discussions about national anthems . . .
>
> Of course there are disagreements, fights, but no one objects. The only bitterness comes from outside these walls, from the jeering crowd of slogan writers who cannot afford the entrance money (Carey, 1985: 599).

This allegory of Australia's future helps us to reflect on some of the dangers facing the nation. An isolationist policy which cuts Australia off from international technological and economic developments would mean increasing backwardness compared with the rest of the Asian–Pacific region. But opening the economy to foreign competition could lead to new forms of dependence, because Australian education, research capabilites, and manufacturing expertise may be too second-rate to compete. The solution can only lie in a cultural opening which provides Australians with the tools needed to make a distinctive contribution to innovation, economic growth and social development.

However, this is an undertaking which is regarded as too risky and demanding by many. Hence the attempts by people like the historian Blainey and Victorian RSL President, Ruxton, to resurrect the myth of a cosy, homogeneous little Australia of a Golden Age lost somewhere in the mists of time around 1925. The calls of the Opposition Leader, John Howard, for a 'One Australia' policy in 1988 were in the same vein. Such appeals are invariably linked to demands for the restriction of Asian migration, because it might undermine 'social cohesion'. They are also based on the desire to abandon multiculturalism and return to a monocultural definition of national identity.

The old 'cultural cringe' mentality, which assumed that anything Australian was inferior to products of Europe or the USA, is still alive in the minds of those who regard themselves as Australian nationalists. It is their interesting unspoken assumption that cutting the umbilical cord to the 'Anglo-Saxon nations' would automatically mean dependence on Japan and other Asian countries. They are resigned to perpetuating outmoded forms of dependence, which they see as the only way of avoiding new forms of tutelage. This nostalgic view of the world is capable of mobilising nationalist and racist sentiments, particularly on the part of those who feel threatened by the economic, social and cultural effects of rapid global changes. But it has little chance of success, because it goes against the realities of Australia's current situation.

International relations

Australia needs to move away from a eurocentric view of the world James R. Kurth has argued that:

> [t]he greatest disasters in US security policy—towards China in the 1940s and 1950s and towards Indochina in the 1960s and 1970s—resulted from the American effort to interpret the Asian reality through the European prism, to squeeze it into the NATO model. Similarly, the greatest conflicts in US foreign economic policy—toward Japan and the east Asian newly industrialising countries in the 1980s—have resulted from the US effort to squeeze these countries into the GATT model (1989: 36).

Kurth argues that Atlantic economic and strategic concepts do not fit the contemporary Asian–Pacific world. He is speaking about the USA, but his comments fit Australia just as well. In the 1960s and 1970s Australia tried to fill the post-colonial vacuum in New Guinea, leading to tensions with Indonesia. The development of a Pacific security system through the ANZUS Treaty was an unsuccessful attempt to imitate NATO. Australia followed the USA and Britain into military adventures designed to contain the perceived threat of communism in Korea, Malaya, Borneo and Vietnam. Australia's economic policy has been based on liberalisation of world trade, and it has been a vocal critic of the European Community's mercantilist agricultural policy.

Such policies need re-examination. Today none of the great powers may have much interest in having Australia as a client state. The relative significance of its mineral resources is declining. Radar and communications centres like Pine Gap are still of military importance for the USA, but the end of the Cold War and changes in technology may reduce their strategic role. Both the USA and Europe have shown scant regard for Australian interests in international trade policies. In the light of Australia's lack of significance, the only realistic perspective might be a regional alliance, which means forming closer political links with Asian countries. And that in turn is only possible in the context of economic co-operation and cultural understanding.

New economic directions

The Australian economy is indeed shifting its orientation towards Asia. By the end of the 1980s, half of foreign trade was with Asian countries. Their hunger for raw materials and, more recently, for foodstuffs, fitted well with Australia's desire for manufactured goods. On the other hand investment by Asian–Pacific countries in Australia was still low—only 12 per cent of total foreign investment in 1987. Investment by Australian companies in south-east Asia was actually declining, with entrepreneurs and fund managers still preferring their traditional links with the USA and the UK (Dyster and Meredith, 1990: 316–17).

The federal government's recent Garnaut report puts forward the view that Australia's long-term economic success (and political stability) lies in binding itself closely with the structure of Asian economies, and in embracing a role which is complementary to that structure. According to Garnaut, this entails the fullest exploitation of our natural resources, the enthusiastic encouragement of Asian capital investment, the promotion of trade with Asia and the maintenance of a large-scale immigration program to draw in 'energetic young migrants with high levels of skill and talents' from north-east Asia (Garnaut, 1989: 6).

But economic openness to Asia is in itself no guarantee of technological advancement or improved export performance. Japanese and other north-east Asian countries have already achieved a high level of market penetration in Australia with their manufactured goods. This has been a major factor in the failure of Australia's attempts to achieve a strong manufacturing sector. At the same time, these countries maintain high tariffs against Australian agricultural products, and use their situation as near-monopoly buyers to control the prices of mining commodity exports. Much current Japanese investment in Australia is in real estate and in the leisure sector. There has been some Japanese investment in research and development in Australia, though mainly where this is required as a condition for major supply contracts to the Australian government. The current economic relationships between Australia and Japan are thus fairly consistent with 'the best pet shop in the world' scenario.

However, Australian production has always been highly integrated with the world economy, and any attempt at absolute independence would be disastrous. Australia therefore appears to be damned if it does open up to Asia but also damned if it doesn't. Somewhere in between are positions which accept the inevitability of integration in the world economy, but look for ways of developing a strong manufacturing base and increasing exports of industrial products. These positions are linked to the interests of Australian manufacturing capital and the trade union movement. For instance the Australian Manufacturing Council report (Pappas et al., 1990) expresses support for the Japanese management model and for integration into world trade, but calls for caution in the pace of change and emphasises the importance of national industrial development. The report is sceptical about Garnaut's enthusiastic hopes for raw materials, and industries based on a high degree of contact with people, such as travel and convention services, sport and leisure, and educational services. It envisages a much greater role for government 'to offset the worst impacts of unlevel playing fields elsewhere' (Pappas et al., 1990: x). The views of the trade union movement were put forward in the report *Australia Reconstructed* (ACTU, 1987), which advocated a social-democratic model for economic management, with a fairly high degree of State involvement.

Immigration and cultural change

The bulk of postwar migrants have come from Europe. Their presence has created the possibility of fertile and vibrant links with those countries—links at first rejected and then to some extent embraced by the Anglo-Australian majority. But today, the European countries are becoming increasingly interdependent. To some extent, this means a closure towards the rest of the world. So while Australia is today culturally better placed than ever before to enter European markets and to attract European capital and migrants, western Europe has erected barriers to Australian exports, shows little interest in capital investment here and is unlikely to provide future migrants. Nor does Australia have much chance of competing with western European capital in the now-opening markets of eastern Europe.

While migration from Europe declined in the 1970s and 1980s, migration from Asia has grown, and now appears as a key part of any strategy to increase Australia's integration in the Asian–Pacific region. Migration can provide skilled personnel for Australian economic development, as well as helping to generate capital investment, exports and growth. Migration also helps develop the cultural understanding essential for closer cooperation. According to the Garnaut report, immigration has an important role in building cultural links and 'in helping Australia to make maximum use of opportunities in north-east Asia' (1989: 32).

All aspects of the opening to Asia have cultural ramifications. But attitudes are still determined by generations of cultural distance, ignorance about Asian societies and racist contempt for Asian people. The Australian education system virtually ignored Asia until the 1980s. Asian languages were not taught at schools or universities, and history and geography teaching were highly eurocentric. The public perception of Asia was one of vast underdeveloped countries, peopled by teeming masses of uneducated and impoverished people. Japan was the exception: an industrious and regimented society, seen as both a military and an economic threat. Asians were regarded as mysterious and traditionalist; their languages were incomprehensible, and their cultures impenetrable. Steps are now being taken to remedy this: the teaching of Asian languages is seen as a task with high priority, and the Garnaut report emphasises the 'need to comprehend north-east Asian social, economic and political institutions and languages' (1989: 3).

The basic contradiction of the Australian condition is that a society established as an outpost of Britain has been cut off from its antecedents by global change, and is now compelled to relate to the Asian–Pacific region which surrounds it. A national identity constituted through insularity and racism has to come to terms with the all-too-obvious decline of white, European superiority. It might be argued that the whole two-century episode of British settlement has been an historical aberration, an accidental conjuncture of colonialism, which will disappear without trace, as Asia develops in the next century. If that proves to be the case, then postwar European immigration and the cultural change it has brought about would have been one of history's blind alleys.

The editors of this book do not subscribe to that view. On the contrary, it is our argument that British colonialism in the Pacific was one facet of the process of historical change which started around the time of the Italian Renaissance. The expansion of long-distance trade and colonialism brought wealth, new commodities, and new ideas to Europe. These provided the basis for the emergence of capitalism, industrialisation and modernity, which spread as a new global culture throughout Europe, and then to the Americas and Asia. The Asian form of industrialisation has a unique dynamic, but it would be unthinkable without the preceding emergence of a world capitalist market. British culture in Australia may have been narrow and exclusionary, but it was only one sub-set of the broad and pervasive culture of modernity.

Nonetheless, the Anglo-Australian culture which had emerged by the mid-20th century might have been incapable of adaptation to the new realities. In 1945, Australia was an insular society, distrustful of anything non-British and with a long tradition of racism and exclusion towards Asians. Mass immigration of Italians and other Europeans undermined Anglo-Australian narrowness, showing not only that there were other ways of doing things, but also that these ways were often more successful, dynamic and rewarding. The processes of integration and community-building described in this book did not only change the immigrants and their cultures; they also influenced Australian institutions, life-styles and world-views. European settlement in the long run made it necessary to shift from assimilationism, based on Anglo-Australian cultural dominance, to multiculturalism, which is premised on acceptance of cultural diversity.

The challenge for multicultural policies today is to ensure that pressures within established ethnic goups (including the Italo-Australians) to maintain cultural integrity do not lead to a new eurocentric conservatism, that excludes Asians and Aborigines. Multiculturalism must therefore move from the model developed in the 1970s in response to the needs of first-generation working-class European migrants, to a more embracing and durable model, which recognises the continuing diversification of the population in terms of origins, life situations and cultural expressions.

Today, Australian multiculturalism can provide a workable answer to a question which affects many countries: how can a diverse population be incorporated within a single nation state? This requires a new definition of national identity, which is not based on national or ethnic origins. It is true that multiculturalism is not universally accepted in Australia, and that some of its principles are more rhetoric than reality. Nonetheless, cultural diversity and the development of ethnic communities challenge the central position of racism in the definition of Australian identity. Without the emergence of multiculturalism and the official rejection of racism, any economic and cultural opening to Asia would be unthinkable. This is not to claim that racism in Australia is dead: it re-surfaces regularly in public debates on immigration and identity, in discriminatory practices against minorities, and in racial violence and harassment, but above all in the continuing marginalisation of Aborigines. But today, racism evokes a response from the organised ethnic communities, from a broad section of the public which welcomes cultural diversity, and from political leaders who see multiculturalism as vital for Australia's political and economic interest.

Thus, it is our conclusion that the Italians who migrated to the Pacific rim not only helped to open Australia to a greater diversity of European cultures—they also paved the way for Anglo-Australian awareness of new geopolitical realities, and in the long run for the opening to Asia. Perhaps this seeming paradox will, in the future, be resolved by new forms of international interchange and co-operation, that may make it possible to move towards a truly global culture. In a time as yet beyond our horizons, humanity may prove capable of developing economic, political and social networks which embody the best of all the great cultural traditions, without eliminating diversity and distinctiveness. Mass migration and the emergence of multicultural societies can help prepare the ground for this development, and history may well judge that the Italians who immigrated to Australia played a small but significant part.

Notes

Chapter 1

1 The Sicilian sailor, Giuseppe Tusa, allegedly arrived in the First Fleet, while Vincenzo Bucchieri and Antonio Jano were among the convicts involved in a major attempted escape from the Van Diemen's Land penal colony in 1814 (Cecilia, 1992).
2 By the 1870s Irish-born people accounted for one-eighth of the total population of the colonies (Fitzpatrick, 1988: 560).
3 The Eureka Stockade was a bloody conflict between the miners and government troops, the climax of months of mounting anger against government regulations and the taxing of the small alluvial diggers. A number of democratic political demands were raised during the protests, and the Eureka Stockade became the symbol of Australian radical nationalism in subsequent decades.
4 The following account about young Italians in the prewar years was written by Ellie Vasta.

Chapter 2

1 See Chapter 12.

Chapter 3

1 Usage of the term second generation varies. Here we use the term in a strict statistical sense, to refer to children born in Australia with over-

seas-born parents. Some people consider that children who were born overseas, but migrated at an early age (for example, less than ten) also belong to the second generation, at least in psychological terms. This issue will be discussed in Chapter 11.

2 Until 1947, there was no separate Australian citizenship: Australians were British citizens. After 1947, Australians got their own citizenship although they remained 'British subjects' until 1973. British immigrants still had all citizenship rights (such as the right to vote in Australia) without naturalisation. This remained the case until 1984. The five-year waiting period was later reduced to three years, and then two years.

Chapter 4

1 BHP is the abbreviation for Broken Hill Proprietary, Australia's largest company, which among other things owns the steelworks at Port Kembla, Newcastle and Whyalla.

2 The situation of Italian women will be discussed comprehensively in Chapter 10.

Chapter 7

1 It was first used officially to describe an informal unpaid leader in the Italo-Australian community in the early 1980s.

2 He was Francesco Calabrò, now a member of the Upper House of the NSW Parliament and the successful head of a million-dollar bus company.

Chapter 8

1 For example, in many parishes of high Italian migrant density certain masses were delivered in Italian; the Catholic Church also established Catholic Immigration Committees or Offices in the 1950s to coordinate welfare activities.

2 These figures may be compared to the 3500 children learning Italian under state Department of Education programs at the time.

3 Information obtained during an interview with *La Fiamma* managing editor Giulio Montagna, 26 December 1989.

4 Recently, in defending SBS against the charge that it caters primarily to a trendy middle-class WASP (White Anglo-Saxon Protestant) audience, an SBS researcher stated that market research showed that NESB people are three times more likely to watch SBS than their Anglo-Australian counterparts *(Sydney Morning Herald,* 15/10/90).

Chapter 9

1 One indication of this is the lack of social-scientific literature. In the 1980s only one book (Jupp, 1984a) and a handful of articles on the topic were published in Australia.
2 This is based on a list kindly provided to the authors by Al Grassby and James Jupp.
3 Based on an interview with Nando Lelli, Wollongong, 2 September 1990. The interview was conducted both in Italian and in English. Other sources for the information contained in this section are: 'The role of migrants in the Australian Trade Union Movement', address given by F. Lelli at the University of New South Wales, 24 October 1988; 'Migrant workers: training and retraining', address given by F. Lelli at the International Centre, Wollongong, 2 December 1988.

Chapter 10

1 For an elaboration of this issue, see Vasta, 1990a or 1991.

Chapter 12

1 The first section of this chapter draws substantially from the text written by Joe Lo Bianco for Chapter 5 of the Italian edition (*Euroaustraliani*).
2 According to the distinction drawn by the American linguist E. Haugen (1953: 334), 'first generation' refers to those born in Italy who emigrated after their speech habits had become fixed, 'second generation', those who emigrated before their speech habits had became fixed (that is, at a relatively young age) or were born in Australia.
3 EFTSU 'effective fulltime student unit' is a measure used by the Australian tertiary system in measuring student numbers.
4 Transcribed from an interview recorded by Mario Bonaccorso during fieldwork undertaken in October 1990 in the western Sydney area among immigrants from the province of Catania (Sicily). The speaker is a 46-year-old woman who migrated to Australia at age twenty and had completed primary school in Italy. Her base speech is Popular Italian. English influences in her speech are marked in bold, dialect influences in italics. The passage may be translated as follows: 'I like to go out on picnics and have a barbecue under the trees. We also go to see a very good friend of mine at Shepparton, Victoria. They live on a farm, a fruit farm. There's more room, more fresh air. I like to go there for a holiday. I like to keep the house tidy . . . my children are very untidy . . . and they make me work a lot. But even if they make me angry I don't worry about it. When they come home they mess everything up.'

Chapter 13

1 The assistance of the Honourable Franca Arena, NSW President of the National Italo-Australian Women's Association, in making the unpublished material available for consultation is here gratefully acknowledged.

2 Gaetano Rando, 'The Australian experience of a south Italian rural community'—research project in progress (interviews conducted January–July 1989). Filicudi is one of a group of seven islands off the north-east coast of Sicily. At the end of last century it supported a population of 1200 people engaged mainly in fishing, farming and seafaring. Over the next 70 years emigration mainly to the Americas and to Australia gradually but inexorably took its toll until by the late 1960s the permanent population was reduced to about 150 mainly elderly people and its traditional social and economic structure was completely destroyed. Since then an increased economic prosperity brought on by tourism has encouraged the resettlement of the island and the return of some emigrants.

3 Hempel characterises the Italian male migrant as an opportunistic person concemed with thrift, hard work and success. According to Hempel (1959: 47) 'a happy migrant is a migrant who has been placed in employment suitable to his level of education and skill'.

Chapter 14

1 The following main sources were used for Argentina in this section: Nascimbene, 1988; Devoto and Rosoli, 1985; Fondazione Giovanni Agnelli, 1987; Raymundo, 1981.

Chapter 15

1 A 'spaghetti palace' refers to an Italian-style double-storey brick house with ornate wrought-iron trimmings around the front balconies. The houses were first built by Italian builders for Italian migrants and have since become popular among other migrant groups and Anglo-Australians who live in Italo-Australian neighbourhoods.

2 Interview with ANEA president Aldo Lorigiola, Sanselice [Pd], 18 February 1991.

Bibliography

Abiuso, J. (1984) *The Male Model and Other Stories* Adelaide: Dezsery Ethnic Publications

ABS (Australian Bureau of Statistics) (1989) *Overseas Born Australians 1988—A Statistical Profile* Canberra: ABS

ACMA (Advisory Council on Multicultural Affairs) (1988) *Towards a National Agenda for a Multicultural Australia: A Discussion Paper* Canberra: AGPS

ACPEA (Australian Council on Population and Ethnic Affairs) (1982) *Multiculturalism for all Australians—Our Developing Nationhood* Canberra: AGPS

ACTU (Australian Council of Trade Unions) (1987) *Australia Reconstructed* Canberra: AGPS

Aguirre, J. M. (1979) 'Influencia de la Immigración en el idioma de los Argentinos' in *La Inmigración en la Argentina* Tucumán: Universidad Nacional de Tucumán

Alcorso, C. (1988) *Migrant Workers and Workers' Compensation in NSW* Sydney: Social Welfare Research Centre, University of NSW

—— (1991) *Newly Arrived Non-English Speaking Background Women in the Workforce Wollongong: Centre for Multicultural Studies for the Office of Multicultural Affairs*

Allan, L. (1984) 'Ethnic transition in inner-Melbourne politics' in J. Jupp ed. *Ethnic Politics in Australia* Sydney: Allen & Unwin

Amati, A. (1886) *Dell' Australia e della fondazione di una colonia con bandiera italiana* Milan

Anon, (1977) *The Story of Mamma Lena* Sydney: St Paul Publications

Andreoni, G. (1967a) 'Australitalian' in *University Studies in History* Vol. 5, No. 1, pp. 114–19

—— (1967b) *Martin Pescatore* Milan: Ippocampo

—— (1971) 'Caratteristiche dell'Australitaliani' in *Quaderni dell'istituto italiano di cultura,* Vol. 4 pp. 301–5 Melbourne: Istituto Italiano di Cultura

—— (1978) *La lingua degli italiani d'Australia e alcuni racconti* Quaderni del Veltro No. 17 Rome: Il Veltro Editrice

—— (1982) *L'Italo–australiano come linguaggio letterario, un racconto documento* Quaderni del Veltro No. 19 Rome: 11 Veltro Editrice

Andreoni, G. and Rando, G. eds (1973) 'Le Relazioni tra l'Italia, l'Australia e la Nuova Zelanda' Rome: [Dante Alighieri Society] in *Il Veltro* Vol. 17, 2–3, April–June

Andreoni, H. (1983) *Non-English Speaking Women in an Isolated Rural Community* Armidale Papers, No. 7, pp. 1–26 Armidale: University of New England

Arena, F. (1985) 'The Contributions of Italian–Australian Women to Australian Society: An Overview' in *Noi Donne Italo-Australiane* Proceedings of the First Congress of Italo-Australian Women Sydney–Melbourne: Associazione Donne Italo-Australiane

—— (1987) 'No More Crumbs' in J. A. Scutt ed. *Different Lives* Melbourne: Penguin

Atkins, G. P. and Thompson, L. V. (1972) 'German Military Influence in Argentina 1921–1940' in *Journal of Latin American Studies* Vol. 4, pp. 257–74

Australian Archives CRS Accession—ongoing

Australian InFo International (1989) *Australian Aboriginal Culture* Canberra: AGPS

Avni, H. (1983) *Argentina y la Historia de la Inmigración Judía* Jerusalem: Editorial Universitaria Magnes, Universidad Hebrea de Jerusalem

Baggio, R. A. (1989) *The Shoe in My Cheese: An Immigrant Family Experience* Footscray, VIC: Footscray Institute of Technology Humanities Department

Bagú, F. (n.d.) *Evolución Histórica de la Estratificación Social en Argentina* Buenos Aires: Instituto de Investigaciones Económicas y Sociales

Baily, S. (1985) 'La cadena migratoria de los Italianos a la Argentina' in Devoto, F. and Rosoli, G. eds *La Inmigración Italiana en la Argentina* Buenos Aires: Biblos

Barzini, L. (1964) *The Italians* London: Hamilton

Basili, F. (1983) *Aspetti del bilinguismo. Influssi sulla lingua degli immigrati italiani d'Australia* Sydney: [unpublished monograph]

Baxter, J. (1970) *The Australian Cinema* Sydney: Angus & Robertson

Bentivoglio, M. R. and Di Leonardo, G. (1984) *Quinto Ercole: Storia di un militante del Movimento Operaio Abruzzese esule in Australia (1894–1953)* S. Gabriele: Eco

Bertelli, L. (1984) *Where to the Italo-Australians? A Profile of Second-Generation Italians in Australia and Some Issues of Concern* CIRC Paper No. 25 Melbourne: CIRC

—— (1986) *A Socio-Cultural Profile of the Italian Community in Australia* CIRC Paper No. 48 Melbourne: CIRC

—— (1988) 'Italian Community Life in Melbourne' in J. Jupp ed. *The*

Australian People: An Encyclopedia of the Nation, Its People and Their Origins Sydney: Angus & Robertson

Bertozzi, D. M. (1984) *Oltre il Mare* Melbourne: Economical Editorial Company

Bettoni, C. (1981a) 'Maintenance or New learning? Italian in Schools' in *Babel* Vol. 17, Nos. 2–3, pp. 25–33

—— (1981b) *Italian in North Queensland. Changes in the Speech of First and Second Generation Bilinguals* Townsville: Department of Modern Languages, James Cook University

—— ed. (1986) 'Studies on Language Contact in English-Speaking Countries' in *Altro Polo. Italian Abroad* Sydney: Frederick May Foundation for Italian Studies and University of Sydney, pp. 61–85

Bettoni, C. and Gibbons, J. (1988) 'Linguistic purism and language shift: a guise-voice study of the Italian community in Sydney' in *International Journal of the Sociology of Language* Vol. 72, pp. 15–35

Beyhaut, G. (1961) *Inmigración Desarollo Económico* Buenos Aires: Universidad de Buenos Aires, Departamento de Sociologia

BIR (Bureau of Immigration Research) (1989) *Australian Immigration, Consolidated Statistics, No. 15, 1988* Canberra: AGPS

—— (1990a) *Australia's Population Trends and Prospects, 1989* Canberra: AGPS

—— (1990b) *Community Profiles: Italy Born* Canberra: AGPS

—— (1990c) *The Economic Status of Migrants in Australia* Canberra: AGPS

Birrell, R. and Seitz, A. (1986) *The Ethnic Problem in Education: The Emergence and Definition of an Issue* Melbourne: Paper for AIMA Research Conference

Bonutto, 0. (1963) *A Migrant's Story* Brisbane: H. Pole and Co.

Borghese, V. (1984) *La Moneta ed altri Racconti* Melbourne: The Author

Borrie, W. D. (1954) *Italians and Germans in Australia: A Study of Assimilation* Melbourne: Cheshire

Bosi, P. (1971a) *Australia Cane* Sydney: Kurunda

—— (197lb) *Blood, Sweat and Guts* Sydney: Kurunda

—— (1973) *The Checkmate and Other Stories* Sydney: Kurunda

—— (1989) *On God's Command, Italian Missionaries in Australia* Melbourne: CIRC

Bosworth, R. (1988) 'Post-war Italian Immigration' in J. Jupp ed. *The Australian People: An Encyclopedia of the Nation, Its People and Their Origins* Sydney: Angus & Robertson

Bosworth, R. and Bosworth, M. (1990) *Fremantle's Italy* Fremantle: Fremantle Arts Centre Press

Bottomley, G. (1984a) *Mediterranean Women in Australia: An Overview* presented to the Symposium of Mediterranean Women's Organisations, Delphi, Greece

—— (1984b) 'Women on the Move: Migration and Feminism' in G. Bottomley and M. de Lepervanche eds *Ethnicity, Class and Gender in Australia* Sydney: George Allen & Unwin

Boughen, H. (1986) 'Towser's Huts, Cobar, New South Wales: Historic

Ruin or Ruined History?' in *Australian Journal of Historical Archaeology* Vol. 4, pp. 67–77

Bourdé, G. (1974) *Urbanisation et immigration en Amérique Latine, XII et XX siécles* Paris

Bourdieu, P. (1977) *Outline of a Theory of Practice* Cambridge: Cambridge University Press

Brunswick Oral History Project (1985) *For a Better Life We Came* Brunswick, VIC: Brunswick City Council

BRW (1990) *Business Review Weekly* 'Rich 200' Vol. 12, No. 13, 6 April

Bullivant, M. B. (1986) *Are Anglo-Australian Students Becoming the New Self-Deprived in Comparison with Ethnics?* Melbourne: Monash University

Burgmann, V. (1978) 'Capital and Labour. Responses to Immigration in the 19th Century' in Curthoys, A. and Markus, A. eds *Who Are Our Enemies? Racism and the Working Class in Australia* Sydney: Hale and Iremonger

Burnley I. H. (1976) *The Social Environment* Sydney: McGraw-Hill Book Company

—— (1988) 'Italian community life in Sydney' in J. Jupp ed. *The Australian People: An Encyclopedia of the Nation, Its People and Their Origins* Sydney: Angus & Robertson

CAAIP (Committee to Advise on Australia's Immigration Policies) (1987) *Understanding Immigration* Canberra: AGPS

—— (1988) *Immigration—A Commitment to Australia* Canberra: AGPS

Cacopardo, M. and Moreno, G. (1985) 'Características regionales, demogreficas y ocupacionales de la inmigración Italiana en la Argentina 1880–1930' in F. Devoto and G. Rosoli eds *La Inmigración Italiana en la Argentina* Buenos Aires: Biblos

Cahill, D. (1986) *The Schooling Experiences of Italian Immigrant Children During the 1950s* Melbourne: CHOMI

Cappiello, R. R. (1981) *Paese Fortunato* Milan: Feltrinelli

—— (1984) *Oh Lucky Country* St Lucia: University of Queensland Press (English translation of *Paese Fortunato*)

Cara-Walker, A. (1989) 'Cocoliche: The Art of Assimilation and Dissimulation Among Italians and Argentines' in *Latin American Research Review* Vol. 22, No. 3, p. 37

Carboni, R. (1855) *The Eureka Stockade The Consequence of Some Pirates Wanting on Quarterdeck a Rebellion* Melbourne: J. P. Atkinson and Co.

Carey, P. (1985) *Illywhacker* St Lucia: University of Queensland Press

Castles, S., Booth, H. and Wallace, T. (1984) *Here for Good—Western Europe's New Ethnic Minorities* London: Pluto Press

Castles, S., Lewis, D., Morrissey, M. and Black, J. D. (1986) *Patterns of Disadvantage Among the Overseas Born and their Children* Wollongong: Centre for Multicultural Studies, University of Wollongong

Castles, S., Cope, B., Kalantzis, M. and Morrissey, M. (1988) *Mistaken Identity—Multiculturalism and the Demise of Nationalism in Australia* Sydney: Pluto Press

Castles S., Collins, J., Gibson, D., Tait, D. and Alcorso, C. (1991) *The Global Milkbar and the Local Sweatshop: Ethnic Small Business and*

the Economic Restructuring of Sydney Wollongong: Centre for Multicultural Studies for the Office of Multicultural Affairs
Castles, S., Alcorso, C., Rando, G. Vasta, E. (1992) *Euroaustraliani: La popolazione di origine italiana in Australia* Turin: Fondazione Giovanni Agnelli
Cavallaro, R. (1981) *Storie senza storia: Indagine sull'emigrazione in Gran Bretagna* Rome: Centro Studi Emigrazione
Cecilia, T. (1985) *Non siamo arrivati ieri* Red Cliffs, VIC: The Sunnyland Press
—— (1992) 'Gli Italiani in Australia 1788–1940 Cronistoria' in S. Castles, C. Alcorso, G. Rando and E. Vasta, eds *Euroaustraliani: La popolazione di origine italiana in Australia* Turin: Fondazione Giovanni Agnelli
Child, I. L. (1943) *Italian or American? The Second Generation in Conflict* New York: Russell and Russell
Cinanni, P. (1974) *Emigrazione e unità operaia* Milan: Feltrinelli
—— (n.d.) *Emigration und Imperialismus: Zur Problematik der Arbeitsemigranten* Munich: Trikont; German edn of *Emigrazione e Imperialismo* (1968) Rome: Editori Riuniti
—— (1979) *Lotte per la terra nel mezzogiorno 1943–1953 Terre pubbliche'e trasformazione agraria* Venezia: Marsilio Editore
Cinel, D. (1982) *From Italy to San Francisco: The Immigrant Experience* Stanford, CA: Stanford University Press
Cipolla, A. (1928) *Il mio viaggio in Oceania, Australia e Insulindia* Milan: Agnelli
Clark, M. (1986) A *Short History of Australia* Ringwood, VIC: Penguin
Clyne, M. (1982) *Multilingual Australia* Melbourne: River Seine
—— (1987) 'Bilingualism and Community Languages: The Educational Consequences' in *Il Veltro* Vol. 31, Nos. 1–2, pp. 57–71
—— (1988) 'Community Languages in the Home' in *Vox* 1 Canberra: DEET August
COASIT (1988) *News (Notizie)* Vol. 2, No. 2, 7 December Ashfield, NSW: COASIT
—— (1989) *Director's Report to the Annual General Meeting* Ashfield, NSW: COASIT
Collins, J. (1988) *Migrant Hands in a Distant Land: Australia's Post-War Immigration* Sydney: Pluto Press
—— (1989) *Cappuccino Capitalism: Italians and Small Business in Australia* Working Paper No. 3, Sydney: KCAE Centre for Labour Studies
Collins, J. and Castles, S. (1989) *Restructuring Migrant Labour and Small Business in Australia* Wollongong: Centre for Multicultural Studies, University of Wollongong
Colosimo, R. (1987) 'Cinema e televisiona. La presenza italiana', in *Il Veltro* Vol. 31, No. 1–2, gennaio–aprile
Concas, L. (1977) *Ballata di Vento* Rome: Gabrieli
—— (1988) *L'altro uomo Poesie 1981–1983* Gorie [BG]: Editrice Velar
Connell, R. W., Connell, W. S., Stroobant, R. E., Sinclair, K. E. and Rogers, K. (1975) *12 to 20: Studies of City Youth* Sydney: Hicks Smith
Coreno, M. (1980) *Yellow Sun* Sydney: Saturday Centre

Cortés Conde, R. (1964) *Corrientes Inmigratorias y Surgimiento de Industrias en Argentina* Buenos Aires
—— (1979) *El Progresso Argentino* Buenos Aires: Editorial Sudamérica
Cresciani, G. (1980) *The Italian Community at the Outbreak of the War* Sydney: unpublished manuscript
—— (1981) *Fascism, Anti-Fascism and Italians in Australia 1922–1945* Canberra: ANU Press
—— (1985a) *The Italians* Sydney: Australian Broadcasting Corporation
——(1985b) *Lo spettro della quinta colonna in Australia, 1939–1942* Quaderni di Affari Sociali Internazionali Milan: Franco Angeli Editore
—— (1986a) *Australia: Italy and the Italians* CIRC Paper No. 42 Melbourne: CIRC
—— (1986b) *Italians in Australia: Past, Present and Future* Occasional Paper Sydney: NSW Ethnic Affairs Commission
—— (1988a) 'Italian immigrants 1920–1945' in J. Jupp ed. *The Australian People: An Encyclopedia of the Nation, Its People and Their Origins* Sydney: Angus & Robertson
—— (1988b) *Migrants or Mates: Italian Life in Australia* Sydney: Knockmore
Cronin, C. (1970) *The Sting of Change. Sicilians in Sicily and Australia* Chicago: University of Chicago Press
Crowley, F. K. (1973) *Modern Australia in Documents* Vol. 2, 1939–1970 Sydney: Wren
D'Aprano, C. (n.d.) *The Swallow* [novel: unpublished manuscript]
David, A. and Wheelwright, T. (1989) *The Third Wave: Australia and Asian Capitalism* Sydney: Left Book Club
Davidson, A. (1988) 'The condition of Italy, 1920–1970' in J. Jupp ed. *The Australian People: An Encyclopedia of the Nation, Its People and Their Origins* Sydney: Angus & Robertson
de Imaz, J. L. (1970) *Los que mandan* Albany: State University of NY Press
de Lepervanche, M. (1975) 'Australian Immigrants 1788–1940: Desired and Unwanted' in E. L. Wheelwright and K. Buckley eds *Essays in the Political Economy of Australian Capitalism,* Vol. I Sydney: ANZ Book Company
—— (1980) 'From Race to Ethnicity' *Australia and New Zealand Journal of Sociology* 1, 16
—— (1990) 'Holding it all Together: Multiculturalism, Nationalism and the State in Australia', *XII World Congress of Sociology* Madrid
De Marco, W. D. (1981) Ethnics and Enclaves: The Italian settlement in the North End of Boston, PhD thesis, Boston College 1980: reprinted in Ann Arbor MI, University Microfilms Research Press
De Scalzo, G. (1938) *La Terra dei fossili viventi Viaggio in Australia* Milan: Ceschina
Devoto, F. and Rosoli, G. eds (1985) *La Inmigración Italiana en la Argentina* Buenos Aires: Biblos
Di Biase, B. (1989) 'Italian in Australian schools and universities' in C. Bettoni and J. Lo Bianco eds *Understanding Italy: Language, Culture,*

Commerce: An Australian Perspective Sydney: Frederick May Foundation for Italian Studies and University of Sydney

Di Nicola, M. (1984) 'The political impact of Italian migrants in Leichhardt, 1961–73' in J. Jupp ed. *Ethnic Politics in Australia* Sydney: Allen & Unwin

Di Pietro, A. (1987) ' "Italianness" in the Australian context' in *Nuovo Paese* November

Di Stefano, E. (1975) *L'Avventura australiana* [novel: unpublished manuscript]

—— (1978) *Voci di lontananza* Sydney: Southern Cross Press

—— (1988) *Se Rimarrà qualcosa . . .* Sydney: Southern Cross Press

Diana, A. (1988) 'Italian Women in Australia' in *Affari Sociali Internazionali* No. 2, Milan: Franco Angeli

DIEA (Department of Immigration and Ethnic Affairs) (1983) *Australian Immigration, Consolidated Statistics,* No. 13 Canberra: AGPS

—— (1986) *Don't Settle for Less—Report of the Committee for Stage I of the Review of Migrant and Multicultural Programs and Services* Canberra: AGPS

DILGEA (Department of Immigration, Local Government and Ethnic Affairs) (1987a) *Australia's Population Trends and Prospects 1987* Canberra: AGPS

—— (1987b) *1986 Census Highlights, No. 2, Country of Birth Data* Canberra: DILGEA

—— (1988a) *Australian Immigration, Consolidated Statistics, No. 14, 1986* Canberra: AGPS

—— (1988b) *Australia's Population Trends and Prospects 1988* Canberra: AGPS

Dingh, A. E. and Menett, D. T. (1985) *Argentina and Australia: Essays in Comparative Economic Development* Melbourne: Clayton

Downer, A. R. (Department of Immigration) (1961) *Citizenship Digest* Canberra: AGPS

Dugan, M. and Szwarc, J. (1984) *There Goes the Neighbourhood! Australia's Migrant Experience* Melbourne: Macmillan and Australian Institute of Multicultural Affairs

Dyster, B. and Meredith, D. (1990) *Australia in the International Economy in the Twentieth Century* Cambridge and Melbourne: Cambridge University Press

Ercole, V. (1932) *No Escape* London: Butterworth

Ermini, L. and Halevi, J. (1989) 'Australia, Italy and the EEC' in C. Bettoni and J. Lo Bianco eds *Understanding Italy: Language, Culture, Commerce: An Australian Perspective* Sydney: Frederick May Foundation for Italian Studies and University of Sydney

Fairfield City Council (1990) *Report 1990* Sydney: Fairfield City Council

Fitzgerald, A. (1981) *The Italian Farming Soldiers. 1941–1947* Melbourne: Melbourne University Press

Fitzpatrick, D. (1988) 'Irish immigration 1840–1914' in J. Jupp ed. *The Australian People: An Encyclopedia of the Nation, Its People and Their Origins* Sydney: Angus & Robertson

Fondazione Giovanni Agnelli ed. (1987) *Euroamericani: Volume One: La*

Popolazione di Origine Italiana negli Stati Uniti, Volume Two: La Popolazione di Origine Italiana in Argentina, Volume Three: La Popolazione di Origine Italiana in Brasile Torino: Fondazione Giovanni Agnelli

——*(1989) Abitare il Pianeta: Futuro Demografico, Migrazioni e Tensioni Etniche* (2 Vols.) Torino: Fondazione Giovanni Agnelli

Gabaccia, D. R. (1984) *From Sicily to Elizabeth Street: Housing and Social Change Among Italian Immigrants* Albany, NY: Sunny Press

Gabbrielli, E. (1992) 'Gli italo-aborigeni del Western Australia' in S. Castles, C. Alcorso, G. Rando and E. Vasta eds *Euroaustraliani. La popolazione di origine italiana in Australia* Turin: Fondazione Giovanni Agnelli

Gagliardi, F. (1881) *Australia: lettere alla Gazzetta d'Italia* Florence: Tipografia Editrice della Gazzetta d'Italia

Galbally, F. (Chairman) (1978) *Report of the Review of Post-Arrival Programs and Services for Migrants* Canberra: AGPS

Gálvez, V. (1942) *Memorias de un viejo* Buenos Aires: Solar

Gamba, C. (1952) *A Report on the Italian Fishermen of Fremantle, Perth* Perth: The University of Western Australia

Garnaut, R. (1989) *Australia and the Northeast Asian Ascendancy—Report to the Prime Minister and the Minister for Foreign Affairs and Trade* Canberra: AGPS

Gastaldo, R. ed. (n.d.) *Italy Toward 2001: An Exploration into Italy's Demographic and Socioeconomic Future* Torino: Fondazione Giovanni Agnelli

Genovesi, P. (1990) 'Lingua e identità culturale' in G. Rando ed. *Language and Cultural Identity Proceedings of the Conference on the Italians in Australia The First 200 Years* Wollongong NSW: Dante Alighieri Society

Germani, G. (1963) 'La mobilidad social en la Argentina' in S. Lipset and M. Bendix eds *La mobilidad social en la sociedad industrial* Buenos Aires

—— (1974) *Politíca y sociedad en un época de transición* Buenos Aires: Paidós

Giadresco, G. (1988) *Dai Magliari ai vu' cumprá* Soveria Mannelli [CZ]: Rubbettino

Gobello, J. (1974) *El Lenguaje de mi Pueblo* Buenos Aires

Graham-Yooll, A. (1981) *The Forgotten Colony: A History of the English-Speaking Communities in Argentina* London: Hutchinson

Guthrie, R. (1983) *What Do They Need? An Inquiry Into the Needs of Aged Italians in the Melbourne Metropolitan Area* Melbourne: COASIT

Halevi, J. (1989) 'FILEF' in C. Bettoni and J. Lo Bianco *Understanding Italy: Language Culture and Commerce: An Australian Perspective* Sydney: Frederick May Foundation for Italian Studies and University of Sydney

Hampel, B. (1984) 'Generations and Class: Sicilian-Australians in Melbourne' in G. Bottomley and M. de Lepervanche eds *Ethnicity, Class and Gender in Australia* Sydney: George Allen & Unwin

Hansen, M. L. (1938) *The Problem of the Third Generation Immigrant* Roch Island: Augustana Historical Society

Harney, R. (1984) *Dalla frontiera alle Little Italies: Gli Italiani in Canada, 1880–1945* Rome: Centro Studi Emigrazione

Haugen, E. (1953) *The Norwegian Language in America* Philadelphia

Hawley, D. S. (1982) *Survey of Students Enrolled in Italian and French Courses in Tertiary Institutions, October 1981* Wollongong: Department of European Languages, University of Wollongong

Hempel, J. (1959) 'Italians in Queensland—aspects of assimilation' in *Quadrant* Vol. 3, No. 4, Spring

Henderson, L. (1978) 'Economic or racist' in H. Reynolds ed. *Race Relations in Northern Queensland* Townsville: University of Queensland Press

Horvath, B. M. (1985) *Variation in Australian English: The Sociolects of Sydney* Cambridge: Cambridge University Press

House of Representatives (Continuous) *Parliamentary Debates* Canberra: AGPS

Huber, R. (1977) *From Pasta to Pavlova: A Comparative Study of Italian Settlers in Sydney and Griffith* St Lucia: University of Queensland Press

—— (1985) 'What will the neighbours say?: honour and shame among Mediterranean immigrants' in M. E. Poole, P. R. de Lacey and B. S. Randhawa, eds *Australia in Transition: Culture and Life Possibilities* Sydney: Harcourt Brace Jovanovich

Hugo, G. (1986) *Australia's Changing Population: Trends and Implications* Melbourne: Oxford University Press

Hunt, D. (1978) 'Exclusionism Unionism: Europeans in the Queensland Sugar Industry 1900–1910' in A. Curthoys and A. Markus eds *Who Are Our Enemies? Racism and the Working Class in Australia* Sydney: Hale and Iremonger

IAC (Immigration Advisory Committee) (1960) *Dovey Report: Progress and Assimilation of Migrant Children* Canberra: AGPS

—— (1963) *Committee on Migrant Women* Minutes of Meeting March 18 Canberra: DIEA

—— (1969a) *Committee on Migrant Women* Canberra: DIEA

—— (1969b) *Committee on Migrant Women* Agenda February 7 Canberra: DIEA

Jakubowicz, A., Morrissey, M. and Palser, J. (1984) *Ethnicity, Class and Social Welfare in Australia* Sydney: University of New South Wales Social Welfare Research Centre

Jupp, J. ed. (1984a) *Ethnic Politics in Australia* Sydney: George Allen & Unwin

—— (1984b) 'Power in ethnic Australia' in J. Jupp ed. *Ethnic Politics in Australia* Sydney: George Allen & Unwin

—— ed. (1988) The *Australian People: An Encyclopedia of the Nation, Its People and Their Origins* Sydney: Angus & Robertson

Jupp, J., York, B. and McRobbie, A. (1989) *The Political Participation of Ethnic Minorities in Australia* Canberra: AGPS

Kahan-Guidi, A. M. and Weiss, E. eds (1989) *Give me Strength—Forza e coraggio* Broadway, NSW: Women's Redress Press Inc.

Kalantzis, M. and Cope, B. (1984) 'Multiculturalism and education policy' in G. Bottomley and M. de Lepervanche eds *Ethnicity, Class and Gender in Australia* Sydney: George Allen & Unwin

Kasnitz, D. (1983) *Work, Gender and Health Among Southern Italian Immigrants in Melbourne, Australia* Vols I and II Michigan: University Microfilms International

Kelly, B. (1983) 'Ethnicity and its Relation to Economic, Social and Political Power in Griffith' in G. Cresciani ed. *Australia, the Australians and the Italian Migration* Quaderni di Affari Sociali Internazionali, Milan: Franco Angeli Editore

—— (1984) 'Ethnic Participation in Australian Political Systems' in J. Jupp ed. *Ethnic Politics in Australia* Sydney: George Allen & Unwin

—— (1985) 'Italian Women's Participation in Community Organisations' in M. E. Poole, P. R. de Lacey and B. S. Randhawa eds *Australia in Transition: Culture and Life Possibilities* Sydney: Harcourt Brace Jovanovic

—— (1989) 'Ethnicity Gender and Unpaid Community Work', in *Unequal Access to Work*—Work Studies No. 4, Centre for Work and Labour Market Studies, Wagga Wagga, Charles Sturt University: Riverina Press

Kelly, M. (1979) 'Problems associated with a parish comprised of Australians of Italian and Irish descent' in *The Australasian Catholic Record* Vol. 56, No. 1, pp. 30–9

Kinder, J. J. (1990) 'Australian Italian: active creation or passive decay?' in G. Rando ed. *Language and Cultural Identity: Proceedings of the Conference on the Italian Community in Australia. The First 200 Years* Wollongong NSW: Dante Alighieri Society

Knott, J. (1988) 'Settlement 1851–1880' in J. Jupp ed. *The Australian People: An Encyclopedia of the Nation, Its People and Their Origins* Sydney: Angus & Robertson

Kobal, I. (1982) *Men Who Built the* Snowy, 2nd edn Sydney: The Saturday Centre

Korn, F. and de la Torre, L. (1987) 'Gli italiani a Buenos Aires' in Fondazione Giovanni Agnelli *Euroamericani: La popolazione di origine italiana in Argentina* Torino: Edizioni della fondazione

Kroll, J. C. and Sábato, H. (1981) *Cómo Fue la Inmigración Irlandesa en Argentina* Buenos Aires: Plus Ultra

Kurth, J. R. (1989) 'The Pacific basin versus the Atlantic alliance: two paradigms of international relations' in *The Annals of the American Academy of Political and Social Science—The Pacific Region: Challenges to Policy and Theory* Vol. 505, Newbury Park, London: Sage Publications

Lampugnani, R. and Holton, R. (1989) *Ethnic Business in South Australia: A Sociological Profile of the Italian Business Community* Paper presented to the Migrants and Small Business Research Workshop, University of Wollongong, 30 June–1 July 1989

Langford-Smith, T. and Rutherford, J. (1966) *Water and Land: Two Case Studies in Irrigation* Canberra: ANU Press

Leoni, F. (1981) *Vocabolario Australitaliano* Armidale: University of New England Publishing Unit

—— (1988a) 'Australitalian: The Language of Italian Migrants in Australia', in J. Jupp ed. *The Australian People: An Encyclopedia of the Nation, its People and Their Origins* Sydney: Angus & Robertson

—— (1988b) Australitalian: The Language of Italian Migrants in Multicultural Australia, PhD thesis, University of New England, Armidale

Lever-Tracy, C. (1984) 'A New Australian Working Class Leadership: The Case of Ford Broadmeadows' in G. Bottomley and M. de Lepervanche eds *Ethnicity, Class and Gender in Australia* Sydney: George Allen & Unwin

Lever-Tracy, C. and Quinlan, M. (1988) A *Divided Working Class* London: Routledge & Kegan Paul

Lewins, F. (1978) *The Myth of the Universal Church: Catholic Migrants in Australia* Canberra: ANU Press

Lo Bianco, J. (1987) *National Policy on Languages* Canberra: Commonwealth Department of Education/AGPS

—— (1988) 'L'insegnamento dell'italiano' in *Il Veltro* Vol. 32, Nos 1–2, pp. 187–98

Loh, M. (1980) *With Courage in Their Cases* Melbourne: FILEF

Lombardo, P. (1985) 'No salami sandwiches for lunch' in *Noi Donne Italo-Australiane* Proceedings of the First Congress of Italo-Australian Women Sydney-Melbourne: Associazione Donne Italo-Australiane

Luciano, G. (1959) *Italians as They Are (Gli Italiani come sono)* Sydney: The Italian Press Pty Ltd

MacDonald, J. and MacDonald, L. (1970) 'Italian Migration to Australia: Manifest Functions of Bureaucracy versus Latent Functions of Informal Networks' in *Journal of Social History* 3

MAE (1862) Ministero Affari Esteri *Grafico al Ministero degli Esteri* Archivio Sardo, serie 11C Busta 47, 17 febbraio 1862

—— (1912) *Bollettino dell'emigrazione*, Rome, Commissariato dell'Emigrazione, 1, p. 127

—— (n.d.) *Affari Esteri* 1861–86, serie IV, Busta 270

Maione, O. (1979) *Bitch* Melbourne: Tusculum

Malpantidis, N. (1986) *Young People From Established Migrant Communities in Melbourne* Melbourne: Report of Ecumenical Migration Centre

Markus, A. (1988a) 'How Australians See Each Other', in Committee to Advise on Australia's Immigration Policies, *Immigration: A Commitment to Australia—Consultants' Report* Canberra: AGPS

—— (1988b) 'Racial Discrimination' in J. Jupp ed. *The Australian People: An Encylcopedia of the Nation, Its People and Their Origins* Sydney: Angus & Robertson

Martin, J. (1978) *The Migrant Presence* Sydney: George Allen & Unwin

—— (1984) 'Non-English Speaking Migrant Women in Australia' in N. Grieve and A. Burns eds *Australian Women: New Feminist Perspectives* Melbourne: Oxford University Press

Martinuzzi-O'Brien, I. (1988) *Australia's Italians 1788–1988* Melbourne: COASIT–Italian Historical Society

McAllister, I. (1988) 'Political Attitudes and Electoral Behaviour' in J. Jupp ed. *The Australian People: An Encyclopedia of the Nation, Its People and Their Origins* Sydney: Angus & Robertson

McHugh, S. (1989) *The Snowy—The People Behind the Power* Melbourne: Heinemann Australia

McLean, B. (1982) *Languages Other Than English in the Primary School: Six Case Studies* Canberra: AGPS

McQueen, H. (1986) *A New Britannia* rev. edn, Ringwood, VIC: Penguin

Menghetti, D. (1988) 'Italians in North Queensland' in J. Jupp ed. *The Australian People: An Encyclopedia of the Nation, Its People and Their Origins* Sydney: Angus & Robertson

MIA (Murrumbidgee Irrigation Area) Agricultural Extension Service, *Annual Reports*, 1948–1956 Griffith, NSW: CSIRO Irrigation Research Laboratories

Miles, R. (1989) *Racism* London: Routledge & Keagan Paul

Ministero Affari Esteri (1981) *Indagine sulle motivazioni all'apprendimento della lingua italiana nel mondo* Roma: Ministero degli Affari Esteri/Instituto della Enciclopedia Italiana

Mistilis, N. (1985) 'Second generation Australians: progress and puzzles' in *The Australian Quarterly* Summer

Mitchell, A. G. and Delbridge, A. (1965) *The Speech of Australian Adolescents* Sydney: Angus & Robertson

Mitchell, G. (1988) *Health Policy for a Multicultural Australia* Canberra: Office of Multicultural Affairs

Munari, P. (1897) *Un Italiano in Australia Note e impressioni* Milan: Tipografia degli Operai (Società Cooperativa)

Nascimbene, M. C. (1988) *Los Italianos y las Integración Nacional* Buenos Aires: Ediciones Selección Editorial

Neals, S. (1989) 'Finance still a problem for new entrepreneurs' *Sydney Morning Herald*, 18 July, p. 67

Nibbi, G. (1937) 'Glossario' in *Il volto degli emigranti (scene di vita in Australia)* Firenze: Parenti, pp. 223–33

—— (1965) *Cocktails d'Australia* Milan: Martello

Nicolaou, L. (1988) 'Trade Union Involvement' in J. Jupp ed. *The Australian People: An Encyclopedia of the Nation, Its People and Their Origins* Sydney: Angus & Robertson

OMA (Office of Multicultural Affairs/Advisory Council on Multicultural Affairs) (1989) *National Agenda for a Multicultural Australia. Sharing our Future* Canberra: AGPS

Ostrow, R. (1987) *The New Boy Network* Richmond: William Heinemann Australia

Pacini, M. (1988) *Italian Cultural Relations within the Euroamerican Universe* Torino: Fondazione Giovanni Agnelli

Palanca, V. (n.d.) 'The development of regional imbalances in Italy: from a bipolar to multipolar pattern' in *Italy Toward 2001: an Exploration into Italy's Demographic and Socioeconomic Future* Torino: Fondazione Giovanni Agnelli

Paoloni, M. (1989) in A. M. Kahan-Guidi and E. Weiss eds *Give Me Strength—Forza e Coraggio* Sydney: Women's Redress Press Inc.

Papalia, G. (n.d.) *Peasant Rebels in the Canefields* CIRC Paper No. 37 Melbourne: CIRC

Pappas, Carter, Evans and Koop/Telesis (1990) *The Global Challenge:*

Australian Manufacturing in the 1990s Melbourne: Australian Manufacturing Council

Pascoe, R. (1987) *Buongiorno Australia, Our Italian Heritage* Melbourne: Greenhouse Publications and Vaccari Italian Historical Trust

—— (1988)*The Recollections of Luigi Grollo* translated by Paolo Bartoloni as *Luigi Grollo: Elementi di memoria* Preston, VIC: Grollo Australia

—— (1990) *Open for Business: Aboriginal and Immigrant Entrepreneurs Tell Their Story* Canberra: AGPS and Office of Multicultural Affairs

Pascoe, R. and Bertola, P. (1985) 'Italian Miners and the Second-generation "Britishers" at Kalgoorlie, Australia' in *Social History* Vol. 10, pp. 9–35

Pearl, C. (1983) *The Dunera Scandal* London: Angus & Robertson

Pettini, R. (1989) *Le Signore di Albion Street: The Ladies of Albion Street* Randwick, NSW: Outreach Randwick College of TAFE

Phizacklea, A. (1983) 'In the Front Line' in Annie Phizacklea ed. *One Way Ticket* London: Routledge and Kegan Paul

—— (1987) 'Minority and economic restructuring: the case of Britain and the Federal Republic of Germany' in *Work Employment Society* 1, 3

—— (1988) 'Entrepreneurship, ethnicity and gender' in S. Westwood and P. Bhachu eds *Enterprising Women* London: Routledge & Kegan Paul

Pittarello, A. (1980) *Soup Without Salt: the Australian Catholic Church and the Italian Migrant* Sydney: Centre for Migration Studies

Platt, D.C.M and di Tella, G. eds (1985) *Argentina, Australia and Canada: Studies in Comparative Development* Oxford: Macmillan

Price, C.A. (1955) *Italian Population at Griffith* Australian National University [Unpublished]

—— (1963) *Southern Europeans in Australia* Melbourne: Oxford University Press

—— ed. (1979) *Australian Immigration: A Bibliography and Digest, No. 4* Canberra; Australian National University

Price, C. A. and Martin, J. (1975) *Australian Immigration: A Bibliography and Digest, No. 3* Canberra: Australian National University

Price, C. A. and Zubrzycki, J. (1962a) 'The Use of Intermarriage Statistics as an Index of Assimilation' in *Population Studies* Vol. 1, No. 1, July, pp. 58–69

——(1962b) 'Immigrant Marriage Patterns in Australia' in *Population Studies* Vol. 1, No. 2, November, pp. 123–33

Pryles, M. and Bravender Coyle, P. (1988) 'Legal Status of non-citizens' in J. Jupp ed. *The Australian People: An Encyclopedia of the Nation, Its People and their Origins* Sydney: Angus & Robertson

Quinlan, M. (1982) Immigrant Workers, Trade Union Organisation and Industrial Strategy, PhD thesis, University of Sydney

Randazzo, A. (1953) *I Canti della valle e d'oltremare* Sydney: Acacia Press

Randazzo, A. and Cigler, M. (1987) *The Italians in Australia* Blackburn, VIC: AE Press

Rando, F. (1973) 'Gioranlismo italiano in Australia' in *Il Veltro* Vol. 17, No. 2–3, aprile-giugno, pp. 115–18

Rando, G. (1967) 'Italiano e Inglese in Australia' in *Lingua Nostra* Vol. 28, No. 4, pp. 115–18

—— (1971a) 'English Loan-word and Standard Italian Original in the Vocabulary of Australian Italian' in *Te Reo* Vol. 14, pp. 74–80

—— (1971b) 'L'Italo-Australiano di Perth' in *Lingua Nostra* Vol. 32, No. 4, pp. 118–20

—— (1973) 'L'italiano parlato d'Australia' in *Il Veltro,* Vol. 17, No. 2–3, pp. 247–52

—— (1983) 'The Founding of 4EB: An Issue of Ethno-Political Control in Queensland' in *Social Alternatives* 3, 3

—— ed. (1983) *Italian Writers in Australia: Essays and Texts* Wollongong: Department of European Languages, University of Wollongong

—— (1984) *A Survey of Multilingual Broadcasting in Australia* Wollongong: Department of European Languages, University of Wollongong

—— (1987) 'Le Associazioni italiane in Australia—oltre 100 anni di storia' in *Marconi News* 20, June–July

—— ed. (1990) *Language and Cultural Identity Proceedings of the Conference on the Italians in Australia The first 200 Years* Wollongong, NSW: Dante Alighieri Society

—— (1991) 'L'esperienza australiana di Raffaello Carboni' (forthcoming)

Rando, G. and Teh, S. (1981) 'Initiatives in Communicating with the Non-English Speaking Migrant: Two Recent Language Programs in the Department of Social Security' in *Social Security* June, pp. 60–5

Ramson, W. S. (1973)'L'influenza dell'immigrazione italiana sull'inglese d'Australia' in *Il Veltro* 16, 2–3, aprile-giugno, pp. 273–7

Raymundo, B. A. (1981) *Argentina 2000: Una Nación Semidesierta* Buenos Aires: Ediciones Lihuel

Reynolds, H. (1987) *The Law of the Land* Ringwood, VIC: Penguin Books

Riccioli, C. (1883) *Australia ed Italia* Naples

—— (1886) *Commerci con l'Australia* Naples

Rimondini, E. (1982) 'The Architecture of the Immigrants' Melbourne: ANZAS Conference

Rock, D. (1987) 'Precursors of Conservative Nationalism in Argentina' in *Hispanic American Historical Review* Vol. 67, No. 2, May, p. 284

Rosoli, G. ed. (1978) *Un secolo di emigrazione italiana* Rome: Centro Studi Emigrazione

Sacchi, F. (1932) *La casa in Oceania* Verona: Mondadori

——'Gli uomini della "ghenga", *L'Italo-Australiano,* 17 October 1925 and *Il Veltro* Vol. 17, No. 2–3 (1973), pp. 374–6

Sack, R. (1986) *Human Territoriality: Its Theory and History* Cambridge: Cambridge University Press

Salvado, R. (1851) *Memorie Storiche dell'Australia particolarmente della Missione Benedettina di Nuova Norcia e degli usi e costumi degli Australiani* Rome: Propaganda Fide

Saunders, K. (1988) 'Pacific Islanders Recruitment' in J. Jupp ed. *The Australian People: An Encylcopedia of the Nationa, Its People and Their Origins* Sydney: Angus & Robertson

Sceusa, F. (1881) *La spedizione del Marchese de Ray e le sue vittime* Sydney: H. R. Woods and Co.

—— (1888) *Hail Australia! Morituri te Salutant!* Sydney: Jarrett and Co.

Scobie, J. R. (1964) *Argentina: a City and a Nation* New York: Oxford University Press

Sebastiani, C. M. (1984a) *Fragilità* Perugia: Guerra

—— (1984b) *L'Approdo (Ashore)* Marrickville, NSW: Southwood Press

Senkman, L. (1986) *El Antisemitismo en la Argentina* Buenos Aires: Centro Editor de América Latina

Smolicz, J. J. (1980) 'Language as a Core Value of Culture' in *RELC Journal of Applied Linguistics* Vol. 2, No. 1, pp. 1–13

—— (1985) 'Multiculturalism and an Overarching Framework of Values', in M. E. Poole, P. R. De Lacey, and B. S. Randhawa eds *Australia in Transition: Culture and Life Possibilities* Sydney: Harcourt Brace Jovanovich

Smolicz, J. J. and Harris, R. (1976) 'Ethnic Languages and Australian Youth' in M. Clyne ed. *Australia Talks Essays on the Sociology of Australian Immigrant and Aboriginal Languages* Canberra: Department of Linguistics, Research School of Pacific Studies, ANU, pp. 131–55

Snowy Mountain Authority (1961) *Annual Report* Sydney: Snowy Mountain Authority

Solberg, C. (1970) *Immigration and Nationalism: Argentina and Chile 1890–1914* Austin, Texas: Institute of Latin American Studies, University of Texas Press

SOPEMI (1990) *Continuous Reporting System on Migration 1989* Paris: OECD

Storer, D. (1976) *But I Wouldn't Want my Wife to Work, Here: A Study of Migrant Women in Melbourne Industry* Melbourne: Centre for Urban Research and Action

Strahan, K. W. and Williams, A. J. (1988) *Immigrant Entrepreneurs in Australia: A Report to the Office of Multicultural Affairs* Melbourne: Productive Culture Australia

Strano, A. (1973) *Prigioniero in Germania* Cittadella di Padova: Rebellato

——(1986) *Luck, Without Joy A Portrayal of a Migrant* [translated by Elizabeth P. Burrows] Fremantle, WA: Fremantle Arts Centre Press

Strano, L. (1964) *Inquietudine* Sydney: Tip. Ital-Print

—— (1986) *Fifty Years Ago* Fairfield, NSW: The Author

Stransky, C. (1988) 'Italians in Western Australia' in J. Jupp ed. *The Australian People: An Encyclopedia of the Nation, Its People and Their Origins* Sydney: Angus & Robertson

Szuchman, M. (1980) *Mobility and Integration in Urban Argentina* Austin, Texas: University of Texas Press

Taft, R. (1975) *The Career Aspirations of Immigrant Schoolchildren in Victoria* Paper No. 12 Victoria: Department of Sociology, La Trobe University

Taylor, B. (1989) 'American, British and Other Foreign Influences in Australian English Since World War II' in P. Collins and D. Blair eds *Australian English: The Language of a New Society* St Lucia: University of Queensland Press, pp. 225–54

Taylor, G. (1984) *Opinions of Sydney Catholic Education Office Personnel Towards Issues Concerning Community Language Education: A Report* Sydney: Macquarie University

Tedeschi, P. (1986) *Senza Camicia* Milan: Editrice Nuovi Autori

Thompson, S. L. (1980) *Australia Through Italian Eyes: A Study of Settlers Returning.from Australia to Italy* Melbourne: Oxford University Press

Totaro, M. (1988) L'insegnamento dell'italiano nello Stato del New South Wales: 1935–1987, MA Honours thesis, University of Sydney

—— (1990) 'The teaching of Italian in the perspective of an Australian national language policy' in *Language and Cultural Identity: Proceedings of the Conference on the Italian Community in Australia, The First 200 years* Wollongong, NSW: Dante Alighieri Society

Triaca, M. (1985) *Amelia, A Long Journey* Melbourne: Greenhouse Publications

Tully, J. (1962) 'Leadership and Integration' in *Australian Journal of Social Issues* Vol. 1, No. 2, pp. 11–25

Valente, R. (1977) The Post-war Leichhardt Italian Community, MA thesis, University of Sydney

Vasta, E. (1979) 'Language and the Second Generation Italian Adolescent' in *Unicorn* January

—— (1980) 'The Second Generation Adolescent at Home and at School' in *New Education* Vol. III

—— (1985) *'If you had your time again, would you migrate to Australia?': A Study of Long Settled Italo-Australians in Brisbane,* DIEA Report Canberra: AGPS

—— (1990a) 'Gender, Class and Ethnic Relations: The Domestic and Work Experiences of Italian Migrant Women in Australia' in *Migration* Vol. 7, pp. 7–31

—— (1990b) Australia's Post-War Immigration Policy: Power, Identity and Resistance, PhD thesis, University of Queensland

—— (1991), 'Gender, Class and Ethnic Relations: The Domestic and Work Experiences of Italian Migrant Women in Australia' in G. Bottomley, M. de Lepervanche and J. Martin eds, *Intersexions: Gender/Class/Culture/Ethnicity,* Sydney: Allen & Unwin

Victorian Ethnic Affairs Commission (1984) *Language Use in Australia* [information paper] Melbourne: Victorian Ethnic Affairs Commission

Visentin, G. (1980) *Australian Parishes and Italian Migrants,* CIRC Paper No. 1 Melbourne: CIRC

Waldinger, R. (1986) *Through the Eye of the Needle: Immigrants and Enterprise in New York's Garment Trades* New York: New York University Press

Ward, R. (1977) A *Nation for a Continent: The History of Australia 1901–1975* Melbourne: Heinemann

Ware, H. (1981) A *Profile of the Italian Community in Australia* Melbourne Australian Institute of Multicultural Affairs and COASIT

—— (1988) 'Origins of Post-war Italian Migrants' in J. Jupp ed. *The Australian People: An Encyclopedia of the Nation, Its People and Their Origins* Sydney: Angus & Robertson

Whitfield, K. (1987) *The Australian Labour Market* Sydney: Harper & Row

Widening our Horizons. Report of the Review of the Teaching of Modern Languages in Higher Education, Prof. R. V. Leal (chair), Draft copy

circulated by the Minister for Employment, Education and Training, Canberra, April 1991
Williams, R. (1962) *Culture and Society 1780–1950* Mitcham, VIC: Penguin
Wilson, K. and Martin, W. A. (1982) 'Ethnic Enclaves: A Comparison of the Cuban and Black Economies in Miami' in *American Journal of Sociology* Vol. 88, pp. 135–68
Wilton, J. and Bosworth, R. (1984) *Old Worlds and New Australia* Ringwood, Vic: Penguin
Wright, E. O. (1982) 'Class Boundaries and Contradictory Class Locations' in A. Giddens and D. Held eds *Classes, Power, and Conflict: Classical and Contemporary Debates* London: Macmillan
—— (1985) *Classes* London: Verso
Wyndham, H. S. (1963) *Citizenship Convention Digest* Canberra: AGPS
Yarwood, A. T. (1988) 'The White Australia Policy' in J. Jupp ed. *The Australian People: An Encyclopedia of the Nation, Its People and Their Origins* Sydney: Angus & Robertson
Zaccari, V. (1986) 'FILEF, Italian Migrant Women and Australian Trade Unions' in *Multicultural Australia Papers* Melbourne: CHONMI

Index